SLAVERY BEFORE RACE

Slavery before Race

Europeans, Africans, and Indians at
Long Island's Sylvester Manor Plantation,
1651–1884

KATHERINE HOWLETT HAYES

New York University Press

NEW YORK AND LONDON

NEW YORK UNIVERSITY PRESS
New York and London
www.nyupress.org

LIBRARY OF CONGRESS CATALOGING-IN-PUBLICATION DATA
Hayes, Katherine Howlett.
    Slavery before race : Europeans, Africans, and Indians at Long Island's
Sylvester Manor Plantation, 1651–1821 / Katherine Howlett Hayes.
        p. cm. — (Early American places)
    Revised version of the author's thesis (doctoral)—University of California,
Berkeley, 2008.
    Includes bibliographical references and index.
    ISBN 978-0-8147-8577-5 (cl : alk. paper)
    ISBN 978-0-8147-2469-9 (e)
    ISBN 978-0-8147-7090-0 (e)
    1. Slavery—New York (State)—Shelter Island. 2. African Americans—New
York (State)—Shelter Island—History—To 1863. 3. Indians of North America—
New York (State)—History. 4. Shelter Island (N.Y.)—Race relations—History.
5. Plantation life—New York (State)—Shelter Island—History. 6. Sylvester
Manor Plantation Site (Shelter Island, N.Y.) 7. Shelter Island (N.Y.)—
Antiquities. 8. Excavations (Archaeology)—New York (State)—Shelter Island.
I. Title. II. Series: Early American places.
E445.N56H39   2013
306.3'6209747—dc23

                                                          2012035346

References to Internet Web sites (URLs) were accurate at the time of writing. Neither the author nor New York University Press is responsible for URLs that may have expired or changed since the manuscript was prepared.

New York University Press books are printed on acid-free paper, and their binding materials are chosen for strength and durability. We strive to use environmentally responsible suppliers and materials to the greatest extent possible in publishing our books.

Manufactured in the United States of America

For Mom and Dad

Contents

List of Figures and Table   xi

Acknowledgments   xiii

Prologue   xvii

1   Tracing a Racialized History   1

2   Convergence   17

3   Building and Destroying   57

4   Objects of Interaction   86

5   Forgetting to Remember, Remembering to Forget   121

6   Unimagining Communities   163

Epilogue   181

Notes   183

Bibliography   187

Index   215

About the Author   221

Figures and Table

Figures

1.1 Coastal/Eastern Algonquian tribal territories (Southern New England and Long Island) at the time of earliest European settlement 27

2.1 Extant Manor house constructed by Brinley Sylvester, 1730s 49

3.1 Sylvester Manor core plantation surrounding 1735 house; additional site areas surveyed and excavated 60

3.2 (a) North Peninsula tested areas; (b) undated photo of Gardiners Creek and southwest tip of peninsula 62

3.3 Cobbled paving associated with early plantation features 66

3.4 (a) Map of plantation period features and overlying midden layer and (b) excavated structure trench 67

3.5 Layer of bone exposed in large waste pit 71

3.6 Geophysical survey interpreted results 74

3.7 Sylvester Manor property map drawn for 1828 Gardiner vs. Dering legal case 84

4.1 Wampumpeague, shell beads 93

4.2 European manufactured pottery, (a) coarse earthenwares and (b) stonewares 96

4.3 Locally produced earthenware in Shantok style,
(a) castellation and (b) partial vessel with handle from
large waste pit feature   102

4.4 English flint, (a) flakes and (b) heavily utilized cores   110

4.5 Cloth, clothing, and adornment materials, (a) pins,
(b) thimble "tinkler," (c) rolled brass beads or aglets,
(d) brass scrap rolled to make tinkler cone, and (e) lead
cloth seal with merchant's mark   114

4.6 Metal items with culturally significant motifs, (a) clipped
coin with etched symbols added on both sides, (b) brass
ferrule with etched bands and cross-hatching, and (c) pierced
silver Charles II penny   116

4.7 Clay tobacco pipes, (a) and (b) Sir Walter Raleigh bowls and
stems, (c) and (d) stems stamped with fleur-de-lis design   118

5.1 (a) Quaker memorial monument dedication in 1884 and (b)
monument detail   146

5.2 Youghco stone monument, with detail of engraved text   150

5.3 Stone monument engraved "Burying Ground of the Colored
People of the Manor from 1651," (a) historic photo of burial
ground, probably late nineteenth century and (b) detail of
engraving   151

5.4 Drawing reproduced in Lamb 1887, thought to be
Julia Dyd Havens   156

Table

2.1 Enslaved individuals identified in Nathaniel Sylvester will
of 1679/80   47

Acknowledgments

Since I started with this project, as part of the UMass Boston team in 1997, I have been amazingly fortunate to participate within a number of different intellectual communities—all of them encouraging, supporting, and critiquing my thinking and writing on Sylvester Manor. The first and most constant of these people have been those of the Fiske Center for Archaeological Research at UMass, who have put much time and love into the project. Steve Mrozowski, the director of the center and the PI for the Sylvester Manor project, poured a tremendous amount of time and energy into the planning, running and intellectual shaping of the project and it never would have gone anywhere without his leadership. Under his guidance, and with a generous donation from Mrs. Alice Fiske, the Andrew Fiske Memorial Center for Archaeological Research was established, and the Center to this day fosters great interdisciplinary research. Steve has been very generous, by allowing me to pursue this project as a dissertation and a book, and I would not be where I am without the opportunities he has provided me. I thank him also for his critical reading of this manuscript. David Landon, Heather Trigg, and Dennis Piechota have all been steadfast friends, collaborators, and levelheaded thinkers in this process, and I hope their intellectual influence is evident in this book, along with the data they generously shared. Their warmth and quiet support have helped me more than they likely know, and they have been role models to me. With Steve, David, and Heather as PIs, this project was also supported for four years by the National Science Foundation, Grant Nos. 0243593 and 0552484.

The fieldwork at Sylvester Manor was accomplished through UMass Boston field schools in archaeology between 1999 and 2006, and I thank the countless students who gave up part of their summer to work with us. I was supported by a Fiske Center Pre-dissertation Fellowship one summer, and given work space and access to the collection for which the Center is responsible over the 2006-2007 academic year. A number of fellow students and colleagues shared the data they generated with their research, for which I am grateful: Sarah Sportman, Craig Cipolla, Ryan Kennedy, and Amy Foutch (with David Landon) for faunal analysis; Jack Gary for small finds and for the use of some of his photographs; Eric Proebsting (with Dennis Piechota) for micromorphology; and Sue Jacobucci (with Heather Trigg) for botanical. Craig Cipolla and Steve Silliman have provided inspiring different perspectives with their own work, and I have been grateful for the opportunities over the years to discuss those with them. Other UMass friends have contributed in various ways, especially Melody Henkel and her photographic eye, but also John Steinberg, Anne Hancock, Kate Lommen, Lee Priddy, Paolo DiGregorio, Dave Brown, and so many others. An earlier synthesis of work to date, to which many of these folks contributed, was published as a special issue of Northeast Historical Archaeology in 2007; Steve Mrozowski was coeditor with me on that, and David Landon was the general editor.

On Shelter Island, the project was pushed into being in part by the persistence and enthusiasm of Mac Griswold. She has been there throughout, has provided an encyclopedic knowledge of the documentary and architectural resources, and most recently has been a sympathetic and supportive voice as we both have brought our own writings on Sylvester Manor to fruition. Mac was instrumental in getting the astounding archive of historical materials out of the Manor's leaky vault and into the protective care of the libraries of New York University. The people of the Shelter Island Historical Society, especially Louise Green and Beverlea Walz, contributed greatly to the project overall. Special thanks—the kind of which I can never give enough—go to the people of the Manor itself. Mrs. Alice Fiske, seemingly delighted when we showed up once a year to put new holes into her lawn right outside her front door, opened her home and heart to us. Gunnar Wissemann and Rose Wissemann have been constant presences and institutional memories of the Manor, even since Mrs. Fiske passed away and the place has begun, once again, to undergo rapid change. The family members of Alice and Andrew Fiske who have supported the project and continue to support the preservation and increasing openness of the estate deserve great thanks, especially the current proprietor Eben Ostby for his commitment to the preservation efforts and Bennett Konesni, who has effectively given his whole life to the future of the place, as the Sylvester Manor Educational Farm. I must also thank the representatives of the Shinnecock Nation, especially Elizabeth Haile, who visited the site and engaged in discussions about our approach.

My work with Sylvester Manor as a dissertation project brought me to a wonderful group of advisors, mentors, and colleagues at the University of California, Berkeley. My committee in anthropology was invaluable in this process, and I thank them for their combined wisdom and guidance: Laurie Wilkie, Kent Lightfoot, Rosemary Joyce, and Jennifer Spear. In addition, Mariane Ferme, Christine Hastorf, Steve Shackley, Maury Morgenstein, and Rudy Wenk were all instrumental in various parts of this research, from the scientific to the philosophical. Friends and colleagues in the labs, classrooms, field sites, and bars helped me more than they will ever know. Liz Soluri and Tsim Schneider, special sources of intellectual inspiration and emotional support, have been like family to me and have kept me going in the transition from California to Minnesota. I must also acknowledge gratefully the financial support for my research I received through the Stahl and Lowie-Olson Funds and the Dean's Normative Time Fellowship.

At the University of Minnesota, colleagues in anthropology, history, American Indian Studies, the Locating Heritage collaborative, and the Early American history workshop have read, heard, and commented on various parts of this work. Special thanks go to Hoon Song for his close reading of my framing of forgetting, and Jean O'Brien for both the enormous inspiration of her own work and for reading multiple chapters. Bill Beeman, my department chair, was extremely generous in finagling time off from teaching so I could work on the manuscript, and Karen Ho championed me through the process of book writing. For critically reading and commiserating I thank David Chang, Jimmy Sweet, Brenda Child, Boyd Cothran, and others in the American Indian Studies Workshop; Lisa Norling, Russ Menard, Demetri Debe, Eric Otremba, and the Early American History Workshop; and Greg Donofrio, Kate Solomonson and Phyllis Messenger of the various IAS Heritage collaboratives. Thanks are also due to my students, graduate and undergraduate, for letting me try out ideas on them and tolerating my writing absences.

Many people at various New York institutions touched upon the project and my work. John Strong of Long Island University and David Bernstein of SUNY Stony Brook offered their expert insight. I am especially indebted to Jenny Anderson of Stony Brook for her scholarly and editorial suggestions. Paul Huey of the New York State Office of Parks, Recreation and Historic Preservation (and Fort Orange archaeology fame) cast his eye for Dutch material culture over some of our finds, which was an enormous help. At New York University, I am grateful for the invitation to present my work in progress to the Humanities Initiative Research Working Group, including Karen Kupperman, Pat Crain, and Marvin Taylor. Debbie Gershenowitz of NYU Press, who saw the potential in bringing an archaeological dissertation to a history series, and Tim Roberts of the Early American Places Initiative have been fantastic in getting me through this process. The suggestions and comments of my reviewers were supremely helpful, and I thank them.

Finally, I could not have done this without the support and encouragement of my family, both Howletts and Matsunagas. My parents, Bill and Barbara Howlett, simply never blinked an eye at anything I said I was going to try to do, from becoming an archaeologist, to teaching at a university, to writing this book—they just believed I could. And to John Matsunaga, who has similarly believed in me, and has listened, read, talked through the project, taken photos and prepared figures, and kept me well-fed and sane as needed, no amount of thanks are enough. But he knows that.

Prologue

These days, as in the past, anyone who wishes to visit Shelter Island must travel by water, for there are no bridges spanning the passage. Sturdy ferries, carrying fifteen or so cars on a trip, make the crossing at the north and south ends of the island. Boat travel to me feels like a sidestep into another time, the gentle rolling motion unlike most modern forms of transportation, despite the fact that you can make the ferry trip while sitting in a car. The ferry ride serves as a temporal rupture, a sign perhaps that history here will not perform as expected.

Arriving at the island, visitors find a quaint but bustling village, especially in the summer, as it is a popular destination for its resorts and summer rentals. But when I turn into the imposing gates to the unpaved roadway of the Sylvester Manor estate, I am immediately enveloped in the quietude of the woods. All sounds of traffic are swallowed on the winding way through thick trees and undergrowth covering a rolling topography created by glacial retreat. It is easy to think that the estate land has not been touched by the modern world, much less a plantation with links spanning the Atlantic world of the seventeenth century. I recall thinking so the first time I came to this place, as part of a team of archaeologists beginning in 1997. After many years of working here, I can no longer see it as a "pristine" landscape; instead, it is gravid with historical associations, some learned through stories and archives, others by visceral experience. I see a rough boulder by the roadway with fading letters engraved on it, marking the burial of servants and enslaved persons. There the road forks, one side leading to a second burial ground and memorial to Quakers, while the other leads to fields where, old farm-hands have told us, countless stone arrow points and pieces of locally made pottery have been churned up by plows. Off deep in the undergrowth, I remember seeing a single piece of clay tobacco pipe emerge with a shovelful of dirt.

Eventually a pair of barns appears as the trees thin, right before the turn that reveals the Manor house built by Brinley Sylvester in the 1730s. It is surrounded not by trees, but by expanses of smooth green lawn, dropping gently to the north and west down to Gardiner's Creek, usually home to geese or swans or Great Blue herons. On the east side of the Manor, however, is the two-acre formal garden, still edged by fence and boxwood hedge, now grown a bit wild. Such a garden elicits the later nineteenth century, a romantic Victorian time of wealthy leisure, tea and croquet, ladies in filmy dresses with servants discreetly positioned in the background. The symmetrical, imposing face of the mansion, groomed lawn, and remnants of ornamental gardens betray neither the plantation infrastructure that preceded it nor the indigenous community who long occupied the island. But just there, in the lawn, I see a depression in the ground marking the place where we uncovered a tremendous pit filled with slaughter waste, brick and mortar, fragments of kitchenwares made in the seventeenth century. In the midst of this trash, like a jewel in the rough ("ya gotta see this," the project director Steve told me, pulling on my elbow), colleagues uncovered the whole rim of a pot, beautifully decorated in a style commonly found at sites of colonial-era Native American occupation. That's impossible, I thought . . . but why?

To my eye, the Manor landscape now holds an incredible history, one that in its prosaic, day-to-day activities never made it into documentary records. But I've come to realize that the mundane nature of the perspective is not the only reason this history has eluded our common narratives. The history has been written in a very different way in local memory, and the landscape has been reshaped to support this well-known story, in which Europeans, Native Americans, and enslaved Africans occupy distinct spaces and temporalities. The preservation and representation of certain histories—that which is consciously remembered—stands in stark contrast to the aspects of the past that have been abandoned, torn down, thrown away, and literally buried—a place where the three groups interacted routinely. Having dug beneath the surface of the contemporary landscape and into the stories that are still told of the place, I can no longer see the plantation past in the same way, nor can I accept ideas about race that are fostered in those stories about our colonial beginnings.

1 / Tracing a Racialized History

When Nathaniel Sylvester and his young bride Grissell came to reside on Shelter Island sometime around 1652 or 1653, they might have spoken between themselves about how they had landed in a lonely place, feeling that the two of them had only one another in this unfamiliar land. Writing to his business colleague, Connecticut Colony Governor John Winthrop Jr., Nathaniel commented about his marriage, "I find my selfe very happie and I hope in God wee may be a Confort unto Each Other [sic]." Their comfort likely came from a shared background, shared values, and a shared understanding of their place in society. In the new colonies and in independent settlements like this one, colonists had to adjust to not only a new environment but also a social order without precedent or tradition. This was partly what they had gone to the New World to achieve, but they perhaps had not anticipated the variety of people that they would also have to accommodate in their society, particularly American Indians and Africans.[1]

Nathaniel, one of four partners who sought to supply their sugar plantations on Barbados, had settled here because of a business venture, but he was the only one of the four who would live on this 8,000-acre island. Located between the two forks of eastern Long Island, Shelter Island was also wedged between the Dutch West India Company settlement based in Manhattan to the west and the Puritan New England colonies which had begun settling on the east end of Long Island in the prior decade. Sylvester had encountered diversity in his life; born in Amsterdam of English Separatists, he had traveled widely throughout the Atlantic world in the 1640s as a merchant in the family business, reaching many areas of Europe, the west coast of Africa, the Caribbean, and Virginia, before settling on Shelter Island to attend to the planter side of the business. He had no love for the Puritans despite his Separatist upbringing, and his wife Grissell was the daughter of King Charles II's auditor, in exile with the king following the monarchy's defeat at the hands of the Puritan Cromwell. Thus, to be surrounded by Puritans, as well as the Dutch West India Company, to which he was no more than competition, was not necessarily a friendly neighborhood. Furthermore, the east end was only recently opened to settlement by the English. Indigenous Algonquian tribes there had previously been isolated from colonizer interference while under the protection of the Pequot, but the Pequot War with the English in 1637 had left the Paumanoc (Long Island) confederacy unhappily resigned to the necessity of dealing directly with the English.

The Sylvesters might have been lonely—far from family and a friendly community—but they certainly were not alone. Not only were there settler villages in Southampton, Easthampton, and Southold and the indigenous Montaukett, Shinnecock, and Corchaug in the lands across a short stretch of water from Shelter Island, but they also had their own retinue of servants and laborers quite literally in their back yard. Archived documents and recorded anecdotes suggest that some of these servants and laborers were indentured, and some were enslaved persons captured from Africa, all perhaps arriving at this place via Barbados. By the time of Nathaniel's death in 1680, he claimed to own twenty-three persons, most explicitly identified as Negro, constituting one of the largest holdings of enslaved persons in the New York colony at that time and larger even than the family of eleven children his wife bore who survived to adulthood. In addition, archaeological excavations have shown that the indigenous Manhanset were part of the labor of the plantation, despite documents and anecdotes suggesting their departure at the establishment of the estate. Their skills, technologies, and crafts contributed greatly to the success of the plantation, though their status as laborers—enslaved, indentured, coerced, or free-- remains unknown. The work of the plantation required many hands: construct buildings, tend livestock, plant and harvest crops, load and unload ships as goods of many sorts passed through often to or from Barbados. Nathaniel Sylvester was there to manage this work, not to undertake it himself. To manage effectively he and his partners assembled a heterogeneous group of laborers—African, Native American, and possibly poor English or Irish. Unlike the inhabitants of the Puritan colonies, on Shelter Island Sylvester was not

surrounded by like-minded individuals who shared a religious foundation or even a similar background; rather, his was a precarious community brought together, by coercion if necessary, to serve his interests.
The nature of his relationship with this community is unknown, but it
cannot have been one of ready identification, as demonstrated in his letters to John Winthrop Jr.; he wrote of his family, business transactions,
and international affairs, but never of the people who were physically
closest to his family.

In this historical context, Sylvester would have sought to establish
control over his place in society by constructing categories of affiliation and difference among the diversity of people who surrounded him.
Indeed, this process is at the very heart of colonialism itself (Foucault
1970; Thomas 1994; Pels 1997; Smith 1999; Spivak 1999; Stoler 2002).
While religion and class were hotly debated in the seventeenth-century
North American colonies, perhaps the most contentious long-term issue
was race (Smedley 2007). The classification and justification of racial categories may have been variously framed by colonists and foreign investors in terms of civilization, spirituality, and eventually blood, but the
effective result of the categories was control over labor and land, through
enslavement and allotment. The discourse of racial difference evolved
greatly over the next three hundred years. But in the earliest years of
the Sylvester plantation, still prior to the enactment of laws defining
race-based slavery, lines of difference and affiliation were inchoate,
open to negotiation. Colonists viewed the enslaved and the indigenous
as different, but how? Was it class, spiritual belief, physical difference?
Or simply an economic need for labor? If it were only a need for labor,
then why did they distinguish between African and Indian—both being
viewed as potential laborers? Perhaps most difficult to answer, how did
the enslaved and the indigenous view one another? The case of Sylvester
Manor's plantation provides a rare place to study not only how racial
categorization emerged and evolved but also, by combining archival and
archaeological perspectives, allows the possibility of interpreting multiple experiences, not just those of the white settlers. Furthermore, the
structuring and representation of racialized relations at Sylvester Manor
have been written and overwritten in so many ways that its history, like
its landscape, is a palimpsest. In this rewriting, we can see the evolution
of attitudes about race.

The case of Sylvester Manor's plantation is also significant because
it pushes back at two prevalent and popular misconceptions of American history: first, slavery was never a true institution of the northern

colonies; and second, American Indians had no connection to the history of plantation slavery and indeed little connection to colonial society as a whole. The effect of these ideas has been to create spurious associations of racialized groups with distinct and separate geographies and temporalities. Thus, according to this historical logic, the roots of white American society lie in New England, the origins of black Americans develop in the southern colonies, and Indians, viewed as a race whose demise begins upon the arrival of settlers, are regarded as irrelevant to the history of either. Each of these misconceptions has been challenged by various historical studies, yet there remains a steadfast belief in the mutual exclusion of racial histories as a rule. Such beliefs have ongoing consequences to the way that race is still conceptualized in American society, namely the notion that racial groups, given their relatively isolated histories, have actually been stable categories until recently. Such an idea underwrites the assumption that race and culture are much the same and that both are generally static rather than actively, constantly renegotiated and reproduced (e.g., Smedley 2007; Berlin 2003; Forbes 1993). The notion of racially isolated histories is profoundly misguided, but when we start to look closely at historical records we see that the idea itself has been actively promoted for very particular reasons. These reasons relate to the struggles of both African Americans and Native Americans (self-identified) for their rights of self-determination and the efforts of colonial planters and later the U.S. government to control the labor and land of these peoples. In other words, our misconceptions of racial histories are not simply products of contemporary attitudes; such misconceptions were also deliberately fostered in the past, by colonial authorities, settlers, and government agencies.

To mitigate this misrepresentation, as well as understand its achievement through specific acts, this book explores the plantation of Sylvester Manor through multiple lines of evidence. Archival resources, the mainstay of historians, can include a multitude of different perspectives on racial categorization, from censuses, court documents, personal letters, account books, and even "ethnographic" descriptions of indigenous and enslaved peoples. These representations may be read for hints and suggestions that the predominant views of settlers on race and diversity were not universally accepted. These records are, however, the views of white settlers, and the active voices of American Indians and enslaved Africans are very rarely and never directly heard in them. Furthermore, the records of the archive are necessarily items that at some point were consciously selected for curation out of the universe of records created, and thus their mere inclusion must be queried for the historical value they represent as well as the perspectives they express. Archaeological remains—the material traces of past buildings, landscapes, daily practices of eating, dressing, labor, and leisure—may be thought of, however, as "records" *not* selected. The bulk of archaeological evidence is derived from excavating structures that have been reduced to rubble or decayed through abandonment as well as the mundane rarely recorded trash from day-to-day activities. Different preservation biases impact these materials, but more importantly the materials result from the efforts of past peoples to cover and discard things that they do not wish to remember. For the Sylvesters and their descendants, the materials excluded from memory included the very structure of the plantation itself, in which such a diversity of people lived and worked.

Thus in combining archival and archaeological evidence, we are often able to juxtapose the conspicuous silences in one (for example, the absence of reference to Manhanset laborers) with evidence of activities in the other. Historical archaeology, using both archival and archaeological remains, is an approach that allows for a critical movement between memory and forgetting, curation and abandonment, representation and embodied experience. This means that we can see not only what the physical and material setting of plantation life was like but also how the physical remains of the plantation have been used or discarded as evidence in the production of numerous historical narratives about the plantation over time. Just as the notion of race as a "natural" category has proven mutable, histories of the colonial period are unstable and contingent representations of the past. Indeed, historical narratives arise from the willingness or desire of communities to remember or forget; subsequent generations must in turn rely on the memory and evidence transmitted to them and their own wishes to remember or forget. Unearthing discarded evidence allows us not only to recover excluded histories but also to investigate *how* and possibly *why* they were excluded.[2]

Remembering race

How communities share memory, with whom they share memory, and how they protect or broadcast that knowledge is culturally and historically variable. Memory practices range from the incorporated or embodied reproduction in ritual or daily practice to the inscribed, textual or representational (Mills and Walker 2008; Van Dyke and Alcock 2003). Commemoration in contemporary Western societies tends toward materially weighty texts and depictions, meant to be evident to wide audiences and with an air of permanence by alienating history from its own history of production (Connerton 1989 and 2009). But memory may also be tied to more intimate groups, evoked in embodied associations, understood not as an independent record but as knowledge handled in careful circulation and dependent upon transmission from person to person. Ethnographic examples from Melanesia (Küchler 2002; Harrison 2004) and West Africa (Ferme 2001) have shown how communities may regard some memory as too dangerous to be permanently inscribed, or too widely distributed, because some associations *must* be forgotten. Contemporary valuation of heritage in our society gives the impression that we do not value or seek purposeful, active forgetting, but many scholars would argue that forgetting is critically constitutive of memory and heritage (e.g., Lowenthal 1996, Rowlands 1999, Shackel 2000), including racial heritage.

As the durability of memory lies in entangled networks of people, objects, and landscapes, forgetting is equally complex. In a plural society with multiple remembrances of the past—not all public or inscribed or even recognized as historical evidence—the process impacts both the ongoing construction of history and memories and the recognition of "subaltern" historicity. In archives, for example, Trouillot (1995) has shown the numerous moments where silences—forgetting through failures of transmission—may be introduced, in the creation of historical facts, archives, and narratives. Material memory may be effaced either by outright destruction or iconoclasm or more subtly by separation or exclusion of important associations (Forty 1999). Forgetting may be commanded, by offering amnesty (linked to amnesia) in exchange for abandoning certain historical ties (Ricouer 2004). The very course of modernity, rupturing associations with tradition and dispersing people from familiar places, has been a strain of forgetting on a massive social scale (González-Ruibal 2008; Connerton 2009; Spyer 2000). Each case introduces an active disruption of the associative basis of memory, sometimes replacing one historical narrative with another. Forgetting is made even more complex in its longer-term effects. Subsequent generations may not recognize that rupture or loss, despite the traces of the past haunting the archive or landscape. Yet conflict over historical perspectives—for example, when degrading representations underpinning racism are challenged--may drive descendants to reassemble those associations found in dusty archival shelves or buried under our feet.

Racialized identity emerges through similar performances of association and exclusion. Race is a distinct category of identity assigned to bodies or persons based on a *perception* of physically evident differences, attributed to some kind of embodied, essentialized, and thus ahistorical quality. Even in historical circumstances when the term *race* was not part of conventionally understood language, there may be evidence of discrimination attributed to some bodily or essentialized characteristic. The source of this personal characteristic has been defined in various ways, such as the lack of a Christian soul, capability for civilized behavior, intelligence, evolution. The process of creating those categories, primarily for the purpose of holding other persons or groups in a subordinate position (see Harrison 1995 and 1998; Frederickson 1988 and 2002), has been termed "racialization" or "racial formation" (Omi and Winant 1994, 55). Social scientists suggest that racial formation takes place in both *representations* of difference and social *structure*. This dual formation is critical for the historical evolution and institutionalization of race categories.

To merely label or represent others as belonging to a distinct group is insufficient to debase those persons if a social structure exists that allows them any freedom to act and to choose. But representations may be used in conjunction with social structures to develop long-term structural inequalities. Racial slavery, for example, elicited debasement through physically demanding labor, punishment and surveillance, malnutrition and the destruction of social supports. Such structures were expensive and difficult to morally defend simply as a means of acquiring labor. The inflicted debasement was thus attributed to the essential nature of the enslaved people, a representation used as a means of justifying their enslavement. Likewise in New England, Indians were subjected to land removal and immoderately heavy fines for small legal transgressions, often preventing their ability to make an adequate living, and in turn their poverty was attributed to their "primitive" and uncivilized nature. This tautology serves to mask the white populace's true reasons for their marginalization, which were fear and the desire for more land. Both the structure and representation over time came to be viewed as "natural," as the conditions of their construction are forgotten. Such racial associations have become so ingrained, so primordial in the imagination of white U.S. society that even now, when bodily or biological explanations are long rejected as a basis for racial differences, the categories continue to have pervasive effects. Critical race theorists point out that neoliberal efforts to neutralize racial representations by adopting "colorblind"

policies ignore the historic social structure of racism (Delgado and Stefancic 2001). As philosopher Charles W. Mills noted (2008, 242), "erasure
of the history of Jim Crow makes it possible to depict the playing field as
historically level, so that current black poverty just proves black unwillingness to work. As individual memory is assisted through a larger social
memory, so individual amnesia is then assisted by a larger collective
amnesia."

The investigation of racial representation has long been a subject for
historians, whether in support or in challenge. Early colonists' observations often explicitly referenced skin color and other physical attributes
when discussing Indians or enslaved Africans (Vaughan 1995). Legal
statutes, census records, estate records, and other forms of documentation provide rich evidence of how racial categories were represented
and negotiated in colonial and early Republic America (Johnston 1929;
Lauber 1913; Porter 1932; Woodson 1920 are early compilations of such
sources). Forbes, for example, offered an exhaustive deconstruction of
racial naming, such as "mulatto, pardo, colored, free colored, negro,
zambo or sambo, mustee and mestizo" (Forbes 1993, 3), and indicated
the multitude of racial terms colonial authorities created to police the
borders of white society. He noted that the uncritical reading of those
terms by contemporary historians has obscured the enmeshed histories of African American, Native American, and European peoples.
More recently scholars have explored intermarriage between racialized
groups by attending to how subsequent generations struggle to define
themselves in wider social settings (Mandell 1998 and 2005; Campisi
1991; Barsh 2002; Miles 2002 and 2005; Parm 2005). These studies show
that gender roles are deeply entangled with and disruptive of racial categories, not least because often intermarriage occurred by necessity, as
selective importation of African men coincided with the decimation of
indigenous men through disease and warfare. Whether born of necessity or not, intermarriage demonstrated that racial differences were not
the basis of exclusion from these marginalized communities. However,
a reactionary effort on the part of colonial and U.S. authorities to regain
control of racial representation can be seen in the ever-expanding legal
codes that clarified the status and categorization of the children of intermarriage or later banned miscegenation (Gross 2008; Pascoe 2009).

Historians have also shown that those communities sometimes born
of mutual support by oppressed groups were not always able to evade
hegemonic racial representations. Native American and African American pluralistic communities, created through adoptions and marriages,

were later subjected to racial categorization as part of nineteenth-century federal and state efforts at detribalization and privatization of communal Indian properties. These efforts ultimately targeted social structures, especially communal ownership of property, but used racial representations to instill dissent and conflict among community members (Mandell 1998; Halliburton 1977; Saunt 2004 and 2005; Sweet 2003; Chang 2010). This complex history, quite evident in the Northeast, plays a significant role in tribal politics even today. Unexamined racial representations still structure the work of some contemporary historical scholars as we continue to presume the association or exclusion of racialized groups with particular objects, places, and times. For example, popular histories reproduce the "invisibility" of enslaved Africans in northern colonies (Melish 1998), of Indians in settings of modernity (Deloria 2006; O'Brien 2010), or of the pluralistic communities forged between them (Mathis and Weik 2005). In fact, their supposed invisibility has less to do with their presence or absence than with our expectations.

Social structure, however, is not only reproduced in discursive representation, but it is also lived in embodied and material realms. Archival records often do contain references to aspects of social structure, but the most habitual and naturalized aspects of daily life are rarely noted. In this arena, archaeological remains can contribute perspectives on the *experience* of racial formation. Archaeological work at plantation sites in southern United States and the Caribbean has not only well demonstrated the repressive structuring of space and daily activities, but it has also shown many acts of resistance and covert cultural maintenance on the part of the enslaved (e.g., Franklin 2001; McKee 1992; Fennell 2007; Wilkie and Farnsworth 2005). These illustrate social structure in planter/enslaved relations. Social relations among disenfranchised individuals and communities have also been addressed in other colonial settings outside plantations. Interethnic/interracial unions have been explored at the household level in Spanish missions and Russian colonial settlements, showing a complex restructuring of living spaces and cultural practices like foodways and bodily adornment (Deagan 1983; Lightfoot and Martinez 1997; Lightfoot et al. 1998). Communities of fugitives from enslavement (maroon or cimarron) were very often assisted by free indigenous persons, or fugitives were simply taken into indigenous communities. Where those places are documented, archaeologists have been able to investigate the material conditions and contexts of their interactions (Sayers et al. 2007; Funari 1999; Weik 1997 and 2009; Deagan and MacMahon 1995). The spatial structuring of the plantation at Sylvester

Manor, where Manhanset and enslaved African laborers worked in close proximity but in spaces designed by the Sylvesters, demonstrates a complex negotiation of social order and tactical resistance between planters and labor. On a smaller spatial scale, certain material items may lend themselves to questions of shared production practices or reuse of goods. For example, Colono-ware pottery, a low-fired locally made ceramic, has been found in many plantation sites and native villages demonstrating a blending of technology, style, and form among African, Native, and European traditions (Ferguson 1992 and 1999; Mouer et al. 1999; Smith 1995). A close examination of locally produced pottery at Sylvester Manor has demonstrated a similar sharing of technological practices, as I discuss in detail in chapter 4.

Representation and social structure may be considered the balancing arms of racial formation, each informing the other. Though archives and archaeological material do not address these as mutually exclusive aspects, the combination of evidence may provide a more comprehensive view of the evolving experience of race than either one alone. Mediating between racial formations and traces of the past are memory and forgetting. Memory is embedded in the habitual and daily practices through which social structure is reproduced as well as selective and self-conscious representations of the past. When social memory is configured through the active processes of replicating associations in multiple media and repetitive action, it is astonishingly durable. But it is also important to recognize that the temporal unfolding of memory is non-linear and that forgetting, whether by benign decay or active erasure, is continually acting upon that process.

I view social memory, the selective transmission and representation of historical narratives through communities and generations, as an important part of the way racial ideologies emerge and evolve, in both the case of Sylvester Manor and the later economic and cultural development of the United States. At Sylvester Manor, enslaved labor was foundational to the plantation and the financial enterprise in which the family was involved at a time when racial categories were still fluid. I argue that the incorporation of Native Americans in plantation settings played a significant role in how colonizers thought about the distinction and status of non-Europeans. In particular, the potential for collaborations between indigenous people and captive African labor came to be viewed as a threat to the control of colonists, who in turn used racial categories as a means to sever those associations. The archaeology has shown that complex entanglements of Europeans, Native Americans, and enslaved

Africans were a daily reality of the plantation. But this social setting has been neither included in local historical memory nor recognized as possible in popular national narratives of colonial society. The subsequent reshaping of the landscape and the commemoration of the plantation residents by Sylvester descendants drastically simplified and separated the remembrance of the early labor populace into distinct racial categories, which may not have been at play at the time. This implicates a process of abstraction and forgetting on the part of Sylvester descendants and the reification of wider national racial ideologies. In the eighteenth century, this reshaping of memory was undertaken by the later Sylvester generations to situate themselves in a more elite class by casting off earlier associations with provisioning and commerce. At the same time, they rejected connections to traditional European hierarchies, as the colony as a whole moved toward revolution. By the nineteenth century, representations of race were inflected with national concerns about slavery and citizenship for African Americans and about the conflicted status of Native Americans as sovereign nations or citizens. Both sets of concerns hinged in part on the ability to distinguish racial categories as readily identifiable and immutable, encoded in bodies. These larger, national discourses were reproduced by the residents of Sylvester Manor, guiding the commemoration and silences in the way the estate's past was remembered.

Thus the way that societies forget, beyond either a passive neglect or an active destruction indicative of struggles for power, has critical implications. Forgetting creates the very conditions for new forms of subjectivity like race. It is only possible to maintain the fiction of immutable, isolated racial categories, if the entangled past has been effaced.

Why does it matter? Citizenship and sovereignty

The representation of race as immutable in historical memory has had real and ongoing effects. Racial categorization has both justified and been reiterated by historical efforts to efface transgressive multiracial communities. Even prior to the introduction of blood quantum measures to state and federal laws, the advent of censuses and other documentary records of racial identification betray the ease with which "documentary genocide" could occur (Herndon and Sekatau 1997) when a multitude of racial distinctions—like Indian, negro, mulatto, mestizo, mustee—become conflated under a single term, such as "colored." Later "colored" might be read in the records as unambiguously black (Forbes 1993). The census or record designation of the same person might also have varied widely over a number of years, being recorded as "negro" in one instance, "Indian" in another, and "mustee" in a third. The documentation of racial designation reflected the perspective of the recorder or census enumerator, not the person in question. For federal censuses, this was true until relatively recently. Such assignments of identity were made based on the recorder's assessment of racial associations: appearance, cohort or family, or status of servitude. Thus, it might be possible for a Native person to be designated a slave, then legally kept in that category through the precedence of the original designation; the equation of slavery with race dictated that, if the person had been documented as enslaved, then he or she must have been black. Such was the power of the colonial legal system to designate the identity and fate of nonwhite people.

By the later nineteenth century, however, racial exclusions took on the character of commanded forgetting. Ironically, systematic efforts, which were most devastating to individuals and communities of mixed ancestry, took place in the wake of the 14th Amendment to the Constitution to extend citizenship to those formerly enslaved. The Jim Crow laws that were enacted by many states following the Civil War afforded a well-known route to categorizing communities and bodies. Without the institution of slavery to determine race relations, these laws dictated the separation of the races, in not only public places and schools but also marriages (prohibiting miscegenation). The execution of Jim Crow laws depended on the ability of authorities to identify a person as of a particular race and, in the cases of mixed ancestry, to determine the appropriate singular category of a person. The laws were predominantly concerned with separating African Americans, although a small number specifically restricted Indians as well (Perdue 2009; Pascoe 2009). Under these laws, people who might have considered themselves part of an Indian community but were perceived to have "black" physical characteristics would have found their cultural affiliations to be inconsequential to the law. Legal historian Ariela Gross (2008, 138) has noted, "Indian communities which had welcomed African Americans at one point in their history, as well as racially ambiguous communities with varied ancestry, faced enormous pressure during this era to comply with the new rules of Jim Crow." The reversion of identity from community to singular racial category had consequences throughout Indian country (e.g., Lowery 2010).

In this same period, many states were in the process of "enfranchising" Indian communities by detribalizing them. The rhetoric employed in these efforts suggested that dissolving the tribal communities in favor of individual rights of citizenship reflected a gesture of civil rights and a desire of the paternalistic white society to bring these wayward groups into the fold of civilized life (Mandell 2008; Plane and Button 1993). This process was tremendously paradoxical: to finally (in theory) sever the association of Indians from their tribal community, the Indians first had to be recognized *as members of that community* because detribalization also meant that tribal lands would be allotted to individuals or families to hold as private property (thus making its sale or seizure for payment of debt subject only to the agreement of the owner, not the tribe), while the state often acquired surplus communal land. But who "counted" as a tribal member in this process? This question was fraught with issues of race and gender. For example, in Massachusetts, the Indian Enfranchisement Act of 1869 was preceded by numerous community hearings in which the question of citizenship and allotment were raised, and tensions over insiders and outsiders fell hard upon households with people of African American ancestry. The Mashpee clarified the issue in their own community: outsiders never came to be considered Indian, although their children, if the mother was Indian, were also Indian. Some African American husbands accepted this, but many did not (Plane and Button 1993). In essence, however, the determination amounted to a rejection or exclusion of non-Indian, particularly black, ancestry.

The Narragansett of Rhode Island were also subjected to detribalization, in 1880. In their case, it became clear that the issue of race was assigned far greater significance by the state committee overseeing the process than by the Narragansett themselves, who instead privileged most highly participation in community. For example, the committee considered race to be a pertinent factor in the decision to pursue detribalization: "there were no more 'pure Indians' and the color ranged from 'Caucasian to the Black race'" (cited in Boissevain 1956). Yet in making determinations of tribal membership, for the distribution of the proceeds from the communal land, race was rejected as exclusionary criteria. All persons who had rights to the use of communal lands were considered Indians, and the committee had to acknowledge that adoption of "outsiders" was a known practice of many Eastern Algonquian groups. Far more problematic was a second criteria--regular engagement in tribal affairs (Boissevain 1956). The strength of the Narragansett community continued despite detribalization and regained part of their reservation land and recognition as a tribal nation by the federal government a century later (Herndon and Sekatau 1997). Indeed, despite detribalization the failure to disappear of numerous native groups, who either have already been re-recognized or are currently petitioning for recognition, indicates the tremendous misapprehension of Indian identity on the part of white New England society (O'Brien 2010, 191–199).

Detribalization and the push to citizenship reached the national level in the Dawes General Allotment Act of 1887. This federal law allowed for the distribution of land parcels to tribal members who were given American citizenship thereby extinguishing communal title, and after an extended period of holding in trust the law allowed the property owner to dispose of the land as he or she wished. Allotment required enrollment, the creation of federally sanctioned tribal memberships, which depended upon identification of lineage or "blood." The law also established standard parcel areas and dictated that surplus land, after parcels had been allotted, must be sold (Wilkins and Stark 2011, 127–128). Racial rhetoric again came to bear in the federal allotment process, particularly among the Five Tribes of the southeast--Creek, Cherokee, Choctaw, Chickasaw, and Seminole--removed by then to Oklahoma. Until the conclusion of the Civil War, some of these tribes had allowed slavery, and some of their communities had fought on the side of the Confederates; the U.S. peace treaty with them had required that they not only free their enslaved people (the last in the country to be so emancipated) but also grant them citizenship in the tribal nations. This citizenship requirement was resented greatly by some in the tribes, and perhaps for the first time the benefits of emancipation, freedom for African Americans, came into direct conflict with sovereignty, the freedom of self-governance for Native nations (e.g., Saunt 2004). Furthermore, like many in the Eastern Algonquian communities, some Five Tribes Indians had either married or had children with enslaved African Americans. For the freedmen and persons of mixed ancestry, the enrollment and allotment processes were critical moments determining how much the perception of race mattered (Chang 2010; Miles 2005).

The enrollment and allotment process effectively enforced an exclusion of ambiguous or heterogeneous communities and instead rewarded those who could claim "purer," racially isolated histories. Although this moment of racial categorization and rending of communities had already happened to many tribes in New England, the execution of the Dawes Act among these larger Native nations brought national attention to the issue of how race (or "blood") and culture had become the same in the minds of most Americans. Jim Crow and tribal enrollment also enacted a widespread forgetting by officially assigning racial identities to large numbers of Black and Indian people, such that history could be ignored. These identifications would be a genealogical or blood standard to which all subsequent inquiries could refer, despite the fact that they were deeply flawed and biased racial assignments, creating the illusion that easy distinctions between racialized populations existed.

Remembering slavery before race, and race after slavery

My goal in this book is to investigate the details of Sylvester Manor's early plantation community, comprised of colonizing Europeans, enslaved Africans, and indigenous Eastern Algonquians, in order to trace the negotiations of affiliation and difference between them and the subsequent replacement of that more complex story with a simpler one reflecting national discourses on race. Thus, my concern is not only to reveal what seems to have taken place there but also to show the many subtle and complex ways that history is forgotten—or at least, forgotten by some. This study is grounded in the social setting and events of the seventeenth century, from settlement of Shelter Island by the Sylvesters in 1652 and establishment of a provisioning plantation to the cessation of the provisioning enterprise, sometime before the turn of the eighteenth century. But the analytical lens that I use to understand the enduring significance of that period is one of memory and forgetting; that is, I trace the representations of the plantation past at Sylvester Manor through the subsequent centuries as well. My explorations of broader national narratives of race relations, as well as the resistance of marginalized communities to them even to this day, take me to events and places beyond the confines of the estate. Those discourses, circulating through the enduring landscape of this place, have inflected the representation of its history.

Thus the exploration of Sylvester Manor begins with the settings most obscured to our modern historical sensibilities, when plantations were diverse amalgamations of people and slavery was ambiguously linked with racial identity, and ends with a setting in which racial categories are adamantly represented as historically isolated *after* the abolishment of slavery. The structuring and experience of the early plantation can be interpreted from the archival material and the archaeological remains, each of the remnants surviving from active processes of destruction undertaken by the children and grandchildren of Nathaniel and Grissell Sylvester. Artifacts and the traces of the past landscape in particular demonstrate clearly that little distinction was drawn between African and Indian, at least in the early years. But my aim is not simply to demonstrate what might have otherwise been remembered if those remains had been kept intact. Those processes of destruction and disregard by subsequent generations of Sylvester descendants worked toward a refinement and revision of racial ideologies, in concert with events far from the estate. This culminated in 1884 with a commemorative landscape; that landscape situated the histories of Europeans, Africans, and Indians literally at a distance from one another and marked each group in its own temporally secluded realm. The weighty stone monuments offer, to this day, a testament to the effort to secure this racially exclusionary history in replacement of the more entangled one lying underfoot and out of sight.

2 / Convergence

Contrary to popular historical depictions, Europeans did not arrive to a find terra nullius in the New World; likewise, history did not begin with their arrival. To understand the relationships and interactions of European colonists and Native Americans in southern New England and coastal New York, we must first look to Native histories prior to European colonization. The social structures in place here played a significant role in the ability of English and Dutch to establish and expand colonial settlements.

Southern New England and Long Island were ecologically rich and diverse environments that, by the Late Woodland period (one thousand to five hundred years before present [BP]) were supporting increasing populations in a variety of subsistence and settlement types. Scholars of historical linguistics suggest that the residents of this area descend from a common group of Proto-Algonquian speakers, dating to the beginning of the Woodland period (ca. 2,700 years BP) (Snow 1980; Ritchie 1980). As there is no contemporaneous archaeological evidence of population replacement, this group was probably created by introducing migrants to the existing peoples, for example through adoption, marriage, and community expansion by incorporating Algonquian newcomers from the west (Bragdon 1996, 32–34). The people of the Northeast were later separated from the wider pool of Algonquian speakers by the influx of Iroquoian groups moving north and west into New York and Pennsylvania; thus the residents of the Northeast are distinguished as Eastern Algonquians (Bragdon 1996; Goddard 1978). Eastern Algonquians throughout the Northeast shared many cultural affinities, likely maintained by a partially mobile population, and some scholars have argued that they also developed social connections with Iroquoian groups who were not of the same linguistic ancestry (Chilton 1998, 137–138), a point that becomes important in understanding the colonial period tribal polities. Within this larger Eastern Algonquian sphere, tribes living in eastern Long Island, including the Manhanset of Shelter Island and the Montaukett, Shinnecock, and Corchaug had closest cultural ties to Southern New England, instead of to their neighbors to the west and south in New York (Solecki 1950, 8–10). The Eastern Long Island groups were recognized in the colonial period as the Paumanoc confederacy (Ales 1979; Tooker 1911, 182–184; see map on page 27).

Much of what we know of these historical trajectories is derived from the integration of archaeological, ethnohistorical, and oral historical sources. These can be summarized through three major themes of cultural change and practices immediately prior to the settlement of European colonists, which greatly influenced the nature of colonial encounters: subsistence, settlement types, and political structures (regional spheres of interaction and exchange).

Subsistence: New England's precolonial history has typically been periodized based on distinctive changes in subsistence strategies. The models that archaeologists have often used are, however, based on quite different, noncoastal areas, like the Paleoindian period seen in western North America or the Archaic and early Woodland periods in Iroquois upstate New York. The Paleoindian period (12,500–10,000 years BP) is characterized by specialized megafauna hunting; the Archaic period (10,000–2,700 years BP) is characterized by diversified, broad-spectrum hunting, gathering, and fishing; and the Woodland period (2,700–500 years BP) is characterized by specialization again, with the introduction and intensification of agriculture, primarily of maize, beans, and squash (Snow 1980; Ritchie 1980). But archaeological evidence, especially botanical remains, interpreted in the past several decades suggests that this model does not fit for the coastal New England/New York area (Bernstein 2006). Very few Paleoindian sites have been recovered in the Northeast, and none in the coastal zones, due to the rising sea- levels. In fact, the earliest coastal sites are dated to sometime between 3,000 and 2,000 years BP (Lightfoot et al. 1987, 27–28). Further inland, environmental studies also increasingly support the notion that a reasonably diverse range of plant species would have been available in addition to the megafauna in the earliest periods of New England human history (Bernstein 2006).

Evidence from coastal sites also often directly contradicts the models that emphasize agricultural development during the Woodland period or more often indicates a difference in the degree to which such intensification occurred. Refinement and synthesis of radiocarbon dates across southern New England and Long Island have shown that prior to 1,400 years BP, adoption of maize agriculture by Eastern Algonquians was rare and isolated, a timing that does not coincide with the beginning of the Woodland period as 2,700 BP (Little 2002). Even when maize agriculture was practiced, its significance in their diet was variable. For Iroquois communities, maize became quite central (Bradley 1987), but in southern New England it may have comprised only one among many contributing foods. A study of bone isotope ratios of a burial population on Nantucket Island showed that in the Late Woodland period, the majority of dietary intake was still derived from marine sources (Little and Schoeninger 1995). Many coastal groups, appearing to have never practiced agriculture, instead relied on gathered plant foods and the rich supply of local marine resources in much the same fashion as they had since the Archaic period (Bernstein 1993 and 2006; Lightfoot et al. 1987; Lightfoot and Cerrato 1988). Why then have archaeologists been so preoccupied with the model positing the development of agriculture? In part, this reflects a continued reliance on the notion of social evolution, in which agriculture (yielding surplus food production) is necessary for the development of complex society. But the observations of early colonial explorers and settlers may also play a role. Bragdon (1996) posits that the preoccupation of regional archaeologists with the idea that agriculture provided staple foods stems from the early explorers' and settlers' emphasis on finding fertile soils to plant, making even rare observations of planting fields central to many of their descriptions of Native communities.

Although there is remarkable continuity of subsistence in many coastal groups, including the people of Shelter Island, this should not be taken to mean that their cultural practices remained static. In fact, the utilization of shellfish became quite important in two later developments in nonsubsistence technologies: the use of shell temper in ceramics, and the production of shell beads, commonly referred to as wampum (Ceci 1990b). Furthermore, contrary to demographic models predicting that agricultural production induces increased sedentism, many groups that continued a hunter-gatherer-fisher subsistence also became less mobile over time. Coastal Algonquians thus adopted agriculture quite variably, but they more consistently relied on particular locations for longer-term residence. Where agriculture was practiced, crops included maize, beans, and squash; in addition tobacco was raised for ceremonial or recreational uses (Strong 1997; Bragdon 1996; Mrozowski 1994).

Settlement patterns are best understood regionally for Woodland period sites, owing to better preservation and larger sites resulting from increased populations. Eastern Algonquians had a clear preference in southern New England for either riverine/river-valley areas or coastal and estuarine areas. As with subsistence, settlement types were variable and do not fit well with generalized models. Riverine areas did support the more expected type of semisedentary settlements, with three-season or year-round occupation and incorporating agricultural produce to a greater degree (Bragdon 1996, 71–74). Coastal and estuarine territories supported people who were less dependent on cultivation and yet were variably mobile. On Long Island, for example, studies of shell seasonality indicate sites with longer occupation cycles in later periods, up to year-round occupation, with an ambiguous or complete lack of dependence on agriculture (Bernstein 2002; Lightfoot et al. 1987; Lightfoot and Cerrato 1988). As there are no identifiable patterns of site types for these environments, an issue among coastal archaeologists has been how to qualify the degree of sedentism exhibited by these Late Woodland communities. Although most sites appear to have been reoccupied, indicating periods in and out of residence, Native movement appears to have occurred between a consistent set of sites; that is, communities were mobile within their estuarine/coastal environments, the boundaries of which may have been determined by political affiliation (Bragdon 1996, 58–60, 77–78). This sort of site grouping has been identified on Shelter Island itself, where a cluster including shell middens, lithic (stone) quarries and workshops, field camps, plant collection and processing areas, and a residential base, taken together, define the broader settlement (Lightfoot et al. 1987, 122–131).

Another ongoing debate among the region's archaeologists revolves around the question of whether larger village aggregation sites existed in this period, especially for those riverine or uplands communities that did implement intensified agricultural production. Models of population growth hypothesize that increased subsistence production and population should lead to larger settlements as part of the evolving settlement pattern of increased sedentism. This has been the case in Iroquois territories in upstate New York, where longhouse clusters were often fortified (Bradley 1987; Ritchie 1980); however, similar sites have not been located archaeologically in New England. The paucity of large settlements has two possible explanations. First, perhaps such sites were never established; instead, as population increased, the density of smaller dispersed sites also increased. Or, second, larger village sites were established, but they are archaeologically inaccessible, given the tendency of encroaching colonial populations to build upon just these sites, simply because they were the most desirable locations (Hasenstab 1999; Ceci 1990a; Thorbahn 1988). Presuming the former, even when southern New England indigenous groups incorporated cultivation as part of their subsistence production, they probably remained fairly mobile. If this were done within circumscribed areas, their "residential bases" may have more resembled the type of settlement described by Lightfoot and his colleagues, for coastal hunter-gatherer-fishers but with planted fields as part of the related sites. This would fit with Roger Williams's early seventeenth-century description of Narragansett practice: "when 'tis warme Spring, then they remove to their fields where they plant Corne . . . when the worke of one field is over, they remove house to the other" (R. Williams 1973, 128). The sole planting site recovered archaeologically in southern New England, at Sandy's Point on Cape Cod, showed repeated reoccupation in similarly light and portable structures, with evidence of shellfish and fish collection and processing at the same location (Mrozowski 1994; Howlett 2002). This suggests that the incorporation of agriculture did not preclude mobility, just as the continuation of hunter-gatherer subsistence did not preclude increasing sedentism. The subsistence and settlement practices likely had implications for the political network that tied the various groups of the area together.

Political structuring: The diversity of resources and relative mobility of southern New England populations suggest that, despite the potential lack of major aggregation sites, a high degree of interregional interaction occurred. Although colonial records and observations best show this, both among the various tribal entities in the coastal region and between coastal and uplands territories extending into Massachusetts and the Hudson River Valley, archaeological materials from earlier periods also support this hypothesis. Indeed, there is a high degree of stylistic similarity of material culture, such as lithics and ceramics, over a rather broad area of New England for much of the Woodland period (Lavin 2002). Great Lakes region cherts, for example, have been recovered in small amounts across New England from sites of any period, indicating long-distance exchange (Luedtke 1993; Calogero 2002; Ritchie 2002). This was once thought to reflect eastern Algonquian adoption of Iroquoian material culture, but more recent approaches have emphasized the variability of technological practices by community, rather than focusing on the stylistic motifs or forms of artifacts (Chilton 1996; 1998; 1999a; 1999b; Goodby 1994). The ceramic material provides a particularly illustrative case, in not only technological variability but also functionality. The Woodland period is sometimes referred to as the "ceramic" period, and the adoption of ceramic manufacture was fairly ubiquitous in southern New England. Although most communities made ceramic vessels, their uses could be quite different. Chilton (1996) has suggested that, coincident with the variability in agricultural practices, ceramic vessels may have been used in some instances for cooking while in others simply for storage. Regardless of use, similar decorative motifs have been found on vessels over a very broad swath of eastern Algonquian territory.

While archaeology supports a pattern of steadily increasing population and interaction through the Woodland period and colonial records document a number of specific intertribal interactions in that later period, we unfortunately cannot assume the specificity of those relationships in the precolonial past. The colonizers induced drastic demographic changes via epidemics that transformed social and political interactions between indigenous groups. Although population estimates vary, archaeologists generally have agreed that 80 to 90 percent of the region's indigenous population died in two major epidemics in 1616–1619 and 1633 (Bragdon 1996, 24–26). In the wake of such devastation, major political voids were opened; ironically, the struggles of the survivors to fill this void provide the most detailed accounting of the tribal entities and interrelationships in the records of Dutch and English colonists. These records hint at the types of social relations that existed previously, if not the specific configurations.

Political leadership was held in the position of the *sachem* (or *sagamore*, in some areas), which was a partly hereditary office, but it is important to note the significant overlap between the ideologies of kinship and political authority. While each community generally had such an office, a higher-ranking territorial sachem might hold political sway over several lower-ranked sachems and their people in relationships that were viewed as tributary by the English (Bragdon 1996, 140–168). The power of such a high-ranking sachem might be acquired via warfare, but colonial observers noted that the offices were more typically obtained and held through persuasion and subtler influence, such as promises of protection or desired materials. Eric Johnson (1993, 1999) has speculated that such a political configuration may have been the result of a more dispersed and mobile population that could "vote with its feet."

These larger confederacies, necessarily smaller in scope than that of exchange spheres, have been categorized by some anthropologists as chiefdoms (Bragdon 1996; see Earle 1987). While the analytical utility of such categorizations has been much questioned, an important aspect of this as gleaned from ethnohistoric observations is that the existence of a sachemship implied hierarchical relations. Such hierarchical relations furthermore appear to have been most pronounced in the coastal regions (Bragdon 1996, 44–49).

These aspects of eastern Algonquian cultural life in the period prior to European settlement—variability of subsistence economy, mobility within circumscribed territories, and political interaction through promises and persuasion—would all become critical in the relationships formed with English and Dutch colonists. As in any "culture contact" situation, there was a high degree of misunderstanding and often the documented interactions emphasized differences between settlers and indigenous. For the new circumstances created, however, it is important to also recognize the aspects that formed commonalities, or "communities of interest" as Siminoff (2004, 3) has termed those interactions. Because of the shared interests, those circumstances of early encounters cannot be said to have been completely controlled by either Europeans or Native Americans.

Dutch and British settlement history

Coastal New England and New York had been explored by a handful of intrepid profit-seeking Europeans in the sixteenth and early seventeenth centuries, notably Verrazano, de Champlain, Gosnold, Pring, Hudson, Smith, and so on (see Karr 1999). These voyages, though not detailed here, were important to the subsequent settlements because they provided colonists with some advance description of the riches and perils to be anticipated. British and Dutch colonists alike were interested in the New World not merely as a place in which to establish a new home but critically as a place from which to extract profit. Reports and maps from these voyages, made available as published texts, were apparently read closely.

Recent historical syntheses of colonialism in the northeast United States, and particularly the southern New England/Long Island Sound region, may be thought of as inherently comparative, simply because the multiple colonies established with different goals very often came into contact and conflict. One effective means of utilizing this comparative viewpoint is the Atlantic perspective: rather than dividing consideration by colonizer nationality, the Atlantic perspective considers the commonalities and exchanges of Atlantic seaboard colonies. As Taylor has noted, this view draws on "the complex and continuous interplay of Europe, Africa, and colonial America through the transatlantic flows of goods, people, plants, animals, capital, and ideas" (Taylor 2001, xiv). The Long Island Sound region saw both Dutch and British colonies established, each of which had to negotiate their enterprises with the indigenous groups as neighbors and trading partners. Furthermore, each colony incorporated a small but important number of enslaved Africans within their communities. A brief overview of the colonization chronology will establish the diversity of these communities, especially the diversity in their aims.

The first permanent colonial settlement in southern New England was Plymouth, established in 1620 by English religious dissenters. Plymouth Colony was followed shortly by Massachusetts Bay (1630), Connecticut (1636), New Haven (1637), and Providence (1636), all established by English settlers. These were hardly a coherent set of political entities at the outset, however. Massachusetts Bay Colony, while founded by Puritans, was established by royal charter, as was Connecticut. Rhode Island was founded by Roger Williams, however, following his expulsion from Massachusetts. Religious beliefs and increase of profits for charter investors were major motivations for colonial expansion at the administrative level, but settlers also arrived with the intention to stay, coaxing other English to come by appeal to potential for personal wealth. Historian Faren Siminoff has proposed that one commonality to the mode of colonization practiced by the English was the mindset of "peopling and planting." Legitimate possession of lands had to consist in both community establishment and in "improving" the land, primarily by planting on it (Siminoff 2004, 36–37). She and others have noted that this philosophy also provided the English with justification for appropriation of lands from the indigenous populations still very much present at this time, as the English understanding of land improvement was scarcely seen practiced by the Native Americans they encountered (Siminoff 2004; Cronon 1983). For the English colonists, the practices of field enclosure signaled productive use of the landscape (see also M. Johnson 1996). English "peopling and planting" clearly did not align with the subsistence and settlement strategies of Eastern Algonquians.

In 1643, in an effort to establish common ground and present a united front, the English colonies established a governing body in the United

Colonies Commission (Pulsifer 1859, vol. 1). In its founding articles of confederation, the colonial signatories declared that "wee all came into these parts of America wth one and the same end and ayme namely to advaunce the Kingdome of or Lord Jesus Christ and to enjoy the liberties of the Gospell in puritie wth peace [sic]" Pulsifer 1859, 1: 3). The articles described the procedures of assembly and also noted that one purpose of the confederation was protection from unruly elements, both foreign (i.e., Indians) and local (i.e., servants and slaves). During the subsequent fifteen years, a tremendous proportion of the Commission's attention was given to the management of Indian affairs, attending to "how all the Jurisdic[tio]ns may carry it towards the Indians, that they neither grow insolent no[r] be injured wthout due satisfac[tio]n, lest warr break in vpon the Confederates through such miscarryages [sic]" (Pulsifer 1859, 1: 6). The Commission assured that the colonies shared the expense and distribution of the Society for the Propagation of the Gospel in New England by supporting Englishmen who would learn the various Algonquian dialects in order to better "encourage" conversion to Christianity and all its material rewards. It did not take long for the diverse English colonies to begin identifying themselves at least in part as a coherent group that needed to stand together in the face of the unknown and frightening Native population.

Dutch colonists established themselves in the area under a somewhat different paradigm than religious freedom, of which they already boasted. The Dutch colony in the Northeast was founded under a corporate charter (rather than a royal charter) as the New Netherland Company, later succeeded by the Dutch West India Company (WIC), which was granted broad monopolistic trading rights by the government of the United Provinces (Foote 2004, 25). The Company's earliest foothold in 1614 was on the Hudson River, in present-day Albany, as Fort Nassau/Fort Orange, a location chosen for its proximity to trade commodities. From indigenous groups in the upper Hudson River valley region Dutch merchants purchased furs, which were then easily transported back to the transatlantic ships (Rothschild 2003, 63–64). To provide further protection for this outpost, the New Amsterdam settlement (presently New York City) was established in 1625, a venture that was strictly controlled by the Company (Taylor 2001, 251–255; Huey 1988, 14–42). Because of these foundations in trade, the Dutch colony's understanding of territorial possession lay not in the English mode of development and control of the land but rather in "touching and trading," claiming title in whatever manner possible and engaging in trade relationships (Siminoff

2004, 34–36). Dutch colonies, although less populous than the English, attempted to lay claim to a much more expansive territory to control trade. The difference in colonization philosophies inevitably lead to conflict between these colonies, over land disputes and relationships with indigenous groups. Of note, the Dutch WIC did manage to arrange an exclusive trade relationship with the Pequot, of the Connecticut coast, for wampum (Siminoff 2004, 28–29). This type of arrangement was typical of the Dutch strategy of controlling territories without occupying them.

Emergence of new Atlantic communities

Another popular but unsupportable perception of the colonization of New England, bolstered by nineteenth-century authors' romanticized versions of "first settlers" history, is that colonial authorities and independent towns were clearly dominant groups and unified in their aims to control new territories. Instead, English and Dutch settlers struggled amongst themselves to achieve their goals and had to negotiate and compromise with the eastern Algonquians they encountered. Although epidemics had taken a toll on indigenous groups, they still approached their encounters with Europeans with confidence that they could control, if not dominate, the situation. As a result, a new hybrid community developed, which Siminoff (2004, 9) described: "neither static, monolithic groups nor interests existed or prevailed in the region; the community rested on and comprised a multitude of groups and interests whose interactions wove a pattern for the emerging Atlantic American society."

European settlers in New England and New York during the early seventeenth century found a reduced but active indigenous presence, following at least one major epidemic that had ravaged the population around 1616–1619. The major groups Europeans encountered included the Massachusett, Pautucket/Penacook, Wampanoag/Pokanoket, Narragansett, Pequot/Mohegan, and Montaukett (see figure 1.1). Some of these groups had established powerful territorial control over their neighbors in the wake of the demographic disasters. The Pequot, for example, holding many groups, including the Paumanoc Long Island confederacy, in tributary status, accepted gifts for which they provided the promise of freedom from harassment and protection from others (Siminoff 2004; Ales 1979).[1] In the regional hierarchy this meant the Pequot leader was a higher-ranked sachem over all others. Such control also granted use-rights over territories, in the manner that lower-ranked sachems wielded power over their own groups, and this right also extended to the power

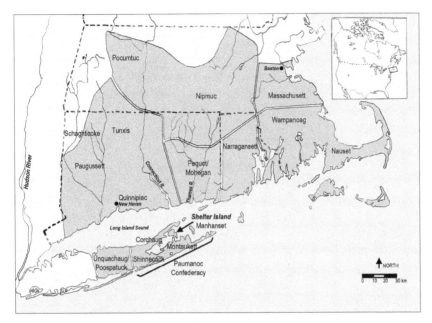

FIGURE 1.1. Coastal/Eastern Algonquian tribal territories (Southern New England and Long Island) at the time of earliest European settlement; settler-named towns and rivers indicated in italics, modern states by dotted lines. Map drawn by John Matsunaga.

to sell land to the colonizers. In some cases, powerful sachems reserved the sole right to negotiate with the English or the Dutch in any sort of transactions, whether an agreement of friendship or trade (Bragdon 1996). If the larger tributary system was an effect of the early colonial demographic changes, then sachems may have begun to maintain their authority through threat or exercise of violence to a greater extent than in earlier times. Under this subordinate status the tributary groups understandably often chafed, particularly the Mohegan, a closely related neighboring tribe whose leader, Uncas, had aspirations of his own (E. Johnson 1996). In the early to mid-seventeenth century colonial world the interdependence of European and Native American interests focused on the exchange of land and wampum for political power and alliances. Despite the population losses to disease, southern New England Algonquians strove not merely to survive, but to emerge as powerful leaders (Grumet 1996; Siminoff 2004); at times they even forged alliances with English individuals and communities.

Perhaps one of the best-known relationships was established between the Englishman Roger Williams and the Narragansett tribe, in the region now known as Rhode Island. Throughout their time together, both Williams and the Narragansett were outsiders, each in their own fashion, to the emerging Puritan society. Williams came to Rhode Island via the Massachusetts Bay Colony after he was expelled for religious heresy (see Rubertone 2001). The Narragansett had become hostile to both the English and other Native American groups that vied for control of the region, especially the Pequot. William's *Key into the Language of America* (1973, original 1643), part dictionary and part ethnographic description, was his attempt to encourage understanding between the English and the Narragansett, biased though it was by his desire to see the Narragansett converted to Christianity (Rubertone 2001). Williams's connection to the Narragansett extended beyond cultural understanding, though, and into mutual advocacy and protection. The Narragansett provided Williams with food and shelter when he was in need, guided him through unfamiliar territories, and alerted him to potential dangers or conflicts with other indigenous communities. In return, Williams often acted as translator and mediator on their behalf with other Englishmen, particularly in the context of the United Colonies commission inquiries. In this respect, their relationship resembled the sort of patron-client agreement in operation in the regional tributary systems of southern New England sachemships, although it is unclear who had the upper hand. Arguably, the Narragansett had sought just such an alliance for their own protection and political advancement within the region (Robinson 1996).

The Pequot, centered around the Thames and Mystic rivers on the Connecticut coastline, also negotiated an early agreement that they hoped would work to their advantage by sealing an exclusive deal with the Dutch West India Company after 1622 to provide wampum (Siminoff 2004, 28–29). While furs were the desired material to ship to Europe for profit, wampum had become the key to eliciting trade with the Haudenosaunee (Iroquoian) people in the northern reaches of the Hudson River valley.[2] The Pequot had by that time gained control over the Montaukett, Shinnecock, Manhanset, and Corchaug of Eastern Long Island, where the richest shellfish resources were and where the highest production of wampum took place. Whoever controlled the wampum controlled the fur trade in the Northeast (Ales 1979, 28–29; Gardener 1897 [1660]; McBride 1994). The Pequots hoped to become the exclusive conduit of European trade goods in the area, while also accruing increased authority through their association with the Dutch. While the alliance did work to their mutual advantage for more than ten years, by 1633 disagreements over specific terms sparked a series of strikes of one group against the other. By this time, the Pequot were in a poor position to negotiate a new alliance with Connecticut's English colonists, who were deeply unhappy with the Dutch incursion into "their" territory, facilitated by the Pequot.

With the failure of this agreement, the Pequots' relationship with the English deteriorated. In 1637, the English launched a massive military offensive against them. It was ironic that one event pushing the colonial English to this point was an unusual case of mistaken identity. Pequot warriors, in retaliation against the murder of one their own leaders by the Dutch, had killed an English sea captain; when asked to atone for this murder, the Pequot spokesman reportedly said,

"Could ye blame us for revenging so cruel a murder? For we distinguish not between the Dutch and English, but took them to be one nation, and therefore we do not conceive that we wronged you, for they slew our king; and thinking these captains to be of the same nation and people as those that slew him, made us set upon this course of revenge." (Underhill 1897 [1638], 58)

Arguably the Pequot were pointing out that, to them, all white people were the same.

The Pequot did attempt to come to some agreement with the English and made particular overtures to the Massachusetts Bay Colony. But the colonial administration, perceiving the advantage in usurping the resources the Pequot had controlled, demanded increasingly punitive terms, including foreclosure of all their land rights and payment of enormous amounts of furs and wampum (Siminoff 2004, 28–32). In the meantime, the Pequot pursued the revenge assassinations that they considered their right, engaging in skirmishes with English soldiers and colonists. In 1637, English militia, supported by Narragansett and Mohegan warriors, attacked the Pequot fort at Mystic, killing most of its occupants and scattering the rest as fugitives (Mason 1897). A number of the fugitives were captured a few weeks later from their hiding place in a swamp and sold into slavery (Mason 1897; Siminoff 2004, 70). The event sent a very clear message to Native communities: the English meant to assume control of the region by holding all others in tributary status. This message was received with variable reactions.

For some, the brutal defeat of the Pequots meant that their biggest adversary had been removed from the playing field. For years, Uncas, sachem of the Mohegan, had attempted to usurp or overthrow the power of Sassacus, the Pequot sachem. Uncas had married Sassacus's sister; when this had not yielded him any additional political weight, he had staged several coup attempts. As the English had grown increasingly unhappy with the Pequots, Uncas had sided with the colonists, providing the militia with information on Pequot locations and sending his men to act as guides for the English. Following the destruction of the fort, the Mohegan continued to aid the English by hunting down Pequot fugitives (E. Johnson 1996). Narragansett leader Miantonomi had also committed his men to the war against the Pequot because they had been enemies; like Uncas, he hoped to ascend to the status of tribute-holding sachem. Following the rout, however, Miantonomi was deeply disturbed by how the English had treated the Pequot, especially the killing of women and children; even before the fight, he had asked Roger Williams to convey to the other Englishmen that he hoped they would spare those who were not warriors (Robinson 1996). That Miantonomi's wishes were so brutally disregarded demonstrated to the Narragansett that the English were not to be trusted, and thereafter the Narragansett maintained barely civil relations with the English only through the efforts of Williams.

On Long Island, the outcome of the Pequot War had several important effects. According to records describing the Native alliances in the territory, all of eastern Long Island had been held in tribute status to the Pequot for at least as long as Europeans had been in the area. As noted earlier, this was a particular boon for the Pequot because of the ability of Long Islanders to produce wampum, which they had done in great quantities with the aid of imported iron muxes (Ceci 1990b). The Pequots in turn had protected the Long Island communities. As long as their agreement with the Dutch West India Company had held, the Dutch also thwarted the efforts of the English to settle there. After the war, however, the Long Islanders were no longer protected (or sequestered) by middlemen. Within three days of the conclusion of the slaughter at the fort, a young Montaukett sachem named Wyandanch arrived in Connecticut to speak with Lion Gardiner, the commanding soldier and engineer of Fort Saybrook. Gardiner recalled:

> . . . He came to know if we were angry with all Indians. I answered No, but only with such that as had killed Englishmen. He asked me whether they that lived upon Long-Island might come to trade with us. I said No, nor we with them, for if I should send my boat to trade for corn, and you have Pequits with you, and if my boat should come into some creek by reason of bad weather, they might kill my men,

and I shall think that you of Long Island have done it, and so we may kill all of you for the Pequits; but if you will kill all the Pequits that come to you, and send me their heads, then I will give to you as to Wequash, and you shall have trade with us. Then, said he, I will go to my brother, for he is the great Sachem of all Long Island, and if we may have peace and trade with you, we will give you tribute, as we did the Pequits. (Gardiner 1897, 137–138)

Wyandanch's brother, to whom he deferred, was the sachem of the Manhanset on Shelter Island, named (in those few records where he appeared) as Youghco or Poggaticut (Ales 1979, 29). Apparently Youghco did assent to this agreement, as Gardiner claimed to have received several Pequot heads from the Long Islanders. By concluding this transfer of loyalty and tribute from the Pequot to the English, Wyandanch and the rest of the Paumanoc confederacy appeared to have had expectations of the same type of protective relationship.

The benefit of English protection did not materialize in the fashion they had hoped. First, eastern Long Island became eligible real estate. Ostensibly, this region was the property of an absentee landlord, the Earl of Stirling, who had been given the land grant in 1636 by the Crown, a gesture meant to initiate English settlement and takeover of Long Island from the Dutch. For all practical purposes, the gesture meant nothing, however, until 1639 when Stirling sent his agent James Farrett to New England, to begin unloading the property for profit. The established colonies were fearful that Stirling's venture would become competition for profitable resources. The colonies were assured, however, that Farrett would only sell the land with advice and approval of Connecticut Colony Governor John Winthrop Jr. Ultimately Farrett was only able to sell three parcels of land, after a fashion: Gardiner's Island to Lion Gardiner, Southampton to a group of settlers from Lynn (Massachusetts), and Shelter Island to Stephen Goodyear of the New Haven Colony (Records of the Town of East-Hampton 1887, I: 1–2; Pelletreau 1874, 9–11). The last of these was purchased with the idea that it would eventually become an expansion of the colony, although it was not immediately settled. When Stirling died bankrupt in 1640, he left his agent stranded in New England and ended his Long Island land sales. Nevertheless, the floodgate to English settlement had been opened (Siminoff 2004, 93–96).

The record of these land sales demonstrates a rather important difference of perception as to their meaning. English colonial authorities quickly came to realize that the land they desired could not be simply coopted from the Native inhabitants, even though the Crown had distributed large land grants from afar. Therefore settlers were directed to obtain dual titles, one from the English grant-holder and one from the Native occupants. If there were no English grant-holder, then settlers were still required to obtain permission from the colonial administrators, who presumably understood the Native polities implicated in each property, before purchasing land. This practice, codified into law by the English by the mid-1630s, had been standard practice by the Dutch since their arrival (Siminoff 2004, 111–114). The English took such documentation to embody the appropriation of sole rights to the property, with no further obligations. It meant something slightly different to the Algonquians, however. They understood that they were effectively signing a quitclaim, but they expected the deeds to act as a declaration of a new relationship with the purchasers, who, as neighbors, would be obligated to engage in mutual aid and exchange. Some communities very quickly learned that the power of such written deeds were more effective when they were very explicit about the terms of that relationship. For example, in Easthampton, Southampton and Southold, all in eastern Long Island, the land-title transfer documents included specific notation of how and when protection and trade would be appropriately provided by each community (Pelletreau 1874, 11–14; Records of the Town of East-Hampton 1887, I: 2–4; Southold Town Records 1882, 363). Another interesting aspect of these land deeds is that they were often signed not only by the sachem of the occupant community but also by the grand sachem of the region.

As tributaries to the English, the Long Island Indians particularly expected actual military protection from the threats of other southern New England Native leaders with aspirations of regional power. Although the Pequot had been effectively vanquished (but not exterminated), the Narragansett and their allies the Niantic had designs on eastern Long Island. They began a campaign of harassment in the hopes that they could gain loyalty through fear or persuasion. For example, in 1640 Narragansett sachem Miantonomi paid a visit to the Montaukett while their leader, Wyandanch, was not there. Miantonomi apparently tried to persuade the Montaukett not to give their allegiance to the English; instead, he urged them to unite with other Native groups against the threat the English posed to their collective way of life. As Wyandanch reported to Lion Gardiner, "he gave them gifts, calling them brethren and friends, for so are we all Indians as the English are, and say brother to one another; so must we be one as they are, otherwise we shall be all gone shortly" (Gardiner 1897 [1660], 142). Tactics of persuasion gave way to physical attacks within ten years. Records of the United Colonies Commissioners indicate that from its inception those Native groups who had placed themselves in such tribute relations with the English appealed to them for protection and lodged their complaints against Native and settler neighbors alike (Pulsifer 1859). In those cases between Native individuals or groups, the Commissioners seemed reluctant to involve themselves in any cases where their own safety or property was not apparently in danger. The regularity with which such cases were brought, however, seems to indicate that the tribute-status Native communities felt it was the responsibility of the English to mediate or protect their interests.

One particularly remarkable act by the Shelter Island Manhanset sachem, Youghco/Poggaticut, illustrates how adeptly Native communities asserted their understanding of governance within the English system. Youghco realized that the English were unlikely to do anything that did not serve their interests unless they were bound to do so by a contract, embodied in a signed document. Thus in 1644, his visit to the Commissioners was recorded:

Youghco the Sachim of Munhausett vpon long Island presenting himself to, the Commissionrs desired that in regard he was a Tributary to the English, and hitherto obserued the Articles of agreement, he might receiue from them A certyficate whereby his rela[tio]n to the English might appeare and he prserued asmuch as might be from vnjust greevances and vexa[tio]ns (*though the Colonies be no way engaged to protect him*) yet herevpon the following certificate was given him [sic]. (Pulsifer 1859, 1: 18, italics added)

Though the Commissioners could not bring themselves to actually promise protection to Youghco, the power of the document became apparent at a later date. The certificate issued included not only Youghco's name, but also that of Wyandanch, Moughmaitow (likely Mandush, sachem of the Shinnecock), and Weenagaminin. In 1653, Ninigret, then sachem of the Niantic and Narragansett, had begun a concerted campaign of harassment of the Long Island communities. He was accused of having sent an assassin to the Shinnecock community to murder their sachem. When this was discovered, the Shinnecock brought the accused assassin to the English in Connecticut for prosecution. English authorities acknowledged the offense and gave permission to the Long Islanders to put the man to death. Ninigret then pursued English authorization to avenge the murder of this man, while sending warriors to Long Island for this purpose. Wyandanch, as the Long Island liaison, appealed to the United Colonies Commission for protection against such persecution, invoking the 1644 certificate given to Youghco. By this time Youghco had died, and the Commissioners were reluctant to involve themselves in what they viewed as an intertribal dispute. At issue was whether to send a platoon of English soldiers to protect the Long Island Indians from Ninigret's persecution. While part of the Commission felt obligated to do so, citing the 1644 certificate, others dissented on the grounds that the certificate had been issued specifically to Youghco, who was clearly not involved. This case is of particular interest because it highlights the intention of Youghco to protect his own community on Shelter Island, as well as the larger group of eastern Long Island Native communities for whom he was considered to be the grand sachem at the time that he requested the certificate (Pulsifer 1859, 1: 18–19; 2: 94–99; Strong 1996).

Whether the failure of the English to fulfill the role of tribute-holder, according to southern New England Algonquian standards, was deliberate, the various groups continued to pursue an array of diplomatic strategies with regard to the English in the hopes that a peaceful coexistence could be accommodated or at least that the Native groups could recoup some political power. The Pequot War had been a clear benchmark as to what would provoke irreconcilable English anger. But the positioning of the Algonquian leaders was far from uniform, and their relations with one another had little to do with their relations with the English. Wyandanch and Uncas, the Mohegan sachem, both worked very hard to maintain close and friendly relations with the English and yet were not themselves allies. In 1650 the two traded accusations of attempted murders via assassination and witchcraft, through formal complaint to the United Colonies Commissioners (Pulsifer 1859, 1: 167). At one point Uncas also made an overture to Wyandanch as the latter struggled with the harassment of the Niantic and Narragansett, by promising to murder Ninigret in exchange for a large quantity of wampum. Wyandanch did send wampum to Uncas, but the promised murder never took place (Ales 1979, 57–58; Strong 1996). Even Youghco, who very rarely appears in the records, complained directly to Massachusetts Bay Colony Governor Winthrop in 1647 that a payment of wampum given to Uncas for delivery to the governor was never received, for which Uncas was censured (Pulsifer 1859, 1: 102–103).

The Narragansett had an even more ambiguous position vis-à-vis the English, who recognized them as the most discontented group and the most likely to instigate a war. Rather than actually attacking the English, Ninigret inflicted his displeasure on the groups friendlier to the English, while presenting the English with reasons for his campaigns that they found difficult to refute. Thus the eastern Long Islanders, particularly the Montaukett and Shinnecock, suffered at Ninigret's hands with little protection by the English (Strong 1994 and 1996; Ales 1979; Siminoff 2004). Another Narragansett tactic was perennial lateness of tribute payments, which the English demanded in fathoms of wampum, or submission of insultingly inadequate payment (Pulsifer 1859, 1: 73–76). In many cases, the English suspected the Niantic-Narragansett of diverting those payments to Haudenosaunee tribes such as the Mohawk, in efforts to instigate further insurrections. Each such charge laid at the feet of an "insolent" sachem incurred more fines payable to the English in wampum, which made it nearly impossible for any group *not* to be in arrears and therefore always suspect in the eyes of the colonial authorities. Roger Williams himself warned the United Colonies Commission of the danger of this situation because he knew that the Narragansett were indeed in alliance with the openly hostile Mohawk (Pulsifer 1859, 1: 116–117).

Eastern Algonquian polities that were less amenable to the idea of paying tribute to the English colonies argued their position partly from the idea that there was no one "grand sachem" to whom they could appeal in person. If pressed to identify such an ultimate authority figure, the English commissioners let it be known that they were all in tribute to the king of England. Narragansett sachem Miantonomi argued of the English colonists, "they are no Sachems, nor none of their children shall be in their place if they die; and they have no tribute given them; there is but one king in England, who is over them all, and if you would send him 100,000 fathom of wampum, he would not give you a knife for it, nor thank you" (Gardiner 1897 [1660], 141). Ironically, within less than a decade, there would be not even one king in England after the civil war that revealed the Englishmen's own conflicting conceptions about the nature of political leadership. The Puritan colonizers of New England were quite embroiled in this process as they supported the demise of both royalty's divine right and the Church of England which they regarded as corrupt and illegitimate (see Schama 2003, 71–140). It is thus unsurprising that the English Puritans and the Algonquians of New England should have very different ideas about what form political authority should take. In some senses, the Algonquian may have had more in common with the English Royalists on the issue.

Youghco's last appearance in the English records indirectly illustrates a failure of the English to provide appropriate protection to their tributaries according to Algonquian standards. In September 1652, the United Colonies Commissioners noted the arrival of Checkanoe (also referred to as Cockenoe-de-Long Island) "an Indian of Menhansick Island" who complained of a Captain Middleton, who had arrived on the island, insisting that he and his partners had purchased it from Stephen Goodyear and that the Manhanset must leave. On behalf of the Manhanset, and presumably of Youghco who was still accounted sachem, Checkanoe reminded the Commissioners of their responsibility to them as tributaries and asked for "justice in the premises" (Pulsifer 1859, 2: 377). The matter was referred to Stephen Goodyear, who was not present at the session but who was one of the Commissioners representing New Haven Colony at the time. It is not known whether the Manhanset felt that "justice in the premises" meant they held the right to remain, undisturbed, on the island, or if they simply desired payment for the property. Some months later, however, Easthampton town records confirmed the transfer of possession:

> Yokee, formerly sachem of Manhansick Ahaquatawamock, now called Shelter Island, did . . . give full Possession unto Capt. Nathaniel Silvester and Ensigne John Booth . . . delivered unto the aforesaid . . . one turfe and twige in their hands according to the usual custome of England; after which delivery and full possession given, the said Yokee with all his Indians that were formerly belonging to the said island of Ahaquatawamock did freely and willingly depart the aforesaid island . . . (reprinted in Mallmann 1990, 17)

In many land transfers effected in the area, later confirmation documents were filed that reiterated the persons and terms, including the payments received. In this particular case, no mention of payment to the Manhanset was made. With this transaction, the provisioning plantation and Nathaniel Sylvester's tenure began at Shelter Island.

The Sylvesters on Shelter Island

Nathaniel Sylvester and his business partners, brother Constant Sylvester, Thomas Middleton, and Thomas Rouse, thought that they had purchased Shelter Island in 1651, from Stephen Goodyear. For that transfer, they purportedly paid "sixteen hundred pounds of good merchantable muscovado sugar" (Mallmann 1990, 15). This was no mean price, as by this time sugar had become a commodity in high demand. The English had just overtaken the Portugese as the largest sugar producers and exporters by capturing profits from both milled sugar and molasses for distilling spirits (Mintz 1985, 38–40). The price paid was quite manageable for this partnership, however, as they had been invested in two sugar plantations on Barbados from early in the explosion of British production there. The motivation for the purchase of Shelter Island stemmed from the same source as the payment, as the four partners intended to develop the island as a provisioning plantation, a place to raise, process, procure, and warehouse supplies for the Barbados plantations where all production efforts were given to sugar. Of the four, however, only Nathaniel Sylvester was to be a proprietor in residence.

The Sylvesters were sons of Giles and Mary Sylvester, who had been English citizens until they emigrated to Amsterdam, where they raised their family. There is no record of the elder Sylvesters' reasons for leaving England; although some sources suggest that they were Anabaptist (Hoff 1994a and 1994b), they were members of a Separatist church in Amsterdam and considered themselves English. Once there, Giles and his family established a profitable business in merchant trade. Sons Nathaniel and Constant in particular were routinely on board for transatlantic trading voyages, as documented in enquiries by the Dutch West India Company because the Sylvesters had evaded the payments of levies and illegally engaged in private trade on the African coast (Griswold 2013). In the majority of documents from the 1650s Nathaniel was titled "Captain," recalling his seafaring days, and he kept the company of associates who also carried naval titles, such as Captain Thomas Middleton, Ensign John Booth, and Lieutenant Seely. Most if not all of the Sylvester children departed Amsterdam to take part in the expansion of their business interests to the New World. Apparently they found that the English colonies held more opportunities for them because they became naturalized English citizens at that time. Constant worked as a London-based merchant in the sugar trade from Barbados before moving to the island to become a producer, while another brother, Giles, returned to London to carry on the business after having spent time first in Barbados and then on Shelter Island (Hoff 1994a and 1994b). Even within the context of the family business, the Sylvester network spanned the Atlantic. Such a broad perspective likely derived from having started in Amsterdam, which was at that time a cosmopolitan center of commerce, international interests, and wealth (Schama 1987).

Such connections were expanded on both sides of the Atlantic with Nathaniel's marriage to Grissell Brinley shortly before taking up residence at Shelter Island. Grissell, married at age sixteen, was the daughter of Thomas Brinley, who had been the auditor for Charles I until the king was dethroned and decapitated in 1649. Brinley then went into exile with Charles II, remaining loyal to him through his restoration to the English Crown in 1660. Grissell's sister had married the governor of Rhode Island, William Coddington, and traveled with Grissell and Nathaniel to New England, via Barbados, in 1652 (Mallmann 1990, 21). Even prior to settling on Shelter Island, Nathaniel's engagement in the burgeoning transatlantic trade likely laid the groundwork for his arrival. From early in his tenure, he exchanged letters with John Winthrop Jr., the governor of the Connecticut Colony and son of the Massachusetts Bay Colony governor, indicating that Winthrop was familiar with much of the Sylvester family in the New World (MHC, Winthrop Papers Collection). The connection may have been through Barbados: the Winthrops were known to have participated in trade between there and New England and had even invested in the slave trade (Trans-Atlantic Slave Trade Database, Voyage ID 25055). Many of Nathaniel's naval associates made the transition to land settlement during that same period. These contacts and associates were extremely important to the Sylvesters when they found themselves at odds with the society of local colonial authorities and citizens in New England.

In 1652 the four business partners signed "Articles of Agreement," not only designating how expenses and profits were to be shared but also establishing some specific guidelines for the physical structure of the plantation. For the household in particular, the contract stated that expenses should be kept at a minimum, with construction only as necessary until profits could bear further extravagance, though necessary was qualified "to wit a house with Six or Seven convenient Roomes" (SIHS, Middleton et al. 1652) which would have been rather large for the time (Cummings 1964). Trade outside the partners' primary enterprise could be undertaken out of the individual's pocket, but only business conducted within it garnered payment of daily expenses. For the business at hand, the island's extant resources and planned infrastructure were noted as assets held in common: pastures, orchards, gardens, estuaries, and a mill. Livestock was a major concern; the agreement referred to instructions given to Lt. Seely on initial stocking and husbandry and further directed that no livestock was to be slaughtered for a term of six years except as necessary for household consumption or in the case that any animal prove to be harmful to the others (as by disease). Later property inventories listed several plows and a pair of millstones, with a cider mill on the island and an unspecified type of mill off the island; thus, the extent to which the partners intended to raise crops beyond orchard fruits is ambiguous.

Nathaniel and Grissell arrived at Shelter Island sometime late in 1652, after having traveled first to Barbados. Their voyage apparently ended abruptly when their ship, the *Swallow* (of which Sylvester was captain but not the owner), ran aground in Narragansett Bay. The ship and most of their possessions were wrecked. Although Nathaniel pleaded with the crew to save as much of those materials as possible, he later sued the ship's owner for theft of the salvaged remains (MHS Winthrop Papers 1947, VI: 284). Following such an inauspicious start, the newlyweds settled into the plantation at Shelter Island, where Grissell had their first child the following year. It has been suggested in later historical narratives that they sent ahead or arrived with some number of indentured servants and slaves from Barbados, necessary for domestic staffing, the development of plantation structures, and field labor (Mallmann 1990, 21). Grissell's will of 1685 later noted that she had brought two enslaved Africans, Hannah and Jacquero, with her as personal attendants (SMA Group I-A, G. Sylvester 1685), but there is otherwise no specific documentation of the "personnel" they may have brought.

The Sylvesters' rapidly expanding family likely soon necessitated additional domestic labor. Following the births of Grissell's first two children, Grissell in 1654 and Giles in 1657, there was a space of three to four years before the ensuing birth. This spacing is based on the records of *surviving* offspring; she likely had additional pregnancies, at least one resulting in an infant death, and perhaps others ending in miscarriage. In the interim between the first two children, in 1655, Nathaniel sent to John Winthrop Jr. a letter in which he sought medical advice for an ailing child whom he noted was only two months old (MHS Winthrop Papers, Sylvester 1655). In the 1660s and beyond, however, the spacing between her pregnancies was clearly only one to two years, meaning that she was nursing her children for much less time after birth. In all, Grissell and Nathaniel had eleven children who survived to adulthood (Mallmann 1990, 177). While not impossible, it is extraordinarily unlikely that this was accomplished without at least some aid in childcare and in particular a wet nurse. That they soon needed such help was indicated in the letter Nathaniel wrote: "I was informed that y[ou] had an Irish woman wch y[ou] would willingly part withall; if so, and shee good for to doe any buseness aboute ye house, I will be your Chapman if y[ou] pleas to lett me have her reasonable [sic]" (MHS Winthrop Papers, Sylvester 1655). While we do not know whether this Irish woman ever came to the plantation, it is clear that enslaved Africans and possibly white indentured servants were integral to the family.

While the Sylvesters successfully established a home and a trade network, they were somewhat less successful at maintaining good relations with settlers in the surrounding area and had only nominal colony affiliations. Because the partners had purchased the property from Stephen Goodyear who, as the deputy governor of the New Haven Colony, intended it to be part of that colony, the plantation on Shelter Island was considered to be within its jurisdiction. As it turned out, the New Haven Colony was perhaps the most stringent in imposing all sorts of constraints upon its citizens and registered the most vehement rejection of Quakers among all the New England colonies, though all of them were fairly intolerant to lesser degrees (Calder 1934, 261–263). Colony statutes demanded stiff fines for merely harboring or entertaining known Quakers. The Quakers themselves, if caught in the colony, faced punishments of whipping and branding before expulsion; if caught returning, they faced possible execution (Hoadly 1858, 238–241; Worrall 1980, 22–24). Whether the Sylvesters were in fact Quakers before their arrival, or were merely sympathizers (who later professed to be Quakers), their leanings drew the ire of the colonial court. As early as 1654, Nathaniel was recorded in the General Court records as confessing that he had made statements offensive to the colonial government:

> as that he should say it was a tyranicall gouermt . . . besides other
> offensive carriage concerning the Saboth, & ordinances, &c., at wch
> court he also shewed much passion and hight of spirit, to the courts
> great dissatisfaction, wch they manifested toward him . . . as also
> for the just offence he gaue at Southold [a nearby town also of New
> Haven Colony] in saying (vpon supposition of an order made to

keepe him out of their towne,) that if any mett him in the streets and medled wth him he would pistol them, and in other respects he hath carried it wth two much bitternes of speech [sic]. (Hoadly 1858, 93)

Although at that time Sylvester issued an apology to the court, in later run-ins he expressed no remorse and often simply failed to appear when summoned. In a 1660 letter to the court, he declared for the record that he did profess to be a Quaker. Because he was also suspected of often harboring other Quakers, the court ordered that 100 pounds sterling of Sylvester's property be seized and summoned him to appear (Hoadly 1858, 364). But a year later, the court noted that Sylvester had been summoned three times and had not yet appeared, and the case did not warrant mention again (Hoadly 1858, 412). The failure of New Haven Colony's authorities to bring Sylvester into their courts demonstrated that the partnership of the plantation had considerable autonomy.

The Sylvesters *were* well-known, as it turned out, for their support and hospitality toward Quakers, some of whom were outspoken leaders of the sect. John Taylor, for one, stayed on Shelter Island on several occasions in 1659. He commented particularly "we were received very kindly by one *Nathaniel Silvifter*, a Captain in the country on the main Land; for this Iſland was his own: And he had a great many *Indians* lived on it, and they were Friendly and sober, and made Serviceable to Friends for Guides, &c. when we travelled into the countries [sic]" (Taylor 1710, 5). He took the opportunity to spend some few days with them and preach to them. Taylor was paid a visit there by Mary Dyer, who had been exiled from Boston and was hanged upon her later return (Worrell 1980).[3] Taylor was last on Shelter Island to await the loading of the ship that would take him to Barbados. George Fox, the founder of the sect, visited the island in 1672, after also spending time on Barbados. During his visit to the plantation, he held several meetings (Quaker services), including at least one with a large number of Native Americans (Fox 1709, 2: 190–191). That Shelter Island became known as a place friendly to Quaker exiles from Boston has figured prominently in local historical narratives. Today a burial ground with a monument to the persecuted Quakers remains on the estate, along with a meeting place.

The business of the plantation was occasionally the concern of the courts and often the subject of private letters. In one isolated 1656 court case, after a mare had died en route to the island, Sylvester sued the men he had hired to transport horses purchased in Southampton to Shelter Island, (Hoadly 1858, 190–194). By the time of his estate inventory, in

1681, there were forty horses on Shelter Island, twenty owned in partnership and twenty owned outright (SIHS, Budd et al. 1680). Sylvester seems to have conducted business with a number of individuals in the region, but little of his correspondence survived. He did, however, maintain a close relationship with John Winthrop Jr., whose archived letters offer some insight onto the Shelter Island plantation operation. In an early exchange (1654), Nathaniel negotiated the purchase of barrel staves and cattle, from or through Winthrop (MHS Winthrop Papers 1992, V: 320, 412–413, 451). Barrel staves would have been essential for the Barbados planters to export produce because that island had very little available lumber. Thereafter, little reference was made to export commodities, which may reflect the stipulation in the Articles of Agreement that no stock be slaughtered for a term of six years, while orchard trees, once planted, would need some time to become productive. In the meantime, Sylvester purchased some additional properties for his own estate (Barck 1927). Much of the correspondence of the Sylvester family to Winthrop included news or discussion of English politics. Many of their letters were delivered by Native Americans crossing Long Island Sound, including Uncas, sachem of the Mohegan, whose presence on Shelter Island was unfortunately not explained. Perhaps he was conducting his own campaign of political persuasion with the Long Island Algonquians.

By 1656, the partnership had been reduced to three when John Booth, who had bought out Thomas Rouse's share, sold his quarter-interest to Nathaniel Sylvester, for £700. The payment was clarified in the following year, when Nathaniel agreed to forgive any debts held against Booth by the partnership and gave Booth possession of half of Roberts Island (now known as Robins Island) near to Shelter Island in Peconic Bay. In this agreement Nathaniel maintained a peculiar kind of control through several stipulations even as he ceded the property: he demanded that Booth must not place the property under any colony's jurisdiction without Sylvester's permission; if Booth were to leave, then he must sell the land back to Sylvester; and Booth must allow "any Indian or Indians belonging to Shelter Iland to fish for shells or Catch any other fish whatsoever about Roberts Iland [sic]" (Easthampton Town Records 1887, 1: 96–99, 104–109). The other half of the island remained in Nathaniel's possession, which he used as pasturage for cattle owned by the partnership. By 1665, he again claimed full ownership of the island in a quitclaim filed with the town of Southold, making no mention of Booth (Southold Town Records 1882, II: 255–258). Although Roberts Island was a small property in Sylvester's holdings, he used it to guard against the unwanted attention of colony authorities.

Having established themselves as outsiders to the New England colonial system, with the exception of their trade relations, the Sylvesters could move toward consolidating their independence. The English Restoration in 1660 marked the turn of political tides in the Long Island Sound region. Of some consequence for the Quakers and the colonies, the Restoration meant that Puritan Calvinists were distinctly out of favor with the Crown and the returned bishops of the Church of England. But Quakers, who had played no part in Cromwell's government and who were reviled by the Puritans, were now regarded with more indulgence by the Crown (Schama 2003, 212). One historian has even suggested that Charles II had been kept apprised of the treatment of Quakers in the colonies through Thomas Brinley, his auditor in exile with him and father of Grissell Sylvester (Lamb 1887, 371).

Eastern Long Island, along with several areas along the Connecticut coast and rivers, had long been contested grounds between the English and Dutch. These disputes were largely brought to a close in 1664 when the English took over the New Netherland Colony, and the entire territory was given to the Duke of York (although the Dutch retook the colony briefly in 1673–1674). To the consternation of the Connecticut and New Haven colonies, this included the portions of eastern Long Island where they had established jurisdiction; residents were required "to surrender their grants or patents and receive new ones from the Duke" (Siminoff 2004, 143). The order opened the door to all sorts of land disputes, which were brought to the new colonial authorities of New York, and often Indian testimony decided the case (e.g., Siminoff 2004; see Fernow 1883, 14: 600–602). The requirement worked very much in the Sylvesters' favor, however, perhaps because Constant and his colleagues had been Royalists, outspoken to the degree that they were nearly exiled from Barbados prior to the Restoration (Smith 1998). Not only did they now receive a new title for Shelter Island from the Duke in 1666, but they were also granted manorial status, rendering them independent of any colonial or town jurisdiction, including payment of taxes, for the low, one-time payment of £150 to the new Governor of New York Richard Nicoll (Fernow 1883, 14: 566; Mallmann 1990, 26–27). Although Thomas Middleton was still one-third owner, only Constant and Nathaniel Sylvester were named as proprietors of the island.

In 1671 Constant Sylvester died, leaving one-third of his share of Shelter Island to Nathaniel and the rest to his two sons. This left Nathaniel as half-owner and majority shareholder. According to Constant's will, Nathaniel owned no property in partnership with him in Barbados, rather Constant claimed all his "lands, plantations, houses, and tenements in the island of Barbados" as sole proprietor (C. Sylvester 1671). Events documented prior to and subsequent to Constant's death suggest that it may have been troublesome to Nathaniel to remain only half-owner rather than sole proprietor of Shelter Island. For example, in 1657, Nathaniel had been involved in a dispute with a ship's captain over payment for supplies being loaded upon a ship. When the captain, Deakins, questioned whether Constant Sylvester would approve of Nathaniel's position (for the shipment may have been bound to Constant in Barbados), Nathaniel replied that he was out of Constant's reach. When Deakins caustically asked if Nathaniel was also out of reach of all authority in both New and Old England, the reply was affirmative (Southold Town Records 1882, 418, 466–468).

Nathaniel's earlier dismissal of New England's colonial power notwithstanding, he did appeal more readily to the New York authorities, perhaps because they were politically more to his liking. The Duke's Laws had been fairly emphatic that all colonists must submit all their dealings with Native Americans to the approval of the colony commissioners. Accordingly, Nathaniel entered two requests at the same time in 1672. First, in his most overtly documented acknowledgment that some Manhanset did still live on Shelter Island, he complained that they "have presumed in their Drink to breed Disturbance, & make Commotions there, the apprehension of the Dangr whereof hath been ye occasion of great ffrights and Trouble in his family [sic]" (Fernow 1883, 14: 671). He requested to be empowered to apprehend the offending individuals and send them to Fort James, the seat of the New York colonial government, to face trial, and this request was granted. His second request was for permission to purchase more land on the south side of Long Island from "ye Indyan Proprietrs," which was also granted, provided he transmitted a survey map of the property to Fort James at the transaction's successful conclusion (Fernow 1883, 14: 671).

As for "unruly" Indians of Shelter Island, it later appeared that the quiet and sober group who so impressed John Taylor in 1657 and for whom Nathaniel had assured access to Roberts Island in 1656 was no longer so friendly. By 1675 New England was embroiled in King Phillip's War, the most violent clash between English and Algonquian since the Pequot, and English colonists were terrified that all Indians would rise up against them (Lepore 1999). The New York colonial council had ordered the removal of all firearms from Long Island Algonquians as a protective measure, but many Indians complained that this order was not only discriminatory but harmful, as they were unable to see to their own defense and livelihoods. The council finally relented for those groups that had demonstrated good faith, "Excepting Easthampton and Shelter Island Indyans, who having paid Contribution to those of Narrogansett, are not to have their Armes for ye Present, but to have equall Justice, & (if quiet) Protection, as others if ye Government" (Fernow 1883, 14: 697). The Manhanset were perhaps hedging their bets on their best source of protection.

Nathaniel Sylvester finally realized the opportunity to consolidate his independent ownership of the island amidst the chaos of Britain's war with the Dutch, which offered Nathaniel fortuitous albeit quite dangerous circumstances. In 1673, Holland briefly recaptured its former colony, and the reinstated Dutch governor declared Constant Sylvester and Thomas Middleton to be enemies of the Dutch state. When the Dutch government ordered their property, including Shelter Island, seized, Nathaniel appeared before the secretary of the Dutch council at Fort James (temporarily renamed Fort William Henrick) to affirm his allegiance to them in order to protect his property. At the same time, he declared that Middleton and the heirs of Constant owed him a great deal of money. In light of this, it was agreed that Nathaniel would pay a sum of £500 to the Dutch, in return for which he would be granted full rights and ownership of Shelter Island and property within, that is, "goods, effects, furniture, negros or whatever else" (text of confirmation reprinted in Mallmann 1990, 28–31). The Dutch left nothing to chance in this transaction; Nathaniel described in his will that the payment was collected by fifty soldiers in a Dutch man-of-war.

> . . . The said Commanders also sending one of theire Men of Warr to Shelter Island where the Captaine Landed with about Fiftie Souldiers takeing possession of the said Moyetie or halfe part of Shelter Island Laid Claim unto by the said Constant Sylvester and Thomas Midleton or what soever in any wise might be there unto belonging and Claimed by them as Owners thereof, and to strike the greater Dread in my familie they beset my house, the better to obtaine the Money which they forced from mee and my selfe Constrained to pay to prevent their Rueing of said Moyetie of Shelter Island and what was there unto belonging unto the said Constant Sylvester and Thomas Midleton as aforesaid. . . . (SIHS, Sylvester 1679/80)

While the Dutch reoccupation of New York was finished by the following year, Nathaniel held to the validity of the transaction. As a means of cementing those terms, however, his will included a detailed accounting of those properties which had been held in partnership, while repeating the reasons why he was at that time claiming them as his own, to be bequeathed as he saw fit to his heirs. As such, the will provided a rich picture of the ventures that Nathaniel pursued, at his own expense, to advance his own interests, as well as the assets of the partnership business, through which he amassed a rich estate.

Nathaniel passed away in 1680, perhaps taken by the illness that he had complained of in letters as early as 1674 (MHS Winthrop Papers, Sylvester 1674). His last will and testament were truly that: an extensive testament to the basis of his claims for sole ownership of his property, and his will that his estate, particularly Shelter Island, should remain always in the possession of his immediate family and their heirs. The property in partnership had included half the island, nine enslaved individuals, a mill and mill-house (which were in Southold), 227 sheep, 20 horses, 60 pigs, and 130 cattle. Individually he had claimed the other half-share of the island plus two or three other properties on the north fork of Long Island, a cider-mill and press, a warehouse, a salthouse, a large supply of bricks, eleven enslaved individuals, a boat, all the contents of the farm buildings and the household, 227 sheep, 20 horses, 60 pigs, and 70 cattle through the will and inventory. Strangely, in the execution of the estate inventory, those properties held in partnership were not accounted in the total estate valuation (i.e., only half the island and half the value of the enslaved and the livestock). Even at that, the estate's value exceeded £1,500, and there was apparently no challenge to his claims by his absent former partners or their heirs (SIHS, Middleton et al. 1652; Budd et al. 1680).

Nathaniel's will also carefully dictated the disposition of his properties among his many children. First, a veritable committee of executors was appointed, including his wife, brother-in-law, son-in-law, cousin, and several others. After assuring Grissell's dower rights to the house and the surrounding forty acres (the rough description of which matches the location of the current house), Nathaniel declared that his eldest son Giles should inherit this central area, while the other sons would be given equal areas of property on Shelter Island on reaching the age of twenty-one, the location of each parcel to be determined by the executor committee. The sons were also to have rights to certain areas in common, such as those described to be commonly held in the 1652 Articles of Agreement. Specific structures were left to sons for their residences. To his daughters he left dowries or allowances should they never marry. For all moveable property, disposal by sale had to meet the approval first of Grissell and then

TABLE 2.1
Enslaved individuals in Nathaniel Sylvester will of 1679/80

Enslaved individuals named in will (by family group)
Tammero and Oyou (married), four children (unnamed)
Black John, daughter Prescilla
J:O and Maria (married)
Jenkin
Tony and Nannie (married); daughter Hester, daughter Grace, daughter Semenie, daughter Aby
Japhet and Semenie (married)
Jacquero and Hannah (married); daughter Hope, daughter Isabel

the other executors. With regard to the land of Shelter Island, however, Nathaniel willed it was *never* to be sold outside of the family, on pain of losing all rights to it. In this respect, the manorial status of the property was regarded as making it entailed property. He asked that upon the death of any son without issue, that son's property would revert to the others. It is evident that Shelter Island was held dearly and personally by Nathaniel.

Another aspect of the will to which Nathaniel gave great attention was the distribution of the enslaved laborers. In all he named or referred to twenty-three individuals total (Table 2.1), three of whom he clarified belonged to his wife. In nearly all references, they are identified with the qualifier "Negro" and in the possessive. But they are also nearly all identified by name and in relation to families. Although each of his children was bequeathed at least one enslaved person (with the exception of daughter Grissell, who was by then married and perhaps had already been given one), in no case was a married couple separated. Children of these couples were given separately, though in many cases they would not have been taken away for some time as they were given to Nathaniel's unmarried daughters who presumably would remain in the same house until marriage. As also identified in the estate inventory, eleven of these individuals were held in partnership. Those persons given to the unmarried daughters and Grissell, including Hannah and Jacquero who were part of her dower's rights, were more than likely domestic staff. The fact that most are named by Nathaniel suggests some familiarity that may have been instilled by household presence. The four children of Tammero and Oyou, who were not named, and several others were among those divided as with land and livestock, suggesting that they were farm laborers.

Much in the will and inventory suggests that Nathaniel had become more of a wealthy gentleman farmer than a businessman engaging in transatlantic commerce. Nathaniel and Grissell's children, moreover, did not follow in the footsteps of the far-flung Sylvester family business network. Instead, they married well, in some cases, and simply lived well as part of the Eastern Long Island communities or the more urban New England areas, like Newport or Boston. The eldest child, Grissell, was engaged to marry a wealthy man, Lattimer Sampson; he died before their wedding, but he had already willed all of his property to her. Young Grissell then married James Lloyd, of another wealthy family of east Long Island and Boston; this union later proved a vital connection for her siblings and relations, as much business was conducted between the families (Mallmann 1990, 32; Barck 1927). Her mother and Nathaniel's widow, the elder Grissell, passed away in 1685, not even reaching the age of fifty. Her own will, in which she poignantly noted herself "taken into consideration the uncertainty of the dissolution of this humans frail life being crazy in body, but of sound and perfect understanding with most serious and deliberate thoughts of my own state and condition," she distributed the household "particulars" to her children. The wealth of the household was apparent: numerous featherbeds and bolsters, "turkie-wrought" carpets and chairs, pewter, brass and silver implements, linens and great chests were items that she bequeathed specifically, with "all else" to be divided equally amongst them (SMA Group I-A, G. Sylvester 1685).

Giles Sylvester, who inherited the bulk of the main estate, had no desire to play the role of the gentleman farmer as his father had. He moved to live in more urban New England areas by the early 1690s and leased the property to tenant operators while directing the accounts mostly from afar (Shelter Island Account Book 1658–1758, East Hampton Library). His dependent siblings either went with him or lived with other married siblings in the area; for example, Elizabeth (Eliza) was recorded on a 1698 census in Southold where her sister Patience lived with her husband Benjamin L'Hommedieu (O'Callaghan 1850, 448). Several names of the Sylvester enslaved individuals were also recorded here, including Maria, Semonie, Tony, Prissilla, Hope, Grace, and Abigail (O'Callaghan 1850, 455). Giles himself, though he married, never had any children, but he apparently did not share his father's sentiment in wishing to keep Shelter Island as an ancestral home for the Sylvesters. He began to sell parcels in 1695, starting with a sizeable portion of Shelter Island to William Nicoll, with a smaller parcel given in 1698 to cover a £500 debt (Southold Town

FIGURE 2.1. Extant Manor house constructed by Brinley Sylvester, 1730s
(photo by John Matsunaga).

Records 1882, I: 407–409). Upon his death in 1707 he willed his property
in part to Nicoll and the rest to his wife Hannah, leaving no portion to
revert to his brothers as his father had willed (SMA Group I-A, G. Sylvester 1723 [orig. 1707]). Giles's nephew Brinley, son of the second Nathaniel, was young at the time this happened, but he later brought suit to
contest the terms of Giles's will to recover at least the core of the original
Sylvester estate where the main dwelling was (SIHS, New York Superior
Court 1735). He won this lawsuit by the early 1730s and apparently tore
down the remaining edifices of the early plantation in order to construct
the elegant Georgian mansion that still stands today.

Enslaved Africans in colonial New York and on Shelter Island

That the plantation operated by Nathaniel Sylvester on Shelter
Island was run in part with enslaved African labor is not only apparent
from his will but also logical given the connections to Barbados sugar
plantations. It is also clear, given the number of individuals named in
his will, that his was a fairly large holding compared to other settlers
in the northern colonies at that time (see Moss 1993). For the most

part, however, Sylvester's documentary remains—the letters, court records, and visitors' observations—contain virtually no comment or reference to the lives of those enslaved individuals. Some generalized speculation about their prospects and experiences can be brought to bear by considering contemporaneous Dutch and English practices of enslavement.

Some of the earliest documented importations of captured Africans were to the New Netherland Colony. In 1626, West India Company records showed that eleven men were brought to New Amsterdam for the expressed purpose of working on the infrastructure of the settlement, such as building construction and farming. Shortly thereafter three women were acquired for labor and companionship for the men (Foote 2004, 36). As the central authority for all of the colony's business, the WIC recognized the severe labor shortage. By 1664 the company had imported a minimum of 467 enslaved individuals, predominantly men, for building, farming, and some military service. Until the 1650s, most of the enslaved were considered WIC property, and few were offered at public auction to independent settlers. While some direct shipments from Africa (Guinea and Angola) and Curaçao were requisitioned (Fernow 1883, 14: 83, 106, 162, 304, 449, 477, 482), an additional unknown number of individuals were brought to New Netherland via captured ships of other nations; thus, it is difficult to identify the places of origin of those individuals (McManus 1966, 26–28).

Despite the control of the WIC, the New Netherlands colony never instituted a formal set of laws establishing the rights and constraints of their enslaved settlers. This meant that the terms of servitude were somewhat fluid, and the enslaved petitioned for additional rights, making the distinction between enslavement and indentured servitude rather vague. Marriages were permitted, some of which took place within the Dutch churches (Kruger 1985, 48). The enslaved also testified in court, petitioned for and received wages, and pressed for their freedom. The WIC administrators compromised to offer some enslaved people a form of "half-freedom" wherein they were free to demand wages and live independently, but they were expected both to pay a form of tribute to the company and to agree that their children remained in bondage (Moore 2005, 43–45). The various reasons for this unstructured approach to slavery in New Netherlands were specific to the circumstances of that colony rather than purely the result of Dutch cultural attitudes (contra McManus 1966). First, the New Netherlands colony had a rather low population density throughout its history. Unlike the English colonies, which were more successful at attracting settlers and indentured servants, few Dutch people were interested in resettling in the colonies, though they were happy to invest in the companies that would reap profits from them. Hence, the need for forced labor was great. Even by 1664, when the English captured the colony, the total population of New Netherlands was only fifteen hundred, of which up to one-quarter were free and enslaved blacks (Moore 2005, 47; Foote 2004, 40).

Second, and related to this, most landholdings in the colony were small, and thus the distribution of enslaved Africans per household was small. In these circumstances, it was not only difficult but also largely unnecessary, from the WIC perspective, to impose strict sanctions on the enslaved (Kruger 1985, 48–53). Third, New Netherland's population was quite heterogeneous by the standards of the time, as a result of both the open societal conditions in Holland and the circumstance of the colony that struggled to attract settlers. This diversity was ironically viewed with concern by the colony directors, who felt that no sense of community could be created among such a population, unlike the single-minded purpose of the English (Foote 2004, 42). Nevertheless, these conditions contributed to a sort of tolerance that made the Dutch more willing to grant additional rights to the enslaved. Interestingly, the Dutch were ambivalent on the issue of baptizing their enslaved: on a personal level they felt that it was only right to offer baptism, yet on a business level they worried that they might be evaporating their labor force as quickly as they imported it because they were uneasy with enslaving Christians (Foote 2004, 43; Kruger 1985, 46).

By the time the English took over the New Netherlands colony in 1664, renaming it New York, there were almost four hundred free and enslaved blacks in the colony. When the new proprietor the Duke of York took over, however, the unstructured and uncodified nature of their servitude came to an end. The "Duke's Laws," which were issued at this time, defined the distinction between lifelong enslavement and limited term indenture. Furthermore, the association of race with enslavement began to be part of the written laws of the land. In 1679, the governor of the colony issued a ban on the enslavement of Indians (Fernow 1881, 13: 537; McManus 1966, 24). Later laws regarding slave status referred to an array of racial identities, including Indian, Mustee, and Negro (Kruger 1985, 71–72; Strong 1997, 281–282), and fugitive slave advertisements reflected this same array of racial descriptors (Hodges and Brown 1994). Barbados planters, many of whom had direct business ties to the English in New York and New England, had begun in 1661 to construct legal codes regarding slavery with explicit reference to "Negroes," a fact that likely did not escape the attention of their northern counterparts (Beckles 1990, 33).

By 1682, the statutes on slavery had been expanded to describe the legal constraints upon the enslaved with prohibitions on their leaving without the enslaver's permission or congregating in groups. Free people were not permitted to harbor or entertain the enslaved (Kruger 1985, 70). It is unclear how the passage of Duke's Law affected free blacks, some of whom had been considered free as far back as the 1650s. Southampton records, for example, document a John Negro being issued military arms in 1657, an act which would have been legal only if he were free (Pelletreau 1874, 155). In the town's 1698 census, however, neither the name John Negro nor anything similar indicating descendants appeared in the category of "male Christians." Under the list of "negro males," a John was counted, but none of the persons counted as negro were given the benefit of a documented surname. Indians were distinguished from this group, but only males over the age of fifteen were documented by name, as "The Sqaus and children few of whom have any nam [sic]." In Southold, where the census distinguished between "Indians, old & young" and "Slaves, old & young," the legal clarification of racial status in the Duke's Laws appears to have taken hold (O'Callaghan 1850, 437–456). The lack of surnames, or any names in some cases, has made it impossible to track whether certain individuals may have been shifted from one racial category to another. The right to a heritable name, at this time, belonged only to whites.

Elsewhere in the English colonies, the association of racial status and slavery was equally indeterminate in practice. While the New England colonies had less dire need for enslaved labor, some small holdings were to be found, and occasional reference to the slave trade was made in correspondence and official records. Emmanuel Downing mused to Massachusetts Bay Colony Governor Winthrop in a 1645 letter that a potential side benefit to the threatened war with the Narragansett would be in exchanging Native war captives to the Caribbean for enslaved Africans: "I suppose you know verie well how wee shall mayntayne 20 Moores cheaper then one Englishe servant" (MHS Winthrop Papers, V: 38). Winthrop also witnessed the sale by Susanna Winslow of an Indian man, who had been her husband's servant, to John Mainford, a planter from Barbados (MHS Winthrop Papers, V: 197). Very often, Native Americans were sold into slavery in the Caribbean simply to get rid of those who were considered dangerous to the colonists (Newell 2003; Hilden 2001). Though the English required less non-European labor than the Dutch had, they pragmatically favored the profitable slave-driven plantations such as were found in Barbados and were eager to reap the benefits of the provisioning trade with those plantations, much as the Sylvesters had done (MHS Winthrop Papers, V: 43, 172). For the New England colonies it was not necessary to enact the legal restrictions on the enslaved like those brought to pass in the Duke's Laws of New York. But in both New York and New England, increasing constraints were placed on the inter-actions of colonists with Native Americans, regardless of the attitude toward their eligibility for enslavement.

The Sylvester slaveholding on Shelter Island was quite unusual in the context of the region in a few respects. First, with twenty-three enslaved individuals in 1680, they had brought a very large number, even after adjusting to the number of adults (eleven) and assuming that those iden-tified as their children had been born on Shelter Island. Generally slave-holdings in New York and New England were small, rarely more than three per household (Kruger 1985, 128–138; Moss 1993, 14–17). By the 1698 census, Suffolk County, which encompasses the east end of Long Island, was accounted as one-fifth black, most of whom were likely con-sidered enslaved (O'Callaghan 1850, 467). But the number of enslaved at the Manor was far larger than the Sylvester family itself. The Sylves-ters' property was relatively large, with eight thousand acres on Shelter Island alone. Rather than rely upon indentured labor, as did many New Englanders who also had connections to Caribbean plantations, the Syl-vesters opted to blend the labor models of their intercolonial concerns, by bringing enslaved Africans to Shelter Island, probably via Barbados. In this respect they perhaps took a page from the Dutch perspective on labor or, in devising a hybrid approach, acted as Atlantic creoles by adapting to the conditions of their new society.

A second point of departure for the Sylvesters was in their apparent support of family units. Four married couples were identified, three of which had children, while a single man was also noted to have a daugh-ter (see Table 2.1). Although family groupings were not unheard of in early colonial slavery, the demographic circumstances in New York and New England made their occurrence rare and difficult to sustain, given a skewed sex ratio heavily preferring enslaved males (Kruger 1985, 128–135). Each of these married couples was indeed bequeathed intact in Nathaniel's will, more in accord with Dutch practices, lending weight to the idea that he was aware of and in favor of the relationships that had been formed. It is perhaps also arguable that the children of these couples, who were instead given to different family members, were not expected to be forever parted from their parents and siblings, as many of the Sylvester children to whom they were bound were likely to remain close. Not all of the enslaved are traceable in the documentary record, but those who are appear to have been sold or moved within a very small community and usually among those related to the Sylvesters, such as the Lloyd family (by marriage to the younger Grissell Sylvester) or the Arnold family cousins (O'Callaghan 1850, 448–456; Barck 1927, 109–111; SMA Group I-A, P. Sylvester 1688 and N. Sylvester 1687).

The naming of individuals in the will also offers some small insights into the possible origins or captors of the enslaved. Most had fairly typical English names (Hester, Grace, Hope, Abby), and a few had potentially Spanish or Portuguese names like Jacquero and Maria, suggesting their transport via those trade circuits. A few individuals had names that may speak to their point of origin, like Oyou who may have been Yoruba—from the Oyo Empire, arriving at the Slave Coast via the Volta River (Hall 2005, 101–2, 111; Gomez 1998, 55). Tammero, Oyou's husband, may have been named for Temne ethnicity in Upper Guinea (Gomez 1998, 88–89; Hall 2005, 30, 37). Two other seemingly English names may also have derived from the alteration of Akan day names: "Aba" for Thursday could easily become Abby (spelled also Aby), while "Kodjo" for Monday could become Jo (spelled also J:O in the will) (Wilkie 1993). Although tenuous assignments, these names do suggest a broad region of the west-central African coast, from Upper Guinea to just north of the Bight of Biafra, from which the enslaved likely were taken. All of these areas were exploited for captive labor by the early Portuguese and Dutch trade (Hall 2005).

No direct records survive of the origins or route of the enslaved Africans to Shelter Islands, but it is very likely that they arrived via Constant Sylvester's plantations in Barbados. The two sugar operations, Constant and Carmichael plantations, were among the largest on the island, where "a plantation of about 200 acres, equipped with two or three sugar mills and a hundred slaves, was considered the optimum size for efficient production" (Dunn 1972, 96). Enslaved labor on sugar plantations was largely dedicated to cultivation of cane and during the harvest of serially planted fields over six months or so the transformation of cane into sugar. The transformation involved cutting cane, transporting it to mills where it was ground to extract juice, boiling the extract in vast kettles to clean and reduce it of water content, packing the resulting granular reduction to drain and cure, and finally packing the end products of crystallized sugar and molasses for export. All of the work was strenuous, but the milling and boiling were particularly dangerous (Mintz 1985, 46–52). Enslaved Africans coming from Barbados sugar plantations might have viewed the shift from cane cultivation and sugar production to the diverse crop and livestock work of Sylvester Manor with some relief. Nathaniel Sylvester, however, having spent time at these sugar operations, would have had expectations of the kind of labor enslaved Africans could endure.

The Sylvester slaveholding may have been unusual in its demographic makeup, relative to the norms of New England and New York, but it was unfortunately all too typical in the failure to allow active voices of those individuals in any documents. Rare anecdotal cases from later generations have survived. For example, Mallmann recounts an uncredited story of two of the enslaved of Thomas Dering (married to a fourth-generation Sylvester), one of whom was caught drinking in the cellar; the second purportedly defended the first by claiming that both the person and the wine were the property of Dering, therefore no net loss of property had occurred (Mallmann 1990, 59–60). Yet the charter generations of the enslaved on Shelter Island were barred from the networks that had allowed some representation of Algonquian voices. The later anecdote of Dering's "property" offers a trope by which to understand what the English in general and the Sylvesters in particular may have held to be a critical component of personhood, in this case that which grants any degree of representation. Though both "Indians" and "Negros" were discursively held separate from the English, Indians had properties which the enslaved did not. These properties were foremost land, and, when they had successfully been disenfranchised from the land, secondary properties were landscape knowledge: how to obtain from the land those resources the English desired but were unable or unwilling to acquire on their own, especially wampum and fur. The enslaved, however, were likely not considered to hold any unique properties, which is precisely how they came to be commodified *as* moveable property. It is apparent from the ambiguities of racial attributions in documents and legal statutes that these categories were nonetheless not mutually exclusive, and one's status could shift over time from one to the other.

This perspective on Sylvester Manor's history, assembled from the remains available in its own archive, the colonial documents of the region, and the ethnohistory and archaeology of early colonial Indian history, already illustrates a complicated social setting, contrary to neat stories of colonial life. The review of the contexts, general and specific, of Sylvester Manor's early plantation has suggested several points: First, there were a multitude of actors and interests at stake, within both the European and indigenous communities, which cannot be neatly segregated into opposing unified positions. Second, these communities held a range of perspectives on several concepts that became important in their interactions, including notions of political authority and control, community networks, property, and personhood. Third, the roles and statuses of enslaved Africans were somewhat ambiguous at this time, particularly in relation to indigenous persons. Moreover, the relationship of enslaved Africans with indigenous people cannot be gleaned from the archival material. These conditions existed at the time when modern discourses on racial difference began to emerge out of colonists' need to clarify issues of labor, property, and sovereignty. At this point, however, there was still significant ambiguity and fluidity to racial classifications. More important, there were spaces like Sylvester Manor in which alternative notions of affiliation and separation could form as enslaved Africans and the indigenous Manhanset came together.

3 / Building and Destroying

Landscapes are not neutral spaces. They are the places of ongoing actions of humans on the environment and the environment on humans, a relationship so constant in its performance that it occurs at a level of bodily habituation. Landscape can include both built structures and natural features, each structuring our experience in such a way that we come to think of landscape as natural. Because of this continuous engagement, documents for historical posterity rarely comment upon historical environments, just as we would scarcely think to record the number of doors we passed through in the course of our day. Yet the doors, walls, yards, open fields, and close overgrown woods all structure us by allowing or denying access, enabling or preventing private conversation, keeping us in sight of or hiding us from others. These features can afford us either power over others or places to evade power. When those landscapes are reshaped or when managed landscapes are neglected, the bodily memory and experience of them may fade quickly, and those who walk the same path later may have none of the same sense of closeness or exposure, access or constraint. When we lack memory or written record, however, archaeologists seek clues in the material traces of building, destruction, the movement of earth, or the growth of trees, crops, weeds, and gardens. Furthermore, to learn more about those residents of Sylvester Manor whose voices appear only secondhand, if at all, in documentary records, those clues become a major source of evidence. How did the enslaved people experience daily life on the plantation? The Manhanset? Even the Sylvesters felt little need to comment upon the place they made for themselves on Shelter Island.

More than three hundred years after the plantation's provisioning operations ceased, the estate's proprietor, Mrs. Alice Fiske, invited a team of archaeologists from the University of Massachusetts Boston to conduct research into Sylvester Manor's past. By that time, the estate's rich archives had been mined to produce heroic and romantic historical narratives. Alice and her late husband Andrew, a descendant of the Sylvester family and an amateur historian, had pondered questions regarding the unremarked or forgotten details of the plantation landscape. Their questions centered on the founding Sylvester: where had he built the original house? And where was he buried? The archaeologists, led by Stephen Mrozowski, were intrigued instead with the lesser-known plantation residents: how did slavery look at a northern plantation? Archives contain remnants of the past that are protected, for one or another, often idle, reason selected from among the many items produced and consumed in day-to-day life. Archaeology, however, deals in the items cast off, as materials of daily life often are consigned to the status of garbage, debris, or rubble. Those materials recovered by archaeologists are reassigned specific meaning, though the history and memory associated with the site have long since undergone change, often drastic. In some instances, those materials can present us with a rupture to our familiar sense of history.

Digging into the plantation, we were presented with just such a rupture. The plantation landscape and material remains indicated not only a setting far more intimate than what we had anticipated, but also the indigenous Manhanset appear to have remained in residence. More than the plantation landscape, we found three hundred years of reshaping, rewriting, and often unsubtle effacement of that past, in an ongoing construction of stories about the people entangled in it—indigenous, enslaved, and settler. That is, the very actions and events that disrupt, distort, or destroy the artifacts and constructions of the past tell us something important about memory. When a building is destroyed, its components reduced to fragments buried under a thick layer of fill, we can interpret those actions in part as detachment, a kind of deliberate forgetting. When buried remains are cut through, a few hundred years later, by contractors laying pipe or electrical lines, we can see that the process of forgetting is complete, for the appearance of artifacts and parts of old buildings are viewed with surprise and puzzlement. At Sylvester Manor, many places on the landscape have attached memories through the transmission of family stories. Archaeological excavation often reveals both the material grounds of memory and the things successfully forgotten.[1]

Archaeological recovery

In archival collections, our universe of historical evidence has already been sampled when someone chose to keep a document or photograph; in ideal cases the location of each of these items is indexed by subjects, historical figures, and dates. The same is true of archaeological remains—a sample of past material worlds surviving processes of decay and destruction—but without the benefit of an index or finding aid. How do we locate those remains? Because complete excavation is costly in time and labor, archaeologists use a number of techniques to obtain hints at what lies beneath the surface before we choose areas to focus on intensively. Having nearly two hundred and fifty acres upon which to locate the plantation remains, we relied on two main survey methods to narrow our focus: shovel test pit survey, in which small (shovel-width) "soundings" were dug out to assess subsurface stratigraphy and artifact presence, and remote geophysical survey, in areas of particularly high potential. Noninvasive geophysical testing generates information about deposits below the surface based on their physical properties, like magnetic susceptibility, conduction or resistance of electrical current, or density.

We selected areas for survey testing based on topographic potential for use (broad flat areas, access to springs or waterways), proximity to historically high-traffic areas, and in some cases local oral traditions. For example, a wooded high ground to the southwest of the 1735 manor house was surveyed, despite its steeply sloped and uneven topography, because a family legend suggested Nathaniel Sylvester was buried there. He was not there, and we found only isolated brick fragments and lithic debris (by-products of stone tool manufacture). We also tested a sample of seemingly unlikely places, however, so as not to bias our perspective. Because these surveys and excavations are time consuming and labor intensive, archaeologists must aim to find small amounts of evidence from many different areas and full recovery of only a few. Thus, material by-products index many daily activities of plantation life even when we were unable to locate the specific place where the activities occurred. The nature of archaeological investigation renders our evidence always partial and fragmentary, given the nature of preservation and postdepositional impacts and the limitations on our excavation resources. My interpretations of Sylvester Manor's plantation are based on both intensive excavations, with full recovery of those areas, and on extensive sampling surveys.

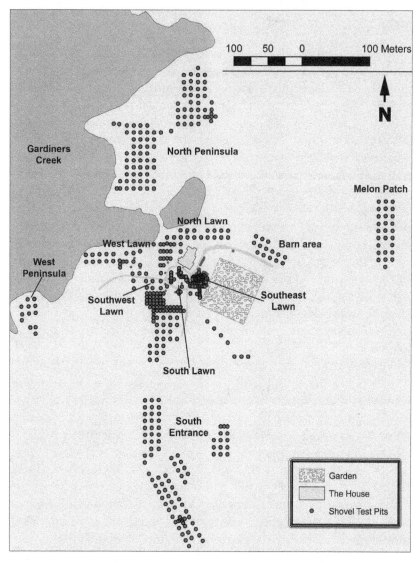

FIGURE 3.1. Sylvester Manor core plantation surrounding 1735 house; additional site areas surveyed and excavated.

Both surveys and intensive excavations are placed on a site grid created by the archaeologist. Imagine laying a very large sheet of graph paper over the site, such that everything recovered as well as the extant landscape can be associated with a coordinate location on that grid. This allows us to record any and all spatial relationships of the artifacts and constructions to one another. The grid also extends to a third, vertical dimension to record depths of deposits, such that lower layers, deposited earlier, are not confused with upper layers, giving us a spatially oriented chronology. We record these depths because complete excavations require that objects and structural remains closer to the surface must be removed to reveal the deeper layers. In other words, as we investigate a site, we dismantle it. Small artifacts may be removed for more careful analysis later, but some finds, like a firepit or a post-hole, must be recorded thoroughly in the field as we dig it out because they can never be so examined again. Thus, we are careful to pass all the removed sediments through hardware mesh to catch the small artifacts and often take small samples of the sediments for even finer-grained analysis. These samples allow us to recover very small artifacts, microbotanical remains, or evidence of anomalous soil chemistry resulting from otherwise invisible residues.

Finally, archaeological investigation consists not just in the buried materials but also in the still-evident features of the landscape, such as the buildings, gardens, roadways, and graded surfaces. The latter are indispensible in helping us understand the processes that have reshaped earlier structures. My focus in this chapter is also on those processes that resulted in the deliberate and inadvertent masking, blurring, or overwriting the past. Archaeology of the Sylvester Manor landscape revealed its layered past—from the precolonial indigenous environment to the remains of the plantation to the extant landscape modifications that have shaped memory. Landscape, in this approach, is twofold: the environment shaped by human activity, and human activity and memory shaped by that environment.

Manhanset landscapes

The evidence relating to Manhanset occupation prior to the arrival and settlement of the Sylvesters is both ephemeral and ubiquitous. That is, scatters of their material culture are found in low numbers across a broad area. Survey work elsewhere on the island has shown that prior to European settlement, coastal Algonquian groups were in residence possibly

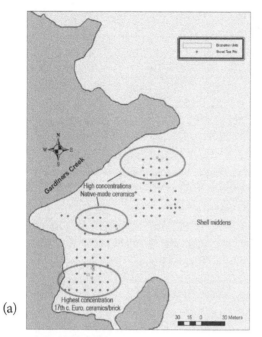

(a)

(b)

FIGURE 3.2. (a) North Peninsula tested areas; (b) undated photo of Gardiners Creek and southwest tip of peninsula (photo courtesy of Fales Library).

year-round, utilizing multiple resource-rich locations. One location may have served as a residential base, preferably near to an estuary, while the Manhanset used temporary encampments at more distant areas with desired resources, like lithic material, plants for food or craft, marine fish and mollusks, or terrestrial mammals (Lightfoot et al. 1987; Lightfoot and Cerrato 1988; Bernstein 2002). The mobility within the island itself indicates that resources were rich enough for them to remain, making use of light and portable structures and periodic encampments that do not leave a substantial archaeological signature. Earlier archaeological survey found no signs of maize agriculture on Shelter Island. If the colonial records of Pequot control over the eastern Long Island Algonquians are accurate, then the Manhanset may have remained in part to use the rich shellfish beds for wampum manufacture.

On the Manor property itself, this portrait of late precolonial Manhanset life was supported by our surveys. Scatters of lithic material, remnants of stone tool manufacture or repair, and locally made pottery were found in many locations, although the highest concentrations were found on the North Peninsula. A rise of land from an estuary in Gardiner's Creek, this area would have been an ideal location for the Manhanset to collect shellfish, where they were well protected from both weather and visitors to either the north in Dering Harbor or Gardiners Bay from which the Pequot might arrive. Few intact features remained here to illustrate the Manhanset's organization of space. Most often, quantities of pottery and lithic fragments were found in deposits on the lower end of a slope, below layers that also contained European-manufactured materials. These materials likely washed down the slope in periods of heavy rain, with later materials coming to rest over artifacts from earlier periods. Dwellings were instead closer to the top of the rise of the land, an area now thickly wooded. Landscape alterations—for example, tree cutting, which destabilizes the topsoil, and forest regrowth—pose serious challenges to recognizing the marks of light, portable structures made of wood, bark, and mats made of woven plant fibers. Such structures were anchored by posts of cut saplings, the traces of which can be indistinguishable from root growth. The most substantial precolonial features of the property were further inland to the east where a more intensive (close-interval and geophysical) survey identified two dense shell deposits approximately 1.5 m wide. One of these was partially evident on the surface, while the second was encountered 20 cm below the surface. A large number of ceramic (pottery) fragments of precolonial Windsor Brushed tradition (Lavin 1998) were recovered from within the shell deposits, as well as a quantity of charred nutshells. Nutshells, because of their relatively short growth span, are ideal for radiocarbon dating. Unlike wood, which may derive from a tree of unknown growth stage or expected age, the date of a nutshell's use is very close to the year of its growth, which can be determined by radiometric dating through accelerator mass spectrometry. In this case, hickory nut shells from two different levels in the deposit returned dates ranging from three to four hundred years before the arrival of the Sylvesters. Column soil samples, taken from one test pit for subsequent microstratigraphic analysis, show that the shell deposits were actually comprised of multiple episodes of deposition that were separated by sterile sediments. In other words, this location was used by the Manhanset time after time, perhaps year after year. Although these features are some twenty meters from the current shoreline, it seems likely that prior to the construction of a land bridge, which cut off part of the creek, they would have been more immediately adjacent to the water (see figure 3.2a). This area may have been one of the Manhanset's preferred locales for shellfish collection, comparable to sites located elsewhere on the island.

These shell middens also contained charred fragments of maize kernels and cupules, the first evidence that the Manhanset may have practiced agriculture. Seeds from weedy field plants in association with the maize support this interpretation (Trigg and Leasure 2007). The finding is resonant with reports from colonial settlement in the area, like Easthampton, where colonists found the "taming of the wilderness" was facilitated by using areas Indians had already cleared for planting (see Gardiner 1871, 13). This may have been the case on the North Peninsula, where a lower southern slope yielded not only the same array of plant remains but also a diffuse scatter of seventeenth-century imported ceramic fragments, the type of assemblage often associated with planting fields. This area perhaps presented itself as a field cleared by the Manhanset and ready to be planted upon the arrival of the Sylvesters. In addition to the evidence of cultivated maize, the hickory nut shells and seeds from fruits, like blueberry and huckleberry, show Manhanset consumption of locally gathered plant resources. Although there is no direct evidence, it is quite likely that they engaged in some environmental management, such as periodically burning away undergrowth to clear the ground surface for planting and to attract game animals. Their familiar landscape was thus associated with available and managed resources more than a built environment: stands of trees, planting fields, estuaries, protected coves, drifts of useful cobbles, or deposits of clay.

Plantation landscapes

Upon the arrival of the Sylvesters, substantial construction com-
menced. Archaeological surveys and open excavations exposed the
remains of some of those constructions, though it is evident that not all
of them are accessible, and there is no specific written documentation
of the plantation layout. What does remain, in the form of structural
footprints, destruction debris, and accumulated waste, gives at least an
impression. In the area surrounding the extant 1735 house, with a later
addition to the north, the sediments beneath the surface contain copious
quantities of artifacts. In some areas, deposition of waste dates to periods
later than the plantation, covering earlier materials. For example, on the
north side of the house, deep deposits of sand and cobble mixed with
nineteenth-century trash lie atop isolated fragments of seventeenth-
century pottery as well as pottery of a style traditionally made by coastal
Algonquians. The distribution of artifacts dating to the seventeenth
century shows that the plantation core stretched from the shoreline of
Gardiners Creek southward through the circular driveway adjacent
to the standing house, an area approximately 75 by 200 meters. Some
portion of this area was created by deep deposits of sand and gravel fill
near the creek shore, perhaps establishing a more substantial dock-side
staging arena adjacent to the early plantation core. The 1735 house, in
the midst of this area, likely covers or incorporates a significant portion
of the plantation footprint. The current location of the two–acre formal
garden to the southeast of the house may also be located on former plantation structures and work areas, but, at the request of Mrs. Fiske (an
avid gardener), this was the only area on the property we were barred
from excavating.

The most intact portions of the plantation core we uncovered were
clustered to the south and southeast of the house. Certain features
appear to date to the earliest phases of construction. A section of
cobble-paved surface is the most stunning of the plantation constructions we found (figure 3.3). It was skillfully made using locally available rounded quartz cobbles, likely collected from glacial till deposits,
creating a pattern of alternating squares of large (~12–15 cm) and small
(~3–6 cm) cobbles. Portions of two intact edges were uncovered, showing the paving to be approximately 3.5 m wide; its total length cannot be discerned as the ends were destroyed, but the intact segment
is approximately 9.5 m in length. The surface may have been used as a
long, narrow dooryard or courtyard or possibly as part of the workyard

FIGURE 3.3. Cobbled paving associated with early plantation features (courtesy of the Fiske Center for Archaeological Research).

with a "clean" surface. The care and time given to creating a patterned surface does, however, suggest an associated structure of appropriately high style and status for the Sylvester family. We found no evidence of such an adjacent structure; thus, the cobble paved surface could have been a roadway. A small intact section of cobbles was taken up to better assess the feature's temporal relationship to the broader area. As only precolonial period Native ceramics were recovered below, we presume this feature was constructed in the earliest Sylvester settlement phase. Unlike other aspects of the plantation core, the surface was not deliberately dismantled, but instead covered by a loam fill. Those portions that were later disrupted appear to have been inadvertently pushed apart by tree planting and growth.

A second early construction was identified as a trench dug for the placement of building posts. The trench appeared as an area backfilled with darker sediments, contrasting with the lighter-colored subsoil into which the trench was dug (6 m in intact length with a corner). Having only one corner of the structure represented, we cannot determine the dimensions of the structure. It was, however, roughly on the same

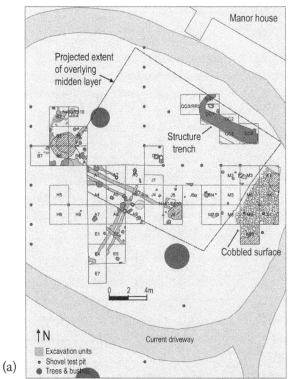

(a)

(b)

FIGURE 3.4. (a) Map of plantation period features and overlying midden layer and (b) excavated structure trench.

orientation as the paving, and if the exposed wall did extend to abut the paving, then the building would have been closer to eight or nine meters on one side, a substantial size for the period. Viewed as a vertical profile, we saw that the trench was covered by layers of mottled and charcoal-rich soil with a mixture of burned and unburned materials. These layers were deposited after the structure was dismantled or destroyed. A faint line of plaster fragments was found to follow the line of the trench at its interior, indicating interior wall plaster. Lower levels of the feature contained several discrete concentrations of burned wood, stone, and brick, showing that a series of posts were set into this trench and partially burned in situ. The charred wood remains from one post showed that they were hewn from oak (Trigg and Leasure 2007). Other segments of the trench lack these remnants, having only backfilled impressions where posts once were before being pulled out. Interior to this trench, there is no excavated cellar, but a lack of accumulated artifacts suggests instead that a floor was built above the ground surface on joists. Thus, we are left with an impression of the structure as built on a frame of oak timbers, with a wooden plank floor and plastered walls, potentially sized to the six or seven rooms suggested in the plantation's Articles of Agreement.

In addition, the apparent method of post-in-trench construction differs somewhat from the more common isolated post-in-ground technique of the colonial period (Neiman 1986). It bears similarities, however, to the technique for Native fort construction, in which tightly spaced posts are set into an excavated trench and backfilled to create a palisade wall (Solecki 1950 and 2006). With this structure, posts were not contiguous; rather, they appear to have been set approximately a meter apart, the bases secured with larger stones and bricks, and the trench then backfilled. While the finished structure would not have appeared unusual, the construction method raises the possibility that either Manhanset laborers assisted in the raising of the frame, or the laborers brought in by the Sylvesters took advantage of the location of existing Native structures when building for the plantation.

Though this structure was possibly the Sylvester residence, the mixture of materials associated with it shows that it was certainly not set apart from the work of the plantation. The majority of the artifacts associated with this structure were recovered from the uppermost layer of charcoal-rich fill, while lower layers had rare fragments of unburned brick, shell, and ceramic, showing that lower levels were intact fill from the original construction, while the upper layer was redeposited or backfilled after the destruction of the building, by sweeping exterior surface materials, like burned trash, into the post-hole voids. This included locally made shell-tempered pottery, rolled copper beads, and waste from wampum production (Foutch 2004; Burggraf 2006) as well as goods manufactured in Europe, dating to the mid-seventeenth century, and a high volume of fish bone and scales. Though the trench appears to have been repeatedly cut into and refilled, leaving the definition of associated posts unclear, it is perhaps our best window into the early plantation phase structures. Most illustrative is the close association, in the fill immediately above the trench, with many small household or personal items, such as copper alloy straight pins used for clothing and cloth drapery. In a residential structure that was otherwise emptied these small items may have been overlooked, or they may literally have fallen through the cracks of the floor. The close association of wampum and fish-processing remains with such domestic items suggests that processing tasks were performed immediately outside the walls of the residence.

Unfortunately, because of the nature of the building destruction, it is impossible to isolate a "household" assemblage for this structure. Was this perhaps a first residence for the Sylvesters? Certain elements seem likely to be of a status and style that the proprietors might have desired, such as interior plaster and the straight pins that would facilitate a proper European matron's dress. If so, the odd post-in-trench construction and the evidence of messy workaday tasks immediately outside show that markers of distinction may have been more selectively deployed *inside* the house, while the outside was associated with the laborers of the plantation. One wonders if this proximity might have imposed restrictions by gender and class upon the women and girls of the Sylvester family, who may have had few outdoor spaces where it was appropriate to spend time.

South of this structure appears to have been an open workyard (see figure 3.4). Several dozen post-holes and post-molds have been recorded here, but no clear pattern indicates a single structure or set of structures. Instead, we can interpret the array as relating to more than one period or configuration of the space. A series of parallel and perpendicular shallow trenches is of clearer orientation. The function of these trenches is not readily apparent, although they could have been sills, fence lines, or drainage. These trenches are cut by several post-holes, and the fill from a few post-holes contained ceramics that crossmended to fragments from the overlying midden fill. Thus at least some of the posts were associated with a later plantation period of use and removed sometime after the accumulation of midden fill. A moderately sized (~50 cm diameter) pit feature near the trenches may be related to either period, though its material inclusions are similar to the fill of the trenches.

The combined residential and working arena included a nearby area for slaughtering livestock. Approximately fifteen meters southeast of the exposed cobbled paving, we located an extensive waste pit. Careful excavation revealed an upper portion measuring approximately four square meters with at least five distinct layers of fill (one layer shown in figure 3.5), each appearing just as excavators believed they had seen the end of the deposit. In all, this pit contained more than twenty cubic meters of plantation-era deposition in dense layers: at top, mortar and brick debris; below, bones from butchered livestock, imported and locally made ceramics, lithics, and more architectural debris; below, burned and crushed shell and clay likely from mortar production; below, more clay with household waste in lower volumes; and lower still a loamy fill with few artifacts. The large size and type of artifacts and recovery of fragments from single vessels across multiple layers suggest that the layers were rapidly deposited. A large number of sizeable locally manufactured ceramic vessel fragments, ballast flint (English stone used as ship's ballast), and a smaller number of European ceramics and tobacco pipes were recovered, among other items. Imagine these layers as nested pans, from narrow openings and shallow depths to wide and deep; these upper materials lay atop even wider, earlier layers of plantation waste. In the lowest levels of the pit, multiple layers of clean sand covered an additional layer of livestock butchery waste approximately 120 to 150 cm below surface. At the bottom of the feature lay a single layer of stone cobbles and a quarry-cut piece of banded gneiss.

The pit itself may have started out as either a precolonial Manhanset feature, such as a borrow pit for clay extraction, or a natural topographic depression, reutilized for waste disposal by the occupants of the earliest plantation.[2] A lack of accumulated materials of indigenous manufacture, however, suggests instead that the pit was excavated by plantation laborers for the purpose of waste disposal, likely using the clean sandy sediment dug out to cover the layers of slaughter waste. Indeed, the lowest layer of animal bone might have been the remains of first shipment of barreled meat to Barbados. One later layer yielded the remains of a minimum of thirteen large, older hogs. These were represented predominantly by "low-utility" skeletal parts, indicating that the high meat-yielding parts were consumed elsewhere, likely cured and barreled for export shipment. This bone assemblage would have yielded approximately thirteen

FIGURE 3.5. Layer of bone exposed in large waste pit (courtesy of the Fiske Center for Archaeological Research).

hundred pounds of dressed meat (Sportman et al. 2007). The pit appears to have been cut and filled in multiple episodes, with the bulk of the butchery waste and sand forming earlier deposits while structural and residential debris was added in later periods. Given the proximity of the pit to the rest of the plantation core, the thick layers of sand must have been a necessary addition to cover the smell of decaying remains and to prevent attracting scavengers.

The uppermost layers, however, contain waste from other activities including more butchery. One of the top (latest) layers contains set mortar and burned brick fragments, while an earlier layer holds dense clay and heavily burned shell, necessary components for the production of hydraulic mortar and plaster. These depositions thus were derived from successive episodes of construction and destruction, perhaps of the structure described above. Other architectural remains include red brick and curved red ceramic roof tiles known as pan tile, nail fragments, and hinges. The layering of the pit, with early episodes of butchery for shipment and later remains of mortar and plaster production suggests that the Sylvesters' priorities lay primarily with the commercial enterprise and secondarily with the creation of a well-appointed home. The confusion of post-holes in the working yard complements this interpretation. This was an organically developing landscape, with ongoing building, renovation, and rebuilding. Certainly, as the family grew, more space was needed, and they may have added rooms to the original structure.

Artifacts of household activities, like cookware pottery, and leisurely pursuits, like pipes for tobacco smoking, were also incorporated to these upper layers. Although they may relate to personal or residential use, it is entirely unclear whose household they came from or how many households are represented. Quantities of locally produced pottery, of a style very similar to contemporaneous eastern Algonquian vessels, were discarded here, including one that appeared to have been dropped whole into the pit. These Indian wares were nestled in the fill alongside ceramics imported from Europe, mostly utilitarian lead-glazed earthenwares. An unusually large number of English ballast flint fragments had been reduced to manageably sized pieces and used as implements for a variety of purposes, like cutting, scraping, and spark production. I explore the role and meaning of these items in more detail in chapter 4.

These items in particular not only shed light on daily life but also help to refine the dating of the layers. Tobacco pipes, with decorative elements that can be dated, are most useful here (Gary 2007; Alexander 1979 and 1983). These clay pipes, while reasonably sturdy when handled appropriately, broke easily when dropped, especially the long stem through which smoke was cooled. As a manufactured commodity, they were inexpensive enough to render repair and careful curation unnecessary. Unlike pottery vessels, which might last for quite some time after purchase, tobacco pipes do not "live" long from their manufacture. The pipes recovered from both this waste pit and the building trench (discussed above) were of Dutch manufacture, though this may reflect availability more than cultural affinities. All of the pipes with identifiable markings had manufacturing date ranges between 1640 and 1700 at the latest, though the bulk of them do cluster in the third quarter of the seventeenth century. As such they evidence a sign that the waste pit and building were likely "closed"—dismantled and covered—well before the end of the century. As central parts of the working plantation setting, the waste pit and a part of the residence facing the working yard may have been deemed unnecessary and unwanted once the Sylvesters ceased provisioning operations, perhaps close to the time of Nathaniel Sylvester's death in 1680.

The paving, the structure, and the waste pit--these may not seem like much of a plantation. They are, of course, what *remain*, not necessarily what *was*. Yet these features together with their associated artifacts can afford us a window into some activities of the plantation. When we look to the broader survey of this core area, we can see additional, vaguer contours of the landscape at that time. For example, at the creek shoreline to the north and west of these features, we combined test excavations in units spaced at intervals on the shore with geophysical survey. Deep layers of sand and gravel with little material culture beyond brick and shell show that the shoreline area has been altered extensively, perhaps to facilitate traffic of goods to and from ships. Further upslope, inconsistent deposits of glacial cobbles and one area of coarse cobbled surface were encountered. At the northeast periphery of this area, a single small boulder was found directly adjacent to two post-hole features, one of which was quite deep (~50 cm), with a coarse sand and gravel fill consistent with that found at the near-shore units. By comparing these small traces to the geophysical survey results, the outlines of extensively built-up landscape begin to emerge (Kvamme 2001 and 2007). In the "interpreted" view shown here (figure 3.6), the areas of abnormally high or low electrical resistance are highlighted to reveal two distinct sets of structural orientation. Perhaps, like the workyard adjacent to the building, this area of the plantation was under continual revision, functioning as a zone to accommodate the traffic of a commercial enterprise: roadways, coarse cobbled surfaces, possibly structures used as warehouses. These constructions lend weight to the family histories claiming that a stone dam, which cuts off the end of the creek and still exists in place today, was built in the plantation period to serve as a landing for ships (Lamb 1887). The extent and scale of this area have made it difficult to pursue these constructions in detail, but the testing has given ample general characteristics for comparison to other working areas of the plantation.

North of the extant Manor house, only the barest hint of the earlier plantation landscape is available. Deep deposits of fill displaced from the construction of a nineteenth-century addition cover a handful of artifacts and a few post-holes dating to the seventeenth century. The condition of the post-holes shows that they were severely truncated, possibly from surface grading. Prior to the construction of the Georgian manor house, the orientation of the working landscape was likely toward the

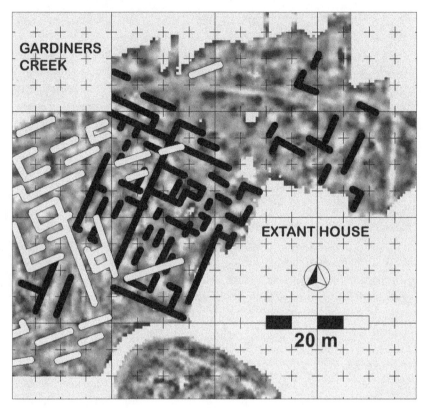

FIGURE 3.6. Interpreted results of geophysical survey, adapted from Kvamme 2007.

water, the sole route of transportation and connection to the sea and the Atlantic world. This area would have been at the face of the plantation. Enough of an archaeological trace remains to suggest that this area played some role, though the degree of landscape modification has destroyed the detailed context. Furthermore, in the eighteenth-century rebuilding of the estate the orientation of the manor was turned away from the water and the Atlantic trade, instead facing toward the interior of the island.

What kind of picture emerges of the plantation from these findings? By synthesizing documentary references with archaeological findings we begin to see a picture. Imagine you are a visitor to Shelter Island in 1673, perhaps one of the Dutch commissioners seeking to negotiate the submission of East Long Island towns to the Dutch or one of the English

Connecticut faction who arrived to declare resistance (see O'Callaghan 1858, 2: 656). Nathaniel Sylvester at that time acted as a go-between, having received assurances from both sides of his sole possession of Shelter Island. Between meetings in Southold, these representatives were housed at what was then Sylvester Manor. Arriving by boats rowed by enslaved Africans, the commissioners would have landed on a shore built upon tons of sand and gravel hauled there by plantation laborers. Perhaps a warehouse looms overhead, a sight that would have been familiar to anyone who had lived in Amsterdam (as Nathaniel had). There is perhaps a reinforced roadbed capable of accommodating cartloads of goods pulled by draft animals. Past the warehouse up the hill stands a sturdy two-story house of oak framing with a distinctive red tiled roof. It is not of high style, but sizeable enough to accommodate Sylvester's large family, as well as the enslaved people who worked as domestic servants. Inside the house one might be surprised at a much more refined atmosphere: gleaming plaster walls, rich carpets and chairs imported for family use, a table set with pewter and simple but serviceable stoneware jugs, and a fireplace.

Taking a stroll outside the house, perhaps smoking a Dutch pipe, you may be reminded again of Amsterdam. The paved dooryard is well swept, and, though there is a working farm behind the house, the yard is a constricted area, perhaps hemmed in on all or most sides by other buildings. Fences to contain livestock, but not the ripe smell of them, run across the yard, which is bare but for some smaller structures--lean-tos to cover goods or shelter laborers at work. The yard appears crowded but neat, although on closer inspection, small fragments of garbage—fragments of shell and coral, small bones, and charcoal—are underfoot. It tends to collect in corners, next to walls, and in uneven spots in the yard, which slopes away toward the water.

The close quarters might feel urban in nature, but when regarding the population and the surrounding environment the resemblance to Amsterdam ends. Sitting in the yard, efficiently cleaning a large fish, perhaps sturgeon, is an Indian woman, while an African man hauls firewood to the house. Between the working structures and into the distance you can glimpse pasturage, an orchard, and likely a barn, perhaps where now stands Alice Fiske's beloved formal garden. The slaughter waste pit may not have been immediately obvious, only a mound in the earth nearby covered in very sandy soil. Though the work of provisioning may not have been in full swing, there was yet a working farm supporting Sylvester's large family and allowing them to be independent while engaging in the wider circulation of Atlantic commerce and finances. As such, the contrast of the house and the adjacent farm may have seemed stark.

Had you been there twenty years before, the place would have seemed busier. The house would have been smaller because there were fewer children to accommodate. A larger number of Indians may have been there, not only cleaning fish but also shaping shells into beads. An enslaved African man may have been at work with the livestock or tending a pile of shells in a very hot fire to make lime for mortar. Those shells may have come from the parts of the abundant local quahog and whelk, which Manhanset residents discarded in making wampum. A cooper may have been at work, assembling barrel after barrel into which cured meats, fruits, or other foods would be sealed. Some of the men might have been down at the shore, transferring cartloads of sand and gravel dug out from some other spot on the island to facilitate access to the creek. Further from shore, the creek is surprisingly deep, perhaps allowing boats of considerable size to land quite close to the plantation. As the main route of connection, much effort was expended upon improvements to this access. In fact, within the first ten years of the plantation, construction must have been continuous and the labor force accordingly large. There was ambition, but not yet a façade of upper-class gentility here.

Landscape of difference?

Throughout the tenure of the plantation operation it seems that the social setting was characterized by close proximity among its diverse inhabitants. Despite owning plenty of land, Sylvester apparently chose not to expand outward as his spatial needs changed; instead, he intensified the use of the same central area, as the evidence of continuous construction and revision of the core shows. Outside this core area of a few acres, archaeological signs of use dropped off dramatically. There may have been extensive pastures, orchards, and planting fields, but there is no indication of *residential* structures outside the core.

While close proximity might breed familiarity and social incorporation, differences can be signaled in many other ways. The closeness of this central compound may have facilitated surveillance. Unlike southern plantations of the eighteenth and nineteenth centuries, with separate quarters for the enslaved (e.g., McKee 1992; Heath and Gary 2012; Deetz 1993; Ferguson 1992), Sylvester Manor does not appear to have included such quarters. If enslaved people were occupying the same house as the Sylvesters, such proximity may have functioned to deny them privacy through differential access: the Sylvesters may have been able to go wherever they liked, but the enslaved could not. Doors could be locked, and apparently they were. Amongst the architectural hardware recovered were lock-plates and keys. The enslaved may have been given access only to marginal spaces, such as an attic, or an exterior kitchen (e.g., Chan 2007). We might suspect, though, that household tasks, such as tending fires and childcare activities, brought them into other residential areas as well.

Outside the house were expansive spaces in which most of the enslaved people likely worked. It is difficult to imagine that they were subject to constant surveillance there. They may have had relatively free passage in fields and pastures, with conditions similar to those described by Garman (1998) in eighteenth-century Rhode Island agricultural settings. There, enslaved African Americans made up a small but critical proportion of the labor force on similar provisioning operations with every person available engaged in production or distribution tasks. With smaller numbers of workers on large properties, draconian physical control was simply not possible. Consequently, farm owners made certain allowances to their enslaved laborers, like small wages or independent farming plots, in the hopes of preventing outright revolt even if resentment was inevitable. In this respect, social relations bore some similarities to indentured servitude. Indeed, local oral histories of Sylvester Manor refer to an area north of the core as the former location of the "Negro Gardens" (SMA, Group IV-A, 3). Survey there showed that this area likely had been planted, but the nature of the archaeological remains makes it impossible to determine when or by whom. Furthermore, because the Manor was on an island, escape would have been difficult, and fugitives would find little refuge except perhaps among local Native Americans. Nathaniel Sylvester must have found those acceptable conditions, and perhaps it was by design that he purchased additional island properties to use as pasturage.

What of the Manhanset at Sylvester Manor? They, of course, knew the landscape better than anyone else on the island and had the option of subsisting far from the plantation core. Likely they did just that, at least part of the time. Yet the unmistakable presence of the products of their traditional technology—pottery, stone cutting tools, and wampum—show that they remained engaged with the plantation community. I do not suggest that this was an entirely free choice. Resources were to be had that the Manhanset may have deemed necessary or at least desirable, and the Sylvesters were happy to exploit that need. Clearly the environment

of Shelter Island was no hindrance to the Manhanset outside the plantation core, but the surrounding Long Island territories may in fact have
been quite dangerous for them. The assertion of friendship of Youghco to
the English documented in 1644 was a form of tribute entailing an obli-
gation of protection, a relationship that may have been transferred to the
Sylvesters themselves. In times of overt Narragansett hostilities toward
the neighboring Montaukett, for example, the plantation core may have
offered the best position of safety from attack. When they were in residence there, the Manhanset appear to have been working, for example
making wampum, within the same plantation spaces as everyone else.

Thus within the plantation core itself, the domestic space and the
close quarters of the working yard afforded the Sylvesters control over
their labor population through surveillance. Class distinctions were
likely signaled within this space through material culture and restric-
tion of access. But there is a distinct absence of archaeological evidence
for structures separating and differentiating between the indigenous and
the enslaved. The potential for engagement with one another away from
the plantation core, as well as the apparently routine opportunities for
interaction within it, raise the question of collaboration and affiliation.

Effacing the plantation

As dramatic a transformation to the precolonial landscape as the
establishment of the plantation was, equally drastic were the efforts given
to rendering the plantation invisible two generations later. This began
with provisioning operations scaling down as early as the last years of
Nathaniel's life. His brother Constant's controversial relationship with
colonial authorities before his death in 1670 likely simplified the decision
to cut ties with the Barbados plantations. Furthermore, in the 1670s, the
increasing tensions between English colonials and many Eastern Algonquian nations culminated in King Phillip's War. In the precursor to this,
Nathaniel's own tolerance for the resident Native Americans with whom
he had apparently lived quietly for many years also dissolved. Shelter
Island Indians were noted at that time by New York colonial authorities to
have been cooperating with the Narragansetts who had earlier subjected
Long Island tribes to such hostility and harassment (Fernow 1883, 14:
697–698). Colonial records show that Sylvester made a notable exception
around that time in allowing Ambusco, "late Sachem of South-hold," to
move with his family to Shelter Island, but all other Indians were barred
from entering (703). Whatever component of his labor force Indians had

made up likely was no longer available to him. In light of this, was the disposal of quantities of their pottery in the waste pit a parting shot? It is undetermined whether they left the island altogether or only the plantation at that time. Anecdotal histories later noted that the Manhanset continued to occupy Shelter Island, in a village on the opposite side of the island, into the eighteenth century (Mallmann 1990, 73).

After Nathaniel's death the remainder of his family began to disperse. His wife Grissell and three of his sons had died by 1696, and his remaining sons chose to live elsewhere, while entrusting their properties to hired managers. Giles, who inherited the core property from his father, spent part of his time in Boston, though a section of a property account book spanning 1680–1701 indicates that he was still managing trade and sale of goods, like barreled meat, cider, orchard fruits, and grains. His waged workers appear to have included a number of Indians, identifiable either by linguistically Algonquian names or racializing qualifiers like "John Indian" or "Squa Hannah," perhaps returning after the conclusion of King Phillip's War (Shelter Island Account Book 1658–1758, East Hampton Library). For some years, the plantation was actually leased to tenant farmers (Suffolk County Deeds, 1693). A comparison of livestock inventories in Nathaniel's 1681 probate inventory and the 1693 lease shows that the scale of operations was quite reduced (Sportman et al. 2007; Mrozowski et al. 2007a). This was only a seven-year lease, with a much smaller resident population in which enslaved individuals do not appear to be part of the labor force. The lease included a provision for use of part of the house. During this time, there seems to have been less care with keeping the working yard clear and accessible. Certainly in the period between Giles's death in 1707 and the resumption of active interest by his nephew Brinley in the 1730s, there may have been little activity there whatsoever. Although it is unclear when the original house was dismantled, the structure trench backfill contained no artifacts with manufacture dates after 1680 (with the exception of Raleigh tobacco pipes, which could have been deposited anytime between 1651 and 1680). This backfill was also completely capped by a later sheet of midden (garbage) that contains materials manufactured significantly later. It is entirely possible that this structure was demolished shortly after Nathaniel's death, perhaps having been an ell or extension of the house.

The presence of a widespread sheet of midden across the working yard indicates more about the way that the plantation core fell into disuse. This deposit, an artifact-dense layer ranging between a few centimeters and twenty centimeters thick, was spread across the majority of the working yard. Given the coarseness and large size of many fragments in the layer, it is highly unlikely that this was an accumulation over the span of the plantation operation, for this would have meant that the yard was impassible. The coarse waste also lay directly over areas where postholes and trenches showed previous walls and fences. Over the course of several seasons in the field, archaeologists removed a large soil block (Piechota 2007) and several sediment cores (Proebsting 2007) for the purpose of studying the stratigraphic development at the plantation core including the midden at a microscopic level. Analyses of these samples and observations from the field tell us that the midden was made up of different piles of material across space and in rapid but punctuated episodes of dumping over time.

Such temporal distinctions are shown in the traces left by hardworking earthworms. In his study of the soil block, Piechota (2007) noted that in the midst of the layer that field excavators identified as the undifferentiated midden there is a zone of earthworm casts, left by their passage through and consumption of organic material in the deposit. Shelter Island's soils are generally far too acidic to see such earthworm activity without soil modification. The inclusion of very alkaline materials in an early deposit of trash—specifically shell, coral, and bone—created a soil environment much more favorable to earthworms. This layer was left undisturbed long enough for the earthworms to process much of the rich organic material available to them, leaving behind a distinct and observable zone of soil alteration. Later a second layer of waste material was laid atop this zone. This "pause" in the deposition of the midden may have several possible causes. Most likely, certain areas of the yard were prone to accumulating trash, as at a fence or structure wall where debris would not present an obstruction to pedestrian traffic. This layer of trash was left undisturbed to earthworms, before the destruction of plantation buildings and piling of debris. The later destruction event was shown by the concentrations of particular types of debris piled in distinct areas, such as brick rubble or smashed mortar and plaster.

Often the debris contained within the midden was burned although the soil around the debris was not, a condition suggesting that the midden is at least a secondary deposit (Proebsting 2007; Sportman et al. 2007), meaning that these materials were first burned elsewhere before being removed to this location. Unburned materials are also mixed into this deposit. It may have been common practice to burn some of the trash, particularly that which may otherwise have rotted. Thus, the midden was likely made not by the gradual accumulation of cast-off items over the years, but by bringing together trash previously deposited elsewhere. This interpretation is bolstered by the fact that some fragments from the same pottery vessels have been found widely distributed, as much as fifty meters apart. Trash was used as a filling medium, smeared across the surface to cover the previous landscape.

When, then, was this mass of debris deposited over the surface of the plantation? Was the material in this layer originally the waste from the plantation itself? The vast majority of the artifacts from the midden layer are poor indicators of date, like the architectural debris. This material could have been either the result of plantation period structures being demolished or later construction waste. At least some portion of the midden layer had accumulated before all the structures were torn down. We found, for example, that once contiguous vessel fragments came from both the midden and post-holes, indicating that the posts had been pulled out and that nearby waste fragments had fallen into the vacated hole in the ground (Hancock 2002). Coral, which we found either in chunks or crushed as a liming agent in mortar, indicates both raw and processed materials. Coral was used as ship's ballast when loading in the Caribbean; when offloaded on the shore at the Manor, it apparently occurred to someone to reuse it as a construction material, perhaps even as late as the 1730s building. In contrast, deposits of mortar recovered from the waste pit and structural feature, dating to the early plantation, were made of a shell-based lime, an evident difference in technology. The widespread midden deposit also contained quantities of coarse red earthenware pottery, suitable for utilitarian kitchen and dairying needs, animal bones, shell, glass bottle fragments, and small personal items like straight pins. These tell us little about date, as even the manufactured goods were produced in similar ways over extended periods of time.

A few items do indicate a range of dates *after which* they must have been deposited. Buff-bodied slipwares, most often manufactured in Staffordshire, were not produced until the later seventeenth century and are not found in North American sites generally until the 1690s. Many of the tobacco pipes were also of styles manufactured around the turn of the eighteenth century or later. A very small number of refined earthenwares, not produced until the mid-eighteenth century, were recovered from the midden. The most precise date represented in the midden material is a George II farthing stamped with the year 1749. These items, a small but significant number, could not have been associated with the plantation, yet were mixed with trash from earlier periods. From an archaeological perspective, this mixing of materials from earlier periods with the beginnings of the Manor's active reoccupation obscures our view of the plantation, as we cannot fully distinguish the debris from each.

When we reconstruct the documentary record of the estate's occupation and the date-diagnostic materials in the midden, it appears that the property was virtually abandoned between Giles Sylvester's death and the reclaiming of the property by his nephew. In the 1730s Brinley Sylvester, Nathaniel and Grissell's grandson, began construction of the manor house that still stands on the estate today, with the intent of residing there permanently (recounted in Mallmann 1990, 47; Duvall 1952, 48–52). The gap in active ownership was important. Brinley had not grown up on the island, had no experience of the plantation setting, and was not shaped by the landscape, only by memories presumably passed down through his family. The house that he built likely stands in the same place where the original Sylvester residence once stood, but facing south, away from the water and toward the terrestrial routes connecting the family to other settlers on Shelter Island. He returned to the estate not to resume the enterprise that had generated so much wealth for the Sylvesters, but to establish a home and setting appropriate to the family's new station. This construction included not only the house itself, an imposing example of formal Georgian style, but also the grounds. In this effort, Brinley, or rather the workmen under Brinley's direction, reassigned the remains of the plantation and all that came after yet again--not simply abandoned *trash* but landscape fill. When construction was complete, the older midden materials and the construction debris were spread across what was now the front yard, filling other low-lying areas with gravel. Like coarse mortar under fine plaster, the midden became the material that filled the uneven and sloped surface of the land surrounding the new house to make a flat and even expanse, while the effect was completed by burying this under an additional twenty centimeters of clean loam. Even the lovely patterned cobble paving was buried.

Brinley himself might not have lived to see the final effect; he died in 1752, and the inclusion of several later-manufactured pottery styles and the 1749 coin show that the underlying midden was still exposed or re-exposed at least in part by that time. By the time his daughter and son-in-law inherited the new Manor house, however, the working yard had been transformed into an ornamental space to frame a gentleman's house. Little but family histories were left to recall the plantation, and those stories were at odds with the new generation's sense of themselves and their status.

Intervening years

Brinley's only child Mary married a businessman from Boston, Thomas Dering. The Dering tenure at Sylvester Manor is poorly represented in archaeological remains of the excavated areas. At some point later a large addition to the north end of the house was added, and the new "working yard" was located at this end, as indicated by the 1828 map of the property (figure 3.7). The map also indicates the garden in its current location, but it is unclear whether this was the formal garden it became in the nineteenth century. An array of outbuildings is shown, including a dairy, a winch-house, a hog-pen, and a cart-house. Archaeological survey located the dairy as it was indicated on this map. The construction of this addition contributed further to the destruction of plantation remains, although the Derings were probably unaware of this effect. By digging a full cellar, their builders unearthed and redeposited enormous quantities of gravelly fill and archaeological materials, mixing artifacts and more deeply burying some remains. Trash in this period was routinely tossed at the northern periphery of this newer working area, into Gardiner's Creek. Today, this material can be seen in heaps at the creekside, mainly glass bottles and fragments of ceramic vessels.

Ironically, the landscape created by the early nineteenth century, which covered the areas worked by the Manor's first enslaved Africans, was still traversed by enslaved people, in the final years before emancipation. In what way, if any, did the new landscape of Sylvester Manor structure their experiences? Lacking a significant archaeological component of the structured space in the later eighteenth and early nineteenth centuries, here we must draw on the existing structures and the documentary record. The Georgian mansion built by Brinley Sylvester is large enough to have accommodated servants, enslaved or otherwise, in its marginal spaces. The attic space, accessible by a back stairwell, provided separation between family and servants. Census records and anecdotal accounts confirm the presence of enslaved African Americans in the household of Thomas Dering (Mallmann 1990, 62–63). Town censuses in 1771 and 1776 both list five individuals under the categories labeled "blacks" and "negroes." Because Thomas Dering later bequeathed individuals as property in his will, we can assume that these were not free black laborers. Gradual emancipation of the enslaved began in New York in 1785. Slavery was becoming a thing of the past at the Manor, although class differences and servitude correlated with racialized identities lingered. In 1829, a new proprietor of the Manor, Samuel Smith Gardiner (albeit still a descendant of Nathaniel

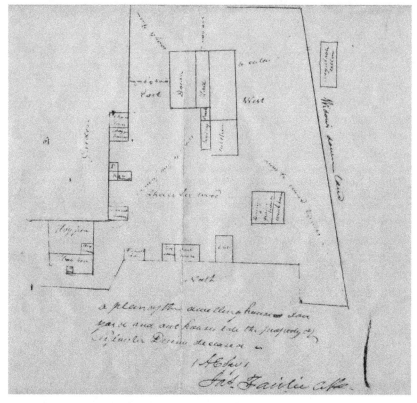

FIGURE 3.7. Sylvester Manor property map drawn for 1828 Gardiner vs. Dering legal case (courtesy of Fales Library, New York University).

and Grissell Sylvester) signed an indenture agreement binding Isaac Pharoah, a five-year-old Montaukett child of Easthampton, to service until his twenty-first birthday (SMA Group III-A, Indenture – Isaac Pharoah 1829). Isaac remained there for the rest of his life. Although the landscape and economy of Sylvester Manor were radically changed two hundred years after the plantation was established, some circumstances had strangely resonated throughout its history.

Imagining the past in the present

Not only the physical effacement of the plantation makes it difficult to find a clear sense of how it was structured, but in many ways our own twenty-first-century preconceptions of a plantation also obscure the view. The archaeology of Sylvester Manor's plantation landscape showed a continual blurring of boundaries, a space through which many people moved and interacted, and thus social distinction had to be performed with little physical distance. But we expect to see stark, rather than subtle, differences and separations—why? In part, because we conflate the representation of racial identity with the structuration of experience. The representation of racial identity did appear in the historical records of the seventeenth century, in town censuses and even in Nathaniel Sylvester's will. But how those differences were "operationalized" in daily life was not clarified. As we attempt to fill in those unknowns, we also see models in the experience of slavery about which we know much more. The "popular" representations of slavery today are drawn from southern U.S. and Caribbean contexts, very often from the nineteenth century. The vast majority of archaeological investigations of plantation slavery have focused on these types of sites, for practical reasons; the more recent, larger, and rural sites are far more likely to have remained intact. Yet this attention reinforces our sense of a plantation's look: separate quarters for the enslaved, distinct deposits of trash associated with households, working areas clearly defined from those of the plantation proprietor (e.g., Singleton 1985; Deetz 1993; Armstrong 1990; Delle 1998; Lewis 1985; Orser and Nekola 1985).

There is also a tendency to associate particular types of persons with temporal or historical eras. In the vast majority of American archaeology, the excavation and study of Native American sites has been the exclusive preserve of prehistorians, while those who worked on colonial or more recent sites were not prepared to recognize indigenous artifacts or landscapes (Lightfoot 1995). African-American archaeologies, however, are the province of historical archaeology. Little archaeological research examines either indigenous presence in plantation settings or the incorporation of enslaved African-Americans into indigenous communities (but see Weik 1997 and 2009; Mathis and Weik 2005). This association of certain categories of people with particular kinds of sites has created an apparent temporal division arguing against the possibility of their interaction with each other (see also Lucas 2004 on disciplinary temporalities).

Landscapes with ambiguous boundaries leave open the possibilities of how people construct their affiliations or build their communities. These spaces, however, only shaped, rather than determined, the potential for interactions. A closer investigation of the detritus from the plantation, the material products of human actions like production and consumption, can help to clarify where or how interactions took place.

4 / Objects of Interaction

Landscape might be the literal grounds for interaction, but very often the material world on a smaller scale—objects portable, intimate, handled, crafted, passed from hand to hand—provides the rationale and locus for people to come together. In chapter 3 I imagined seeing the early plantation core setting, arriving from the water, viewing the house, walking about the compact arrangement of buildings forming a compound, and gazing past the buildings to the more open lands. Recall a few of the historical actors in that scene--an Indian woman processing fish in the yard and an enslaved African man bringing firewood to the house. With what particular materials did they work? What tools and resources allowed them to complete those tasks, and for whom are their products intended? How did the Indian woman cut up the fish, with an iron blade acquired from the Sylvesters or with a stone blade she made herself? Do we imagine that objects "belong" exclusively to individuals? Or are all of these tools and materials the subject of daily negotiations among the plantation residents?

Another interpretive approach we may take to the plantation experience involves thinking through a few mundane materials of daily life, as well as a few potentially less mundane, to ponder how certain objects and materials can bring people together or keep them apart. Sylvester Manor's landscape was a setting of both spatial proximity and an ongoing negotiation of social distance. Much of the disposed material was once instrumental in enacting social relations of labor and production. Access to resources and the use of end-products might be strictly controlled, but the production of food or goods for export required many steps in a process and many contributors to that process. Some items, imported for particular purposes, were put to novel uses while caught in multivalent realms of meaning and adapted to new communities. In the tension between proximity and the efforts of settlers to establish separate social categories like race, certain materials become a focus for transgressions of the emerging social order by demanding interaction and intimacy. As I explore these objects and materials, consider not just what they are, functionally or representationally, but their own "life histories" as they were handled, circulated, and consumed by many historical actors (Kopytoff 1986; Hoskins 1998; Thomas 1991). Those object biographies contain within them the thousand small acts and gestures of people through whose hands they passed.

Acts such as these are what, over the long term, created the structures of inequality, according to the desires of the Sylvesters but executed by laborers who built the plantation landscape. But not all acts were in the service of the Sylvesters' vision of orderly society, even after the physical structures were built. Although the plantation environment imposed constraints upon its laboring residents, spaces, some of which were outside the plantation core, still existed where individuals could pursue their own interests. Even within the plantation, however, small actions might pass unnoticed or unremarked; small opportunities to engage in a community were perhaps not completely but still partly of a laborer's own choosing. These comprised the tactical practices theorized by Michel de Certeau (1984); while the "proper place" and end production operated according to the Sylvesters' desires, the movement and engagement of their laborers within that "proper" structure formed a social space unto itself—hidden in plain sight. Exchanges and associations made through the circulation of material culture, particularly of small items or temporary concerns, are easily hidden or ignored. Such engagements passed unremarked in the curated records and transmitted memory of the Sylvesters. The material traces of these acts were constituted as garbage (as suggested by Lucas 2002), not durable reminders.

I use selected types of material recovered in archaeological excavations to draw out the possible grounds for interaction they provided. Sometimes these interactions are evident in the material, but in most cases I infer more information from the artifacts' location in the larger context. Much of this material, coming from the core work-yard of the plantation, seems to have been entangled in the laborers' lives, although by proximity these experiences are also tied to relationships with the

Sylvesters themselves. Not all of the recovered artifacts are subject to this discussion; for example, the masses of architectural debris of the midden, from which the landscape perspective of chapter 3 was partly inferred, are not revisited here.

Faunal remains: food and labor

Food provisions were a central concern of the plantation. One main goal of the operation was to provide consumable supplies to the Barbados sugar-producing properties. As such, some business-related documents of Sylvester Manor explicitly mention the scale and kind of animal husbandry undertaken as part of its commercial operations. Not all provisions were exported, however; some were consumed locally by the plantation residents.

Faunal remains, the durable elements of animal organisms, were major components of the waste deposited at the plantation core, but this should not be taken as an indication that meat comprised the majority of the food the family consumed, only that preservation favors bone and shell over other goods, like plant remains, starches, and fats. The animal bone assemblage recovered from the early plantation deposits and the blanketing midden layer was dominated by domestic livestock: sheep, cattle, and swine. Lesser quantities were identified as domestic and wild fowl, fish, shellfish, deer, canine, small wild game such as raccoon and squirrel and reptiles (Sportman et al. 2007; Kennedy 2008). The domestic livestock was at the heart of meat provisions because it was bred for bulk and manageability, but some animals served other purposes as well by providing milk and wool and muscle to pull plows and wagons. Horses, not generally bred for meat, were also documented as valued commercial resources. Nathaniel Sylvester's estate inventory of 1680 enumerates the animals (and their value) he and his financial partners owned, indicating a tremendous amount of wealth on the hoof: 427 sheep, 200 cattle, 120 swine, and 40 horses, for a total value of £350 and approximately 20 percent of the value of the entire estate. That the "property" held in partnership is comprised almost entirely of livestock and enslaved individuals speaks to the nature of the enterprise.

Care of these animals prior to their slaughter or live export entailed pasturage, allowing them to roam and forage for food as provided by the island environment. Pasturing animals requires a relatively low number of caretakers, and we might infer that those seven persons noted in Nathaniel Sylvester's estate inventory as being owned in partnership were responsible for the care of the livestock. While the island, circumscribed by water, naturally contained grazing animals, some effort must have been given to prevent the animals from either disrupting other valuable resources, such as planted fields, or wandering into dangerous areas like swamps. The sheep and cattle herders likely benefitted from close communications with the Manhanset who held an intimate knowledge of the island's environments and may have even been employed in the work themselves. The Manhanset probably also were concerned with the intrusion of grazing animals on their own preferred resources, like particular hunting grounds, plant collection areas, or planting fields. Livestock damage was a common point of contention between settler and indigenous communities in the colonies (Cronon 1983, 129–139). Account book entries from the 1680s noted payment to a number of laborers for cutting wood and "railes" which may have been for fencing (Shelter Island Account Book 1658–1758, East Hampton Library). The tasks of livestock herding and care may thus have brought the indigenous and the enslaved into communication and potential conflict with each other, not only within the plantation proper but also in areas at a distance from the plantation core. Robin's Island, for example, was reserved by Nathaniel as both pasturage and fish and shellfish resource areas for Manhanset use (Easthampton Town Records 1887, 1: 96–99, 104–109).

Although herding, pasturing, and feeding were constant low-labor tasks, livestock entailed periodic bursts of intense work (Trigg and Landon 2010). Laborers cut, dried, and bundled hay for feed in the summertime. Sheep needed shearing in the spring, and the resulting wool might be cleaned and sold or kept to be spun. The age profiles of the caprine (sheep or goat) bones and teeth found in the midden deposit suggest, however, that few sheep were kept for more than a few years; that is, they were primarily raised for meat, not wool. Sheep raised for export of meat were likely shipped live or "on-the-hoof" because cured mutton did not preserve well. Other animals, like hogs and cattle, raised for meat export were slaughtered on-site. Periodically, larger numbers of animals would be butchered, salted or otherwise cured, and packed into barrels for shipment. The large pit that was excavated at the plantation core held, in one layer of bone, the remains of thirteen large hogs, likely yielding considerably more than a thousand pounds of meat and thereby representing a significant amount of work. The bulky, low-utility parts of the hogs (cranium and feet) were discarded rather than shipped, allowing quantification of meat production through their remains. The cattle, appearing in great numbers in documentary records, were not similarly dressed, as their skeletal remains were recovered with representation of all parts. Given that the plantation kept such a quantity, some must have been exported. Most likely, the cattle found in archaeological deposits were likely consumed there, while the animals slaughtered for shipment were packed with all parts included on the bone (Sportman et al. 2007; Kennedy 2008; Trigg and Landon 2010). It is unclear whether livestock slaughter and barreling would have been a task that the Manhanset would participate in, although enslaved persons likely had no choice but to do as directed.

Meat from domestic livestock was, of course, consumed by plantation residents as well. While hogs were quite evidently processed for export, there was little sign that any pork was kept for local consumption, with the exception of the low utility crania and feet. These were found in not just the deposit of slaughter waste but also the midden and residential waste deposits, perhaps used by the enslaved to supplement their diet. Beef and mutton, the preferred meats in an English diet of the time, were well represented in the midden deposit and residential fill lying over the slaughter waste. There was no preferential or skewed distribution of skeletal parts of the cattle, but there was preference shown in some parts of mutton, such as the desirable upper hind quarters, which were proportionately better represented in the midden than in other deposits (Kennedy 2008, 56–57). This skewed representation likely stems from a subtle level of distinction drawn between the Sylvesters and their laborers: although all might eat the meat of the same animals, they did not all eat the same cuts.

Domestic livestock dominated the remains recovered from the plantation, yet a small but significant set of remains indicate as well consumption of wild species, including white-tailed deer, fox, squirrel, raccoon, rabbit, fish, and wild bird species such as swan, Canada goose, crow, and pigeon (Kennedy 2008; Sportman et al. 2007). Mirroring the skewed distribution of mutton skeletal parts, wild species were recovered from all plantation deposits, but the upper deposit lying over the slaughter waste pit contained a greater proportion and diversity of these species than the others. As all of these species were candidates for the traditional Manhanset diet, this overrepresentation may be the result of proximity to their own dwellings, perhaps located to the east in the unexcavated formal garden. Alternatively these remains may have been acquired and sold by the Manhanset to the Sylvesters or acquired by enslaved Africans themselves, for diversity and supplement to the diet (e.g., Franklin 2001).

A few of these species would have been particularly desirable to the Sylvesters themselves. Swan was considered a delicacy in England (Wilson 1991) as was dolphin (Sim 1997), of which a single bone specimen was found, and sturgeon. Remains of both bone and scales (scutes) of sturgeon were found in several deposits, including the slaughter waste and the structure trench, which contained a large number of scales of many unidentified fish, and some were quite large (having scales over one-half inch wide). A great majority of the fish bones and scales could not be identified to a species, as these remains exhibit notoriously poor preservation, but the Atlantic coast was well-provisioned with larger species, like cod, that might have been desirable. This distribution suggests not only that sturgeon may have been consumed by a number of different plantation residents but also that larger fish species could have been brought in by the Manhanset as another export commodity (Kennedy 2008). The Manhanset were recognized for their skill in deeper water fishing; in 1675, for example, a petition was lodged by Jacob Schellinger of Easthampton to hire four Shelter Island Indians for whaling, despite their sanction for unruly behavior earlier that year (Fernow 1883, 14: 707–708).

Shell material, the durable remnant of bivalve and gastropod marine mollusks, comprise another type of the faunal remains recovered from Sylvester Manor. Shell had an even more complex circulation among the plantation residents than animals because it played a number of roles as food, as raw material for durable construction, and as currency. Yet shellfish acquisition and use was completely absent in the documentary records of the plantation, a silent economy. A number of species were plentiful in the waters around Shelter Island and the greater Peconic Bay, including hard shell clam or quahog (*mercenaria mercenaria*), soft shell clam (*mya arenaria*), knobbed and channeled whelk (*busycon carica* and *canaliculatum*), Eastern oyster (*crassotrea virginica*), scallop (*pectinidae sp.*), and mussel (*mytilidae sp.*), all of which have been recovered from Sylvester Manor's plantation period deposits. All are edible and could represent an additional food resource, although they likely were not considered particularly desirable by the Sylvesters, with the possible exception of the oysters, which were incorporated into a number of English dishes (Wilson 1991; Thirsk 2007). Thus, the bulk of shellfish may have been left to the enslaved or other laborers to consume. Two of these species, quahog and whelk, dominate the assemblage, both of which are the source material for producing wampum, or shell beads. These quantities suggest that the shellfish may not have been solely, or even primarily, collected as a food resource.

Wampum, from the Algonquian *wampumpeague* and alternatively called *seawant* by the Dutch (Beauchamp 1901), has a complex history entangled with the early Dutch and English colonies surrounding Long Island Sound. These small beads of white or purple/black shell were produced by coastal Algonquians prior to European colonization, although the archaeological evidence for them is scarce. The beads were observed, however, as trade items in circulation by a number of European early coastal explorers (McBride 1994; Ceci 1990b). Following colonization, however, the production and circulation of wampum increased dramatically, for several reasons. First, the use of European-manufactured iron awls, often referred to as "muxes" by Algonquians, rendered the production process much faster. Second, the beads were prized by the Haudenosaunee of northern territories in the upper reaches of the Hudson River and the eastern Great Lakes. Dutch entrepreneurs quickly realized that a steady supply of wampum would create a steady source of furs from their Native trade partners in those northern regions, so much so that it was referred to as "the source and mother of the beaver trade" (cited in Jacobs 2009, 108). This reliable trade value and a general lack of available coin currency thus led both English and Dutch colonies to adopt wampum as an acceptable and regulated form of currency, in which they valued the white beads (made from whelk) generally at half the value of the purple/black beads (made from a portion of the inner quahog shell). Among the Algonquians, wampum became a common tribute payment, accounted in strings of standard fathom length, and increasingly demanded as a payment for fines levied by English colonial authorities (Siminoff 2004; Beauchamp 1901). The quantities turned over as payment, ranging in the hundreds of fathoms, would not only have been extraordinarily lucrative to the English but also elevated wampum production to a nearly continuous occupation of collecting shells, reducing them to their usable portions, shaping them with abrading stones, and drilling bore-holes.

This production process was taking place in the plantation core of Sylvester Manor. Although a small number of beads was found in the later midden deposit, the vast majority of the evidence of bead production was in the form of shell in various stages of reduction, found in the early plantation deposits in the structure trench and above the slaughter waste layer (Foutch 2004). Manufacturers removed the outer plates of whelk shell to extract the central columnella, which was then sanded to produce a smooth, straight, and rounded length of shell. To make a purple bead from quahog, the interior colored segment of the shell was extracted, and the lengthwise segments were sanded to a rounded

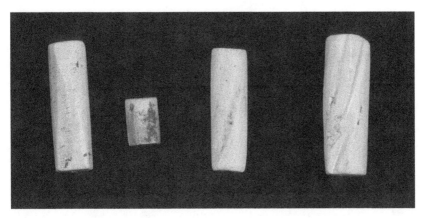

FIGURE 4.1. Wampumpeague, shell beads (photo by Melody Henkel).

column. These blanks were cut into smaller lengths from 5mm to 2cm, although larger examples have been documented (Beauchamp 1901, 368). Finally, the beads were bored through by using a stone drill or iron awl. Two such awls were recovered from the extensive midden deposit. The completed beads were strung on lengths of fiber twine or thread if it was available. Fathom-length (six foot) strings are estimated to have held about 330 beads (Ceci 1990b).

Coastal Algonquians did not consider wampum to be currency, strictly speaking. While it could be used to pay tribute, it was regarded more as a politically laden gift. Women might make belts or collars of multiple strings, patterning the white and purple beads to create designs in the finished field of attached beaded strings. High-status individuals wore these at the neck, head, or waist, or as smaller bracelets or ear adornment. The Haudenosaunee also used either single strings of wampum or elaborately fashioned belts of multiple stings as materials essential to diplomatic relations and declarations of alliance or war (Beauchamp 1901; Hough 1861). Routine negotiations or visits between coastal Algonquians might require one or more strings of wampum as gifts. Thus, the strings were much more than money; they were material instantiations of a relationship. Why was wampum being produced at the plantation? Although there have been rare documented cases of non-Indians producing wampum (Peña 2001), in all likelihood this was a Manhanset tradition in practice. If they were paying tribute to the Sylvesters for protection, then this was their medium for marking the obligations of the relationship. For the Sylvesters, the beads were a financial boon, an opportunity for Nathaniel to engage in trade, perhaps without his financial partners' knowledge.

The enslaved Africans might well have understood the concept of shell money also. In a number of coastal West African societies, cowrie currency had long been in circulation. Similar to wampum use, some societies drilled the cowrie shells and strung them for easy enumeration. Cowrie currency was, however, a true currency, exchangeable for commodities, and the shells themselves were not local acquisitions but instead imported from the Maldives and East African coast on the Indian Ocean. The shells formed a small denomination in a larger system of currency including gold, iron, and imported copper alloy (Johnson 1970; Adebayo 1994; Hogendorn and Gemery 1988). The concept may have been similar enough, however, to spark recognition and perhaps a willingness to participate in the hopes of generating their own wealth. The enslaved were at least witness to the wampum production and likely a part of the circulation of shells, for either the edible components or the unwanted fragments used in producing tremendous quantities of mortar and plaster.

Two distinct deposits dominated by shell in the early plantation deposits illustrate this latter use in mortar and plaster production for building construction. Set and broken mortar, with evident chunks of burned shell, was recovered from those deposits. Shell is composed largely of calcium carbonate (calcite), a hard and durable mineral. Cements, like mortar, can be made by breaking down the calcite mineral, then making it reactive to form new calcite crystals. The calcite in shell can be broken down by burning it at a high and consistent enough temperature to release all of its organic carbon. The resulting decarbonized shell can be crushed into a powder called quicklime and mixed with water and filler materials like sand, gravel, or larger chunks of shell. The reaction will form new, hard calcite crystals; if it is also mixed with a reactive silicate like clay or quartz sand, the resulting mortar will be resistant to water (Wenk and Bulakh 2006). The shell material, whether by-products of meals or wampum production or acquired for this particular process, was burned in great quantities to fill and plaster the walls of the original Manor house. Burning such quantities sufficiently was a dirty, overheated process, which likely fell to the enslaved. But the waste from this production was located, just as the wampum waste was, at the core of the plantation, and it is hard to imagine that the various shell productions, close at hand to one another, did not inspire curiosity, exchanges, or sharing of materials and methods. Shell, in its circulation, was a major factor in drawing the Manhanset into the operation of the plantation.

Pottery: imports and local production

Ceramic (pottery) fragments are commonly recovered in archaeological excavations because ceramic material is so durable. While archaeologists rarely find whole vessels outside of ritual or mortuary contexts, fragments of vessels that have broken and been discarded are nearly ubiquitous in settled residential areas because pottery, being a malleable and relatively inexpensive medium and a craft practiced by people all over the world, is so frequently used for a wide variety of purposes. Moreover, as fired clay, the finished product becomes like stone in its resistance to decay or degradation, as opposed to the many organic materials used in daily life that do not survive for us to examine. The ceramic items used at Sylvester Manor were both imported and locally produced varieties, indexing different realms of circulation among the residents.

The imported pottery was typical of wares produced in Europe from major potteries in England, Holland, and Germany. European pottery production in this period was already a specialized industry (Noël Hume 2001; Watkins 1968; Pearce 1992; Schaefer 1998). Rather than support a potter with the kiln and extensive production materials he would need, the Sylvesters relied upon commercial sources for imported wares. The assemblage of pottery fragments that were found in the early plantation features represents a fairly small number of items, generally used for food storage and cooking as well as beverage jars or mugs. The food vessels were mostly coarse red- or buff-bodied earthenwares, glazed on at least one surface in order to reduce porosity so that they could be used to hold liquids (figure 4.2a). When we were able to identify the original vessel form it appears that the most common were jars and pipkins or the Dutch *grapen*, legged and handled cooking pots (Gary 2007; Janowitz 1993). A few additional fragments were from fancier tin-enamelled wares, with a distinctively thick white glazing and blue, purple, or multicolored painted designs. Sometimes referred to as "delft-ware," these vessels were generally valued for their bright surface color and painted decoration that made them showy items, broadly resembling the much more expensive imported Chinese porcelain. In the main, however, the imported pottery likely was kitchen ware, used in food preparation or storage. A larger number of these vessels found in the later midden deposit also suggest their use in dairying, including several milk pans, broad and shallow vessels ideal for cooling and separating milk.

Unlike one predominant use of pottery today, these vessels were not used for dining. As Deetz (1996) has noted, the use of matched sets of

FIGURE 4.2. European manufactured pottery, (a) coarse earthenwares and (b) stonewares (photos by Jack Gary).

individual ceramic plates was not widely seen until the eighteenth century in North America. The absence of food-serving pottery, combined with the recorded 1680 probate inventory, does suggest clues as to what would have been used instead. The inventory noted "280 pd of pewter" as well as an additional four "dozen of plates." The pewter, undifferentiated by form, probably represented a wide range of vessels, including cups or flagons. The large number of plates could have been ceramic, but just as likely (for a wealthy household, as Sylvester's was at the time of his death) may have been silver. Pewter and silver were more expensive than pottery, but they were also more durable and thus far less prone to accidental breakage. Pewter is made of malleable metals that could be repaired or recycled, and so such vessels were less likely to end up in trash deposits. The valuation of the four dozen plates at £2 8s, however, when compared to other inventories of the time, is certainly too low to be silver and may even be too low to have been pewter. The Sylvesters themselves probably ate from the pewter at a very stylish table. The plates referred to may have been trenchers, made of hollowed wooden slabs, used by their laborers and domestic servants; they might also have used porringers, more bowl-like dish forms with or without handles. One dozen porringers were enumerated on the inventory, though without a description of their composition. Wooden dishes are unlikely candidates for long-term curation; they would not survive in an archaeological deposit, or they may have been burned as part of trash disposal practices. Our interpretation of the food preparation and serving materials in this case must be as much informed by absence as by presence.

Imported ceramic beverage containers of the seventeenth century were often stoneware, a ceramic that is fired at a higher temperature than the coarse earthenware cooking pots in order to render them more vitrified and less porous. Although no stoneware vessels were found in the early plantation deposits, at least twenty-nine were found in the midden (Figure 4.2b). Their potentially early manufacturing dates and sturdy construction suggest that some may have been used in the plantation setting. These vessels were mostly jugs or tankards; most were of German manufacture, though a few were English (Gary 2007). As drinking vessels, these were probably supplemented by the higher-style pewter, as earlier suggested. The stoneware jugs were part of a larger suite of bottles, most notably glass bottles containing spirits. The earlier plantation features contained very little of this glass, but numerous fragments from wine bottles and case bottles, square-sided containers for harder liquors like gin, were found in the midden.

These few imported ceramic items had a circulation that could have included any of the plantation residents moving through the house. But as with the house itself, access and ways of using those materials would have been dictated by a person's status and role. Fine pewter or silver items may have only been for the Sylvesters' use, but the fine pieces were undoubtedly also handled by domestic servants. Cooking and storage wares, however, were routinely used by those servants and perhaps less by the Sylvesters, though the latter may have selected them for purchase. With the exception of vessels related to dairying, few of these items would have been circulated outside the household and its immediate environs.

The locally produced pottery enjoyed a rather different kind of circulation and recognition among plantation laborers and the broader network of coastal Algonquian people. The process of pottery *production* either on-site or nearby meant that a greater diversity of people may have seen, handled, discussed, used, and--more importantly—had a hand in the *making* of these vessels. The finished items are technologically and visually quite distinct from the imported wares: they were neither glazed nor painted, were hand-built rather than wheel-thrown, and were fired in a pit or bonfire rather than a kiln. The style of this pottery was much in the tradition of indigenous manufacture, which was a household undertaking rather than specialized production. Yet who was included in that production, in the context of colonial interactions with a diversity of people? One way to investigate that question is to examine the traces of the manufacturing process itself, rather than simply categorizing the finished product. Those traces index a multitude of actions, some of which are choices among many possible actions. When the craft was practiced by households, pottery-making techniques were shaped by the traditions of past generations.

In this particular case, the skills of small-scale pottery production were tradition only for the indigenous and the enslaved Africans. West African sites of the seventeenth and eighteenth centuries demonstrate that a household potting tradition existed and employed a variety of techniques (DeCorse 2001; Stahl 2001; Kelly 2001 and 2004). Further, Caribbean (Hauser and Armstrong 1999; Hauser and DeCorse 2003; Meyers 1999; G. Smith 1995), Chesapeake (Mouer et al. 1999; Emerson 1999; Deetz 1988), and Carolina (Ferguson 1992 and 1999) plantation sites with distinct spaces for the enslaved have yielded many examples of locally produced, open-fired coarse earthenwares. Given the evidence of this tradition, we can infer that the enslaved Africans at Sylvester Manor were quite familiar with the kinds of production practices employed by the Manhanset. Enslaved Africans may well have had related skills, such as fire temperature control learned through ironworking and sugar-boiling and the chemically related production of mortar and plaster that could be transferred to the pottery-making process. As for the Manhanset, the evidence of their skills and traditions can be found within ambling distance of the plantation core, dating back at least a thousand years. Only the European residents of the plantation had no traditional skills to offer in this process.

There are a number of essential stages in the production of pottery. Raw clay material must be collected and processed, often by mixing it with aplastic "tempers" that strengthen the clay and prevent the vessel from collapsing as it dries and shrinks. A potter then shapes this mixture by using one of the common techniques for building a vessel like coiling ropes of clay, pinching a slab of clay into the desired form, paddling clay over a form, or using a potter's wheel. Decorative elements would be added after building, by attaching shaped clay forms, impressing, incising, or stamping the surface, or coating the surface with paint, glaze, or slip. The vessel is left to dry before firing it in order to convert the clay particles into a bonded, inert substance. As noted earlier, the temperature at which pottery is fired impacts the physical properties of the finished product, like hardness and porosity. At every step, the potters make choices of technique, based on prior knowledge or memory of the process and the desired effects.

If you were to examine the finished product, many of these technical gestures would be evident: the shape of the vessel, the decorative elements, or large fragments of tempers added to the clay. Many actions are not so readily apparent, however, and to assess those requires additional analytical methods. The chemical and mineralogical characteristics of the pottery may indicate the source or type of raw materials, including tempers of small grain size. The process of firing the vessel introduces specific changes in mineral structures that are progressive with increasing temperature ranges. Methods for processing clays and tempers are often most evident when viewed at the microscopic scale. The locally produced ceramics at Sylvester Manor were analyzed using techniques that allow the characterization of chemical and mineralogical properties, including x-ray fluorescence spectroscopy and petrographic microscopy (for detailed description of these studies, see Hayes 2008, 141–190; Hayes 2013).

The question that arises for the locally produced pottery found in the plantation contexts is whether the manufacturing practices are consistent with those evident either in the periods preceding colonial settlement or in contemporaneous Algonquian fortified sites. Pottery production is considered a conservative tradition. In a society where, as ethnohistoric observations suggest, women were potters who taught their craft to daughters, abrupt changes in manufacture might be related to broad social disruptions, including interactions with people having different traditions that may seem innovative. Alternatively, conformity of style and manufacture in a period of social upheaval might be an expression of orthodoxy, a conscious reproduction of tradition in defiance of pressures to change. In the ceramic materials at Sylvester Manor, a combination of both responses was in action.

Tradition and change in eastern Algonquian pottery practices has been a process over the long term, as described by archaeologists who have found their pottery at sites dating from the Early Woodland period (2,700 B.P.) to the period of European colonization. This entire span is represented in the pottery recovered from numerous locations at Sylvester Manor. In the earliest periods, potters produced thick-walled (8–12 mm), mineral-tempered, and rough-surfaced vessels owing to the coarseness of the paste and the practice of paddling to seal the coils. Cord-wrapped paddles were most frequently employed. These ceramics had little to no decorative elements and plain, wide openings without neck constrictions (Lizee 1994, 57–74; Lavin 2002). Later vessels had similar morphology but more frequently were decorated by shell-stamping (linear, rocker-stamp, and dentate) on the upper vessel portions close to the lip. Low-density shell-temper was occasionally used, usually in association with coastal occupations. By the Late Woodland period (roughly 1000–500 B.P.), several shifts in practice are widely recognizable. First, potters made the vessel walls increasingly thinner, while using a smaller temper grain size; the two elements are likely connected. Decorative elements were elaborated, particularly on collars built over constricted necks on the vessels. By the end of the Late Woodland period, potters applied decorative motifs with incised lines rather than shell-stamping, although they still used dentate stamps to leave small angular impressions. Finally, later ceramics were predominantly well-smoothed on surfaces (Luedtke 1985; Lizee 1994).

The ceramics produced in the early colonial period by Coastal Algonquians were the most elaborate of all, with the addition of modeled castellations. This style was originally associated with the Mohegan because of the great quantity first found at the Fort Shantok site excavations (L. Williams 1973; Rouse 1947), on Mohegan land in Connecticut. Archaeologists still refer to this style as "Shantok-type." Since that early find, a great many other areas, including Fort Corchaug in Southold (Smith 1950; L. Williams 1973) as well as Sylvester Manor, have yielded similarly collared, decorated vessels. In this colonial period, a proliferation of manufacturing techniques resulted in a wide variety of collar and castellation morphologies (for example, high-relief vs. low-relief), and limited chemical composition testing indicates that the vessels were produced in many locations rather than from a single source (Lizee et al. 1995). At the same time it has been noted that the decorative motifs themselves became more standardized, mostly a narrow range of variations of triangular designs framed by incised banding (Lizee 1994, 233–234). A second common characteristic was the use of a dense shell temper, quite evident even when looking at the surface of the vessels. The combination of visually prominent standardized characteristics (pendant triangular motif and dense shell temper) with wholly unstandardized building techniques has been interpreted by some archaeologists as a style signifying increasing Algonquian alliances, as potters from numerous tribes chose to represent the same motif (Goodby 1998 and 2002; an analogous case from the Pueblo Revolt is presented in Liebmann 2008). The representation of this emblematic style at the plantation core of Sylvester Manor thus indexes the continued engagement of the Manhanset in the wider indigenous political networks (figure 4.3).

Based on these superficial traits, largely referencing decorative styles, the Sylvester Manor Shantok-type pottery, found only at the plantation core, might easily be attributed to the continued presence and persistence of Manhanset traditions only. But large quantities of these vessel fragments were found throughout the plantation deposits, in the core area where landscape clues describe a close and well-used work-yard. To whom else was the manufacture and circulation of these pots meaningful? Here, Paul Connerton's (1989) distinction between *inscribed* and *incorporated* memory is useful. Intended as a heuristic device for the analysis of social memory, he described *inscription* practices as those that are either written or recorded in some fashion perhaps outside the body (as in text or images) or verbalized in repetition and mnemonic reference. Inscribed practices emphasize the sedimentation of ritual in repeated and constant forms, which can be made portable as ideological coda. The emblematic motifs on the pottery were an inscription of this sort. *Incorporated* practices, however, are centered in the body, as postural or technical gestures but without being "permanently" inscribed so that the memory of such social identifications must be carried and transmitted in person. Rowlands adds that in incorporated practices, secrecy and exclusion are important aspects of such knowledge and identity (Rowlands 1993). The invisible or nonrepresentational gestures that went into the making of the pottery would thus be part of an incorporated memory, available to the exclusive group of those participants.

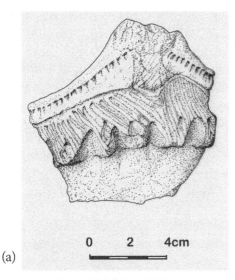

(a)

FIGURE 4.3. Locally produced earthenware in Shantok style, (a) castellation (drawing by Elaine Nissen) and (b) partial vessel with handle from large waste pit feature (photo by author).

0   2   4cm

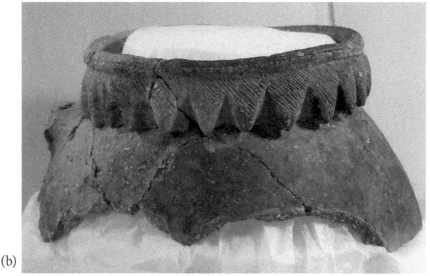

(b)

The basic clay-temper mixture and the processes of vessel firing were gestures of an incorporated knowledge. The evidence for these lies in the chemical and mineral composition of the pottery. The chemical composition varies most significantly on strontium and calcium, reflecting the use of shell temper. When comparing the Late Woodland period vessel fragments to those from the plantation, the latter demonstrates at least three times the elemental strontium over the former. Pottery samples from Fort

Corchaug and Fort Shantok had similarly high levels of strontium and calcium, but within a much smaller range of variation. This change in density
of shell is evident in simply examining the sherds of the pottery. However,
the calcium carbonate (calcite) of the shell can play a significant mechanical role in the body of the ceramic material. The amount of calcite and
the method of processing the shell can dramatically change the way that
pottery is fired and the strength of the finished product. A small number
of pottery fragments were selected as representatives of these tempering
"groups" from both plantation and precolonial areas at Sylvester Manor.
These nineteen pieces were cut transversally, affixed to a glass slide, and
ground down to a thickness that would allow their examination under
a petrographic microscope that allows light to pass through the sample
(optical petrography). The distortion of the light through a mineral crystal,
along with its structure, can be diagnostic of specific minerals. An examination of a complete cross-section of pottery allows for the characterization
of the pottery on the basis of the presence and volume of specific mineral
particles. Although this method entails cutting artifacts, it allows a richly
detailed characterization of how the pottery was made, including both its
ingredients and the heat to which it was subjected. This evidence in turn
offers clues about the pottery-making traditions in use at the plantation.

The importance of exploring changes in firing techniques was suggested by the centrality of adoption of shell temper to changing manufacturing practices over time. The use of shell as a temper can confer
greater thermal shock resistance to a ceramic vessel because of its lower
thermal expansion coefficient than, for example, quartz (Rice 1987, 229;
Feathers 2006, 92). This would be a beneficial property for vessels used
on or over cooking fires (Chilton 1998). Shell prevents both complete
vessel failure from rapid particle expansion and progressive failure by
inhibiting the propagation of small cracks that naturally form. Because
of the behavior of the calcite in shell in response to higher temperatures,
however, considerably more care must be taken with the firing temperature and atmosphere to prevent the failure of the vessel in firing. Calcite
($CaCO_3$) decomposes on reaching temperatures in the range of 750° to
850° C, to lime (calcium oxide) and CO_2 (Rice 1987, 410). If combined
with reactive silica as in clay, then the lime can produce cement minerals, which significantly increase the strength of the fired vessel, but only
if it does not absorb too much water and carbon dioxide from the atmosphere on cooling. The reabsorption of excessive moisture will cause
spalling or complete fracturing (Wenk and Bulakh 2006, 551; Rice 1987).
To prevent this, shell-tempered ceramics must be either fired below the

decomposition temperature or prevented from exposure to the air during cooling. Furthermore, finely crushed shell can maximize the beneficial recombination of calcium oxide (Feathers 2006, 92). Thus, by incorporating such a high volume of shell, potters were obligated to change the way that they fired their pots; if they did so, then the vessel would not only be stronger but possibly also more watertight (Budak 1991).

A microscopic view of the fabric of the ceramic shows that a tremendous range of methods were attempted by the plantation potters. The amount of shell added varied widely, as did the fragment sizes of the shell. Some of the shell temper was preburned, while some was not. The very finely crushed shell was indeed acting as a cementing component, in the same way it would act in the hardening of mortar or plaster; the mineral formations matched those in the mortar from one of the plantation deposits. Firing temperatures and environments also ran the gamut, ranging from low temperatures with little oxygen (indicated by significant organic carbon retention) to 800°C or higher temperatures with plentiful air to oxidize or redden the pottery. Many of these vessels displayed the mechanical failures of improperly fired or cooled calcium oxide. Others struck the correct balance, thereby creating superbly strong pottery. The tremendous variation and combination of techniques suggests technological experimentation, with potters trying different recipes. The hybridizing of pottery was more overtly on display in one vessel of traditional Shantok style that incorporated a handle attached to its side, an element unique in the regional indigenous pottery of this period or before (figure 4.3b). The handle form resembles examples of both European and African American or Caribbean manufacture (Ferguson 1992). Such a vessel form is a poignant suggestion of sharing, with a handle that literally reaches out to those who might otherwise be unaccustomed to managing such vessels. Yet, this vessel was found to have been dropped whole into the large waste pit, perhaps a sign that a gesture of sharing or inclusion was not appreciated by all.

The changes in these two production elements, firing and temper processing, point to the contribution of skill knowledge of enslaved Africans in the production of the ceramics. At the very least, mortar production was a task most likely undertaken by the enslaved labor force, as it is labor-intensive and potentially dangerous in the burning of shell to quicklime. They likely also contributed pyrotechnology, skill in control of fire temperatures. It is probable that at least one, if not more, of the enslaved originated from a central West African community that engaged in the widely practiced crafts of iron smelting and/or ironworking (e.g., see

Schmidt 1996). Increasing that possibility, those who had experienced labor on one of the Barbados sugar plantations may have been forced to work with the boilers and furnaces (Mintz 1985, 49–51), requiring the maintenance and control of high temperature fires. Mortar and plaster production itself involves pyrotechnology, in the production of quicklime through burning (Kingery et al. 1988). Furthermore, the production of mortar, plaster, and lime washes were common house construction and maintenance practices in many areas of West Africa and used for housing of the enslaved of many southern and Caribbean plantations (Crain 1994; Vlach 1993).

Although there is archaeological evidence of neither ceramic production in the core plantation area nor other pyrotechnological practices (like a blacksmith's shop), geological and documentary information show where these two activities may have been more closely associated. Shelter Island itself has little clay available for ceramic manufacture. The highest clay-bearing soils contain less than 11 percent (USDA Soil Conservation Service 1975), and there are no known exposures of the much older Gardiner clay stratum below Manhasset formation and Wisconsin drift glacial tills on the island (Fuller 1914). The closest exposures can be found on Robins Island and in Southold, a town west of Shelter Island on the North Fork of Long Island. Southold also was a town closely associated with Nathaniel Sylvester's business interests, and he had a mill there at one point (SIHS Records, Sylvester 1679/80). It is possible that he also had a blacksmith's shop there, or at the very least some of his enslaved laborers worked there periodically. The possibility that some or all of the ceramic production was taking place off-site makes the presence of such a quantity of locally produced ceramic at the core plantation all the more intriguing. That is, the places where interactions and technological collaborations between Manhanset and enslaved Africans took place were distributed more widely, thus creating stronger associations. Just as livestock care may have created spaces for interactions, so too may have pottery production. Though the style of the pottery reflects a continued connection of the Manhanset with other indigenous communities, the new techniques also tied them to the plantation.

Lithics: make your own tools

Stone (lithic) tool manufacture is not often considered important in the context of European-colonized sites. First, stone tool manufacture (also referred to as flint-knapping, or stone knapping) is considered a

Native American skill, not one practiced by Europeans. Second, stone tools are thought to have been abandoned by Native Americans in favor of iron or steel, universally recognized as a superior technology; this is an assumed but deeply problematic reason. In other words, lithic manufacture is thought to have been a premodern primitive technology unimportant in the world of European colonists. However, an abundance of utilized stone was recovered from the early plantation deposits and the later midden at Sylvester Manor, but precious few iron tools. Although the Sylvesters were wealthy, iron was quite expensive; imported iron implements could only be bought at great cost, and local efforts to establish an ironworks in the colonies did not fully succeed until the late seventeenth century (Regan and White 2010). The very real need for alternative materials is evident in the stone tools with heavy use-wear and damage patterns, though they are less apparent with respect to who was using them and for what purpose. Clearly, stone tools—used for cutting as well as spark production– had a role to play in the work of the plantation, and the need for these items necessitated their local manufacture. It is useful to reconsider what kinds of manufacturing skill would be expected of the plantation's various inhabitants.

European utilization of chipped-stone materials in the colonial period was almost exclusively for the production of sparks: gunflints and tinderflints. Flintlock firearms were first produced in the late sixteenth century, but they were not manufactured in great numbers commercially until approximately 1625. Non-Native early to mid-seventeenth-century sites have yielded "do-it-yourself" chip flints, crudely produced gunflints of minimal retouch (Kent 1983). Luedtke (1998) examined some of the knapping characteristics of these types of flints from the Aptucxet site in Massachusetts and proposed that European colonists were employing bipolar percussion techniques (smashing cobbles between a hammer and anvil) on ballast flint nodules in order to glean usable flakes. Given their limited skill, however, colonists generally spent little effort in rejuvenating flints with worn edges and would instead simply bash out a new one. Gunflints may vary greatly morphologically and still be as effective, given a proper edge to strike the steel frizzen (Luedtke 1999); thus, there is little expectation that gunflints would be of a standardized form until industrial production started. Despite this variability, gunflints may be identified by the presence of residues resulting from spark production, particularly ferrous adhesions from molten steel, and edge-crushing from striking the steel (Kenmotsu 1991). Tinderflints, fragments struck freehand against a firesteel, demonstrate the same type of residues.

Evidence for West African traditions of lithic manufacture is extremely limited. As with most North American historical archaeologies, African historical site publications do not generally discuss recovered chipped/ flaked lithic materials and only rarely note ground stone tools beyond milling stones. One rare reference to stone artifacts from the site of Savi in coastal Benin noted the presence of gunflints, a small number of which were reworked, but other stone material and bottle glass from the same site was determined to show no evidence of secondary retouch or cutting use-wear (Kelly 2001). The Savi researchers felt that "the lack of stone or glass cutting tools is a strong indicator of the degree to which the inhabitants of seventeenth- and eighteenth-century Savi relied upon iron implements, and is indicative of a pre-European-trade iron supply sufficient to meet coastal needs" (Kelly 2001, 93). This lack of evidence suggested that little traditional skill in stone-knapping would be part of the technological repertoire of the enslaved Africans at Sylvester Manor, beyond perhaps gunflint shaping. It is interesting to note, however, that later sites have revealed glass-knapping practices in African American contexts in the nineteenth century (Wilkie 1996), perhaps an indication of entrepreneurial or creative acquisition of technique. These artifacts were largely low-retouch scraper-type tools, based on the larger edge angles and use-wear, rather than cutting tools.

The group most obviously associated with skilled lithic tool manu-facture at Sylvester Manor was, of course, the native Manhanset. The toolkit associated with Eastern Algonquian archaeological sites dating to the Late Woodland period include the beautifully refined triangular Levanna projectile points, used for hunting, as well as a suite of other utilitarian items, such as scrapers, blades, perforators/drills, and mul-tipurpose flake cutting tools (Ritchie 1980). The assemblage recovered from precolonial sites at Sylvester Manor is consistent with this toolkit. For Shelter Island in particular, the only locally available materials for chipped-stone tools are quartz and quartzite cobbles from glacial till. Quartz is an especially difficult material with which to work, given its hardness; thus, a fair amount of skill and practice might be inferred from the presence of fairly refined quartz projectiles. Given the multiplicity of tool forms in use at least through the colonization period, the Manhanset were skilled in a broad range of manufacturing techniques, including the ability to produce large, thin flakes for expedient cutting tools or for sub-sequent refinement to projectile points (i.e., expedient core technology). This does require familiarity with certain incorporated knowledge: how particular rock types will perform, how to prepare the rock surface to strike, and what angle and placement of the blow is needed to produce a useful flake rather than a blocky chunk (Whittaker 1994). Many archaeologists have interpreted the proliferation of tool-types as a sign that stone-knapping was not a singular skill; instead, they claim it was part of a suite of material practices employed by most individuals in indigenous communities (Cobb and Pope 1998; Sassaman 1998; Luedtke 1997; Gero 1991). Such a commonplace skill would not quickly be replaced, even with the introduction of iron tools, simply because there were more tool-use tasks than there were new tools brought into circulation. The large volume of lithic debris recovered from the plantation deposits supports this idea, although, as with the locally produced pottery, we cannot assume that this remained a solely Manhanset practice.

A comparison of the Sylvester Manor lithic assemblages in the Late Woodland period deposits and plantation period deposits reveals some definitive changes in practice (for detailed description of this analysis, Hayes 2008, 191–228). Though quartz was consistently used in the precolonial periods, the plantation supply of ballast flint arriving in merchant ships was taken up quickly as the preferred material for tool production. Quartz was still used for occasional flake tools, but it was mainly introduced to plantation deposits in the construction of the cobbled paving surface. While this construction was not, strictly speaking, stone tool manufacture, it did entail some of the work involved in lithic practices: the procurement of appropriately sized cobbles of quartz from exposed glacial till and fracture of some of those cobbles to ensure their fit in the patterned surface. Manhanset participation may have in part allowed this accomplishment, as they were knowledgeable about the source collection areas.

The ballast flint, however, was an introduced material, easier to shape into usable tool forms than quartz, especially to those who may have been inexperienced in stone-knapping. Flint was used by plantation laborers by first preparing cores, often from heat-treated nodules, and then opportunistically removing usable flakes from the cores for expedient and low-retouch flake tools and gunflints. The gunflints do not present a morphologically or technologically coherent group; rather they demonstrate a range of manufacturing techniques, from expedient spall flakes to expertly crafted bifacial flints. A number of long, thin, and sharp-edged flint flakes attest to the presence of a skilled stoneworker, capable of producing expedient cutting blades. A great many fragments, however, appear to have been made for multiple other uses--for example, both for chopping and for use with a firesteel. These multiuse tools were often quite large and thick. This could have been the result of little need or ability to prepare a thinner flake with a very sharp edge. It may also reflect a lack of concern for scarce material. The damage observed on these tool edges, however, shows that they were used repeatedly and strenuously before their discard, in some cases showing signs that they were reworked in an effort to produce a new, sharp edge.

One class of material displaying a spectacular range of damage is the flint cores, nodules of material from which smaller, usable flakes could be extracted. Ordinarily not considered tools, spent cores (too small to yield usable flakes) could be worked into bifaces. Flint cores at the plantation, however, are large, and most do not appear spent given their size. Despite this, these cores show signs of having been repurposed as tools: between 15 percent and 100 percent of their available edges were crushed or marked with bifacial microflaking, mostly at ridges between flake scars. Three cores also retained ferrous residues. Given the similarities of damage to that accruing on gunflints, one explanation might be that the cores were being occasionally used as tinderflints. The metal residues might also have resulted from the use of a metal tool as a percussor. This type of effort would not be unexpected from a novice or inexperienced stone-knapper learning to create usable flakes, often missing the correct platform target or trying to use edges that are not appropriately angled. In this case the novices may have reached for whatever tool was at hand to use as a percussor.

One other observed type of damage potentially supports this scenario. At least seven flint fragments showed Herzian cones resulting from percussion damage, not at the expected edges of the fragment but rather on faces. This may have resulted from either failed blows to the fragment, by missing the platform completely or deflecting from the platform to strike the face, or unsuccessful attempts at bipolar percussion. Although the number of fragments showing such facial percussion marks is low, taken with the range of core damage they point to the likelihood of novice plantation stone-knappers, potentially learning by observation or direct instruction how to produce usable flakes. Perhaps the introduction of heat-treatment for the flint, a completely new technique in the scope of Manhanset tradition, was also part of this effort. Heat-treatment of some types of stone can reduce the hardness, making it easier to get a flake of the material from the core (Luedtke 1992).

Compared to the range of manufacturing techniques seen in the precolonial quartz assemblage, the plantation material shows a greater variability of techniques and skills. Certainly this range of variation

(a)

(b)

FIGURE 4.4. English flint, (a) flakes and (b) heavily utilized cores (photos by author).

could have been produced by a labor population that brought quite different backgrounds and traditions in the use of stone for tools. Why was it even necessary, though? Very few spent or broken iron blades, awls, or chisels were found in the plantation deposits. A wealthy operation like the Sylvesters could have afforded plenty of tools for their laborers, and Nathaniel's 1680 probate inventory listed iron tools, chains, and pots, but their estimated value was enormous. Iron tools appear to have been tightly controlled items, perhaps necessitating the apprenticeship of other laborers to the Manhanset, who were able to make what they needed with the materials at hand.

Small finds

Certain kinds of artifacts are found in low numbers, a seemingly insignificant proportion of the total, yet their numbers do not reflect their importance as meaningful items. Many small finds in the plantation deposits present great disruptions to our sense of who the historical agents were, even if only to raise questions that are impossible to answer. The most evocative of these finds are personal items, used for either dressing and adornment of the body or leisure and amusement. These items, perhaps more than any other, help us to envision the historical actors.

In every society, clothing is a rich locus of human experience and expression, encompassing cultural norms of bodily exposure and beauty, essential protection in a particular environment that is adapted to one's expectation of activity or leisure, and an active element of identity signaling (Loren 2001, 2008, 2010). Sumptuary laws, determining what kinds of clothing and adornment individuals could or could not wear according to class or moral imperative, were common in both Europe and the colonies during the plantation era. Ways of dressing would have been silent but tremendously important signifiers in the relationships among the Sylvesters, the enslaved Africans, and the Manhanset. Yet most of the materials of clothing, from textiles to leather from animal hides, are scarce in archaeological remains, being prone to the rapid decay of organic matter. The cloth in use at the plantation is indicated only by a few lead "tags" or seals once used to mark the manufacturing source of cloth sold and shipped (figure 4.5e).

What survive are the durable metal, glass, ceramic, or stone items that were used in a variety of small ways in dress and personal adornment. Sylvester Manor's early plantation and later midden deposits held quantities of metal clothing fasteners. The most common of these were copper alloy straight pins of a wide variety of sizes (figure 4.5a). The large quantity of pins likely reflects both their common use and the ease of their loss, as they dropped through floorboards and were simply difficult to see once fallen. Seventeenth-century Euro-American colonial dress, for both men and women, might require a dozen pins on one's person, for cuffs and collars on men or aprons, hats, head cloths, lace insets, and stomachers for women (White 2005; Beaudry 2006). Pins served as the closures where cloth ties and lacing were not used. For men of means in the period, buttons of brass or other showy metals were popular clothing fasteners, sometimes attached simply for show. But poorer, laboring men made do instead with the pins, nearly invisible on the person and thus leaving the appearance plain. The early plantation deposits contained no buttons of brass or other bright metal, only fragments of pewter or tinned buttons, and one copper alloy ring which may have been the frame for a cloth-covered button. There were also a small number of hook-and-eye type fasteners—like pins, fairly common for both men's and women's clothing (White 2005, 74–75). Also like pins, hook-and-eyes were invisible closures, tiny metal loops sewn to the edges of clothing. We might infer that, as women's dress required more fasteners and the number of recovered pins was in the hundreds—as Beaudry (2006, 28–34) has pointed out, pincushions and cases were ubiquitous female possessions--women were quite active in the labor of the work-yard. According to the gendered demographic of the enslaved and their association with the Sylvester daughters referenced in Nathaniel's will, a number of the enslaved were at least partially occupied in domestic service. The Sylvesters likely provided them with clothing of the plainest sort considered appropriate for servants in a European household.

The midden layer, reflecting a less restricted depositional source and a later end-date, did contain a small number of more expensive items of personal adornment. Brass buttons, for example, appeared in its mix, as well as a variety of buckles, larger for shoes and smaller for fastening breeches at the knee, neck-cloths, or hat-bands. The midden also yielded a silver stick-pin, topped with a fleur-de-lis, and a small fragment of gilded chain that may have been part of a necklace or bracelet. It is possible that these were cherished or hidden items belonging to the enslaved; however, the midden in other respects appears to have been a deposit originating from a distinct location separate from the early plantation features, and these items more likely were lost remnants of Sylvester family members' clothing.

Did the laborers of the plantation then have no resources for personal adornment? Certainly it appears that only a few inexpensive buttons and buckles were among the items of typical European-style elaboration. But some artifacts do suggest a resourceful use of materials to fashion useful or symbolically meaningful touches to their otherwise plain garb. Sheet brass, likely cut from kettles or other pans, was rolled into 1 to 2 cm long tubular beads, by crimping the copper around a cord (figure 4.5d). Beads of this style were commonly manufactured by Native Americans, using American-sourced copper, cold hammered into sheets prior to the availability of manufactured European copper alloy items, but native copper was a scarce resource. Brass kettles were thus a tremendously popular trade item, though they were relatively expensive to import as ore sources and production centers were scarce in seventeenth-century Europe also (Day 1991; Rehren and Martiñon-Torres 2008). Indigenous trade partners valued the material itself, rather than the kettle into which it was shaped. Numerous Algonquian and Haudenosaunee sites of the sixteenth and seventeenth centuries held the remains of brass kettles refashioned into beads, pendants, tinkling cones (so named for the sound they produced when attached close to one another on clothing), arrowheads, scrapers, and numerous other forms (Ehrhardt 2005; Bradley 1987). Artistic reuse of imported copper was also practiced by West African people, for both crafts and adornment (DeCorse 2001). A concentration of rolled copper beads and scrap sheet copper was buried in the fill layers around the structure trench from the early plantation, while others were found at the surface of the work-yard and in post-holes. Sewn in rows on clothing, with or without other types of beads (glass or shell), some of these rolled copper pieces were likely a decorative embellishment worn by a Manhanset person, perhaps lost while working on wampum manufacture indicated by the associated shell remains.

Yet the beads were more than just a marker of an indigenous aesthetic. Some examples still retain remnants of a spun white yarn (protected from decay by the copper), suggesting an additional use on clothing laces, perhaps inspired by Manhanset copper refashioning. Another bead demonstrated a slightly different approach, being made from a fragment of a thimble and rolled into a more conical form with the dimpled surface faced outward. The conical form evokes a second resemblance to the tinkling cones commonly manufactured and worn by indigenous people throughout the Eastern Woodlands. The crimped copper of the beads is identical in functional form to lacing tips (also called points, or aglets, like the ends of modern shoelaces),

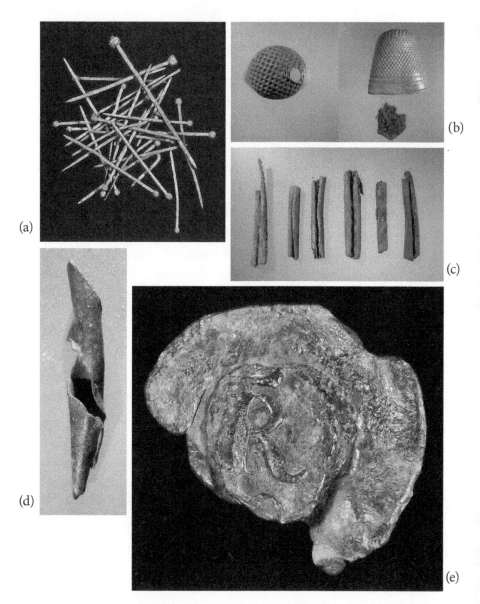

FIGURE 4.5. Cloth, clothing, and adornment materials, (a) pins, (b) thimble "tinkler," (c) rolled brass beads or aglets, (d) brass scrap rolled to make tinkler cone, and (e) lead cloth seal with merchant's mark (photos by Jack Gary and Melody Henkel).

used to protect the ends of clothing laces from fraying and to facilitate passing the lacing through clothing eyelets (White 2005). Laces were common closures for shirt or dress fronts, breeches at the stomach or knee, or for affixing hose and stocking tops. For well-to-do European customers, lacing tips could be manufactured in precious metals, or in flashy styles. Here, however, a Manhanset tradition of reuse and manufacture seems to have been adapted to the plain garb worn by other plantation laborers. Some small items needed little alteration to serve as adornment; for example, a complete thimble was pierced through its crown, likely to allow a thread or cord to pass through, and held a bark fragment wrapped in plant fibers to keep the thimble from sliding off its cord (figure 4.5b). Scrap copper sheeting was found, both in early plantation and later midden deposits, in a variety of forms: large flattened or folded segments, cut to lengths similar to the beads, or partially rolled (figure 4.5c). Given these indications of its potential value to many people working at the plantation core, scrap copper was likely collected, traded, or shared.

Sheet copper and other metals were also used to fashion decorative elements, notably featuring designs of ambiguous tradition, and thus they were potentially sites for creating shared meaning. Two items, a small clipped silver coin fragment and a copper alloy ferrule (figures 4.6a and 4.6b), were etched with design motifs that are similar to those in many cultural traditions. The silver coin clipping retains a small portion of its original stamping: One side is stamped with a cross, and a worn spot bears etched figures resembling the Algonquian manitou (or divine beings) Cautantouwit and Hobbomok, represented as the thunderbird, drawn as an X within a triangle, and the serpent, a hatched line to the right (Bragdon 1996, 187–190). The opposite side bears a single X or cross. While the cross and manitou have apparent links to Christian and Algonquian beliefs, the X-markings may also have been meaningful as a cosmogram to people of West African traditions, such as those with Kongo beliefs. Similar markings have been found in a variety of media, especially pottery, on plantation sites in South Carolina (Ferguson 1992 and 1999). A second etched piece, perhaps once part of a handled tool like an awl, was encircled by two narrow linear bands with the space between crosshatched to form diamonds and triangles. This design has many analogues on other plantation materials, including the abundance of locally made pottery decorated with pendant triangles below bands (see figure 4.3) and fleur-de-lis icons stamped within diamonds, found on many smoking-pipe stems.

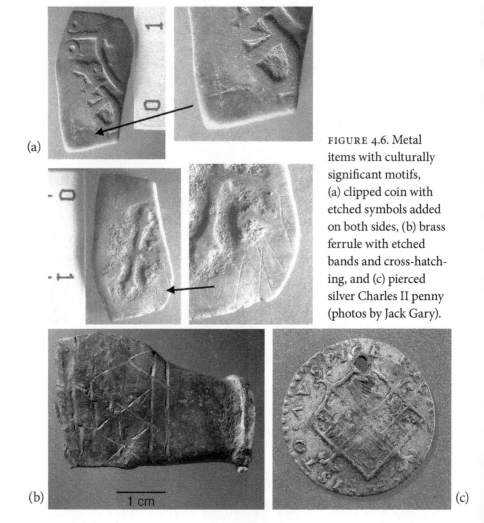

(a)

(b)

(c)

FIGURE 4.6. Metal items with culturally significant motifs, (a) clipped coin with etched symbols added on both sides, (b) brass ferrule with etched bands and cross-hatching, and (c) pierced silver Charles II penny (photos by Jack Gary).

These motifs may have been abstract enough to open common grounds, symbols that were easily transferrable among people of different symbolic traditions. Anthropologist Grey Gundaker (1998) has traced the durable association of diamond shapes or other emblems of four symmetrical repetitions from widespread use in West African societies through African American usage (also Fennell 2007). Diamonds evoked eyes of protective deities, or the doubling of eyes marked spiritual or supernatural sight. In other words, abstract geometric designs may have found the widest possible audience appreciation because elements of each evoked some tradition. A pierced silver Charles II penny, recovered from the later midden, may also have found such a wide appeal with its square crest subdivided by crossed bands. The location of the piercing centered over one corner of the crest, rather than a random placement, shows that the design and its orientation did matter to the coin's owner. The piercing allowed its use as a pendant, perhaps viewed as a charm. This practice could be tied to nearly anyone on the plantation; Native Americans have been documented utilizing coins in this fashion in numerous instances during the colonial period, but the use of coins worn on the body has also been noted in both English and African American folklore as an apotropaic device (Chireau 2003; Davidson 2004).

A final class of artifacts speaks to another practice that breached social or cultural boundaries at the plantation: tobacco smoking. The durable remnant of that practice, the clay smoking pipe, provides archaeologists with valuable temporal information, by associating the short-lived pipes with distinct manufacturing periods. From a social perspective, tobacco smoking marks a leisured, or ritual, but certainly congenial habit in the colonial period. In the broad temporal view, this was a practice that Native Americans introduced to Europeans, who then introduced it to West Africa in the sixteenth century (Emerson 1999; Rafferty and Mann 2004). For coastal Algonquians, tobacco smoking was once a ritually prescribed practice but had become more widely adopted in the demographic and social upheaval of the early colonial period (Nassaney 2004). A small number of locally manufactured pipe fragments, smoothed and burnished, some with incised bands around the bowl, were found in early plantation features, showing Manhanset indulgence at the plantation core. More than one hundred fragments of identifiably Dutch or English manufactured pipes and several times that number of fragments, identifiable only as imported, were recovered from the early plantation and later midden deposits. Because pipes were relatively inexpensive and smoking was a common activity, the Sylvesters may have made imported pipes and some allotment of tobacco available to their laborers, as has been occasionally documented on southern and Caribbean plantations (Handler 2009, n37; Genovese 1974, 644). Smoking was a social activity, indulged in groups, and the commonality of the practice would have made it an easy place to begin forging associations among those who found themselves working together in the yard.

The imported pipes also bore some decorative embellishments that may have made them appealing. The diamond-framed fleur-de-lis motif found on many of the pipestems was a very popular Dutch style, perhaps

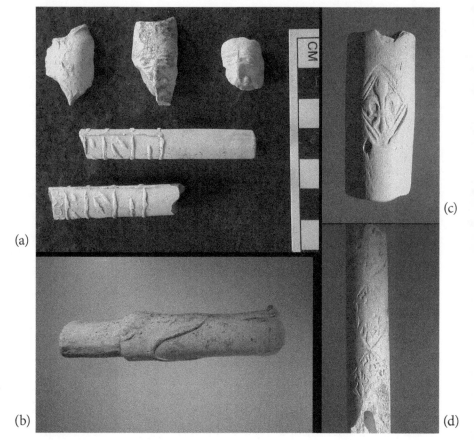

FIGURE 4.7. Clay tobacco pipes, (a) and (b) Sir Walter Raleigh bowls and stems, (c) and (d) stems stamped with fleur-de-lis design (photos by Jack Gary).

appropriated by the Dutch pipe makers to associate a typically French sign instead with the English export tobacco (Dallal 2004). But it has also been found, through archaeological recovery, to have been very popular as a trade pipe to Indian communities. This may stem from a dominance of Dutch trade with Haudenosaunee Indians, but it may also have related to a preference for the diamond motif (Bradley 1987; McCashion 1979). As noted earlier, the diamond motif would have been significant to enslaved Africans as well. Sir Walter Raleigh pipes (a satirical representation of Raleigh's head on the bowl with a crocodile, who would not eat him because he stank of tobacco, on the stem) might have struck the Manhanset as an amusing kind of effigy pipe, or a representation of Hobbomok in serpent form, giving the pipes an altogether different meaning for them. It has been suggested that the Raleigh pipes were also interpreted as Jonah and the whale (Dallal 2004, 217–219), a biblical reference that might have been appealing to the Sylvesters as a means to proselytize, by distributing the pipes to the indigenous and other laborers. Sylvester men, or one of the visiting Quaker figures, may have used the social setting of pipe smoking to engage the laborers. The recovered smoking paraphernalia included one fragment of a "smoker's companion," a metal device for tamping tobacco and picking up hot coals to light a pipe (see Alexander 1979), more of a specialty item, perhaps left behind or given as a gift. Whatever the case, tobacco smoking as an activity provided openings for affiliation and opportunities for potential social connections.

Associating things with people

Archaeologists will, from time to time, slip into a way of talking about artifacts that identifies them singularly by their place of origin or tradition of manufacture. We may speak, for example, of Dutch pipes, English stoneware, European alloys or Native pottery. These labels are shorthand metonymic terms, a substitution of one characteristic part of the object's history that stands as a representation of the whole. Although these terms are easier to use, they mask the fuller biography of the artifact: what role did this item play, by who was it used or shared, what different meanings did it have for those who made it or used it and those who merely saw it? In this respect, these identifiers are like the racial descriptors we find in historical documents, meant by the author perhaps to convey something essential about the individual, although it only conveys something about that author's view of others. Upon reflection, readers know that this descriptor tells nothing about the person, that we must know more about his or her biography, at least to know their community, their material world, if not their own voice, to better understand them.

Artifacts have rich life histories. Like landscapes, people's lives are fashioned by things, even as they fashion those things. In the plantation setting, the enslaved were restricted in their food options by what the Sylvesters had directed them to produce and further by what, of that production, were apportioned to them. Yet the enslaved might have added diversity to their diet by sharing in the wild species of animals and plants that the Manhanset were accustomed to eating. The choices of clothing and adornment were also constrained by what the Sylvesters made available to them. Nevertheless the plantation's diverse residents seem to have found ways to fashion their own subtle expressions from the materials and technological traditions found in their own community, often different from, or even in opposition to, the Sylvesters' expectations. To simply label these items as European or Native closes out these fashionings and covers a much more complex social history. For the enslaved Africans in particular, such narrow definitions erase their existence altogether. In essence the shorthand terms or metonymic references create an epistemic blankness, disallowing certain stories. In similar fashion, these blanknesses or silences introduced to the archive and the burial of the plantation landscape and materials allowed for some very peculiar and simplified histories to be written about Shelter Island and the Manor in subsequent years.

5 / Forgetting to Remember, Remembering to Forget

The physical face of the plantation and its complex human geography were nowhere to be seen by the end of the eighteenth century. A new landscape, a succession of generations with new political concerns, and the dispersion of the descendants of the indigenous and the enslaved undercut the durable materiality and means of transmitting social memory. Yet today, Sylvester Manor and Shelter Island are places steeped in their own history, where residents pay particular attention to the time of settlement by the first generation of Sylvesters. How is the story of that time told? What parts are remembered, and what is forgotten?

As I investigate these questions, I rely on a particular set of ideas about what memory is and how it relates to the construction of historical narratives. History, like memory, is a construction of associations. Historical narratives may be written to make explicit connections to larger themes and discourses that are valorized. That is, if a local event is compared or related to more famed historical movements, then its importance is amplified, and a connection is forged in the minds of the readers between the local and the more global (Sahlins 2005). But narratives may also be written to sever certain associations, especially if they either raise uncomfortable questions or are linked to infamous events. O'Brien's (2010) exploration of "lasting" narratives is a prime example of this separation. Accounts of the "last of the (tribe name)" are frequently found in local histories, arguably as a means of distancing local identity from present discourses that were unwanted, difficult, or distasteful to Anglo-Americans, such as heterogeneity in the community on the one hand and uneasiness with the treatment of American Indians on the other. Likewise, the taint of racial prejudices or support of slavery was deflected by either ignoring the practice of slavery in northern colonies or claiming the distance of time from when the "last slave," who very often conveniently disappeared into the mists of history, was freed (Melish 1998). In New England and New York, specific historical narrative forms were created to disassociate the region from those troublesome and ongoing events in other regions of the new nation, like slavery and Indian removals, as though there were never a time when the founding figures of New England engaged in such morally suspect practices.

According to Maurice Halbwachs (1992), even individual memory is bound up in one's community. That is, without a community in which memory can circulate and be strengthened, personal memory is fallible and ephemeral. But if a community is needed to maintain and transmit memory, then changes in a community over time impact the perspective and selective transmission of memory as well. Rather than a static storage of an objectively descriptive narrative, memories transmitted from the past (including both oral transmission and the creation and maintenance of archives) are actively incorporated into narratives that perform values or identity. Philosopher Michel de Certeau argued that narration and practice are fundamentally associated. Narration itself is a practice wherein one's histories or actions are made coherent to oneself through a performative act of narration. The point of the narration is not what it describes, but the act of giving structure to that which is learned or experienced. He draws a distinction between description, which merely represents, and narration, which actually produces, quite often in a goal-oriented strategic or tactical manner. For example, he points to "the recitation of the oral tradition . . . it is a way of re-telling the consequences and combinations of formal operations, along with an art of 'harmonizing' them with the circumstances and with the audience" (Certeau 1984, 80). Thus, any particular historical narrative involves the selection of elements of the past lending authenticity while performing a specific set of associations with which to identify.

Historical memory is enacted through a complex negotiation among a community of transmitters and their concerns. By considering the drastic refacing of the eighteenth-century plantation landscape and material culture we now have a better understanding of what kinds of material traces or reminders were lost or destroyed. The community also was disrupted by its virtual abandonment, breaking the links of generations who would have experienced the plantation even through its transformation.

Not all aspects of the plantation were forgotten, however. A significant documentary archive has accumulated, and some stories seem to have been transmitted from one generation to the next, occasionally committed to paper without provenance. Not until the nineteenth century did anyone make a concerted effort to construct a coherent historical narrative, either of the eastern Long Island region or Shelter Island and Sylvester Manor. This process involves even more of a winnowing of memory, selecting among those traces to shape a particular story.

Thus far I have contrasted the curated documentary remains with the abandoned materiality of the archaeological landscapes and artifacts, but neither of these sources constitutes history unless someone chooses to use them in constructing a narrative. In telling the history of colonial Long Island and Sylvester Manor, local historians have chosen certain historical facts, while others are made to hide in plain sight—in the quiet recesses of archives—because they are not selected for the iterations of the story at that time. Still other facts were not available, having literally been buried beneath the placid Manor landscape until archaeological excavation reconstituted them as facts, from which many stories can be written. By the end of the nineteenth century, a particular version of the story prevailed and received its own materialized place in the landscape. By reading these narratives in the context of national events contributing to racial discourses, and in some cases considering the position and motivation of individuals who wrote them, we may be able to trace the processes and reasons for forgetting the more complex history of the plantation.

Forgetting the past in the eighteenth century

Lowenthal (1985, 71–73, 105–106) has noted that, in considering the urge to commemorate one's forebears, it makes a difference whether those one remembers are parents or more distant ancestors, for the relationship with parental figures may be too personal, too close, and too fraught with tension. This certainly may have played a role in what was curated and what was abandoned at Sylvester Manor. Nathaniel Sylvester's children were not interested in carrying on his grand vision for an entailed estate. Several of them sold off portions of the island property not long after his death in 1680, including the eldest, Giles, who resided at Shelter Island only when he sought to avoid his Boston creditors (Griswold 2013, chapter 12). Though the subsequent generation did return to Shelter Island, nothing of the original plantation infrastructure was preserved. Even in the archive of family documents, very few were apparently carried forward from the plantation itself, and those kept were of legal necessity in determining property ownership, like wills, property sales and use agreements, and the important grant of manorial status given in 1666. Although we may hold preservation dear today, the cavalier disregard of the "founding" Sylvester generation by the second generation bespoke a growing disaffection with colonial authority. Certainly, Nathaniel had little love for those authorities, yet he undoubtedly benefited from a grant of administrative independence from the English crown. Shelter Island's manorial status exempted the estate from the tax and military obligations for which other communities under the English colony were responsible. In a rejection of both that privileged status and the explicit dictates of Nathaniel's will, much of Sylvester's estate had been sold outside the family by his sons. By the time the new Manor house was built, Shelter Island had been incorporated as a town--not only subject to taxation and the New York colonial authority, but also regulated at the local level by the people who had purchased the property in the decades after Nathaniel's death (Mallmann 1990, 38–46). The eighteenth century leading up to the American Revolution was a time of forward thinking and of breaking with the traditions of the past, in particular the tradition embodied in the British empire. Rejecting the past meant rejecting the tyrannical control over the colony in order to create something novel.

During the latter half of the eighteenth century, Anglo-American sensibilities underwent great changes, particularly to the sense of where the individual fit into the broader society. This change is attributed by many scholars to the rise of mercantile capitalism, demise of feudal societies and guilds, and eventual turn toward wage labor. In this kind of economic regime, individuals, rather than a corporate community, made their fortune and accumulated wealth through their own efforts in the new open markets created in the colonies. This process of fashioning the self was also accomplished through acts of consumption, in a marketplace increasingly oriented toward a myriad of choices (Breen 2004). In anthropological terms, the construction of a *person* was decoupled from the network or community and instead one's status in the world was attributed to individual will. Materially, such an attitude shift can be seen in the way that living spaces were segmented with increasing distinctions of public and private space or in the multiplying numbers of dishes, utensils, chairs, or other possessions that were used by individuals rather than shared (Deetz 1996). Certainly the second Manor house embodied this arrangement, with private rooms protected from public disruption by large hallways, and any outbuildings and working areas placed at a greater distance from the house. The deposits of items dating to the eighteenth and nineteenth centuries were dominated by specialized tablewares, meant for individual place settings, rather than the smaller number of commonly used bowls and jugs.

A contributing factor in this shift also came from religious resurgences, such as the Great Awakening, which "democratized American religion by shifting the balance of power between minister and congregation" (Ruttenberg 1993, 429). The Sylvester descendants were active participants in this evangelical movement, several times hosting George Whitefield, the hugely popular revivalist minister who traveled North America preaching until his death in 1770 (SMA Group II-Oversize B, G. Whitefield letter 1764). Discourses of citizenship, investing both rights and responsibilities in individuals as parts of a society, figured as prominently in the churches as it did in the political philosophy of the revolution. Coastal Algonquians also hoped that the Great Awakening would provide a route to freedom through equal footing as well, through the redemptive re-creation of souls that an evangelical interpretation of Christianity provided (Schneider 2003; Rubin 2005; but see Fisher 2012 challenging the degree of Indian conversion in New England). Amongst Indian communities, questions of citizenship tinged by race became important with respect to rights in communally held property, as they struggled to retain the land they had (Mandell 2005; Parm 2005; O'Brien 1997; Sweet 2003, 171–182). The evolving meaning of citizenship (Kerber 1997) and the relationship of this meaning to property rights have been recurrent issues for those communities through the present day. In this kind of an atmosphere colonial or creole communities gave less focus and attention to the weight of history, which had favored a more caste- and status-driven society, except when it could be used as a cautionary tale.

On Shelter Island, the Revolutionary War itself was a quite literal effacement of the earlier landscape. Like the whole of Long Island, Shelter Island was occupied by the British for the duration of the war, during which time the island was stripped of much of its timber and other resources to provide fuel and food to the British. Although Thomas Dering and his family, the residents of Sylvester Manor at the time, were able to flee to Connecticut, many other residents of Shelter Island were subject to the martial law imposed by the occupation. Dering played his part for the revolution by serving as delegate to the New York congressional convention, while one of his sons, Sylvester Dering, rose to the rank of Brigadier General in the Rhode Island militia (Mallmann 1990, 54–57, 64–65).

Following the colonists' successful conclusion of the war, a new relationship with the past became necessary. Members of the new republic had the self-conscious sense of being agents of history, and the valorization of the "Founding Fathers" demanded that their contributions be remembered by future generations. As David Lowenthal (1985, 74–75) noted, "late eighteenth-century North American tensions over patrimony had an explicitly political focus, and opposing views of the past as guardian and as tyrant engaged a substantial segment of the population." Narrative description of the new nation's short history served to both document the exceptional and unique character of American society and to help shape the character of citizens and communities in the new republic through idealized examples (Conforti 2001). These aims were built into a number of historical overviews that were written in the years immediately following the end of the war, as in the work of David Ramsay (1791) and Jedidiah Morse (1790). These authors built in the notion of the independent citizen in their histories through particular tropes that rested upon a separation of racialized groups. For example, Ramsay was of the opinion that colonial communities established through the direct purchase of property from Native groups were more appropriate than the Crown's sweeping claims to land by royal right; without such purchase, colonists had no right to expect Natives to leave. An underlying assumption to this statement is that rights to property are equally available to any free individual, unrestricted by sovereign claims (whether English or sachem). He claimed also that colonial societies, especially those in New England, were equitable because of the industry of individuals as freeholders, a status given by individual responsibility to and improvement of property (Ramsay 1791, 1: 32). By contrast, the southern colonies in his view suffered from the vice of idleness (1: 24): "The political evils of slavery do not so much arise from the distresses it occasions to slaves, as from its diminishing the incitements to industry, and from its unhappy influence on society." The unique equal playing field demanded by the new nation was best derived, in Ramsay's view, from small, *homogenous* communities.

These narratives often relied on the teleological argument that the founding of the United States was providential or divinely ordained (Messer 2005; Cheng 2008). Unlike the Puritan sense of predestination based on individual grace, these authors believed in a broader divine

approval of the nation itself, indicated by ultimate success of the autono-
mous community model that became the republic. Native Americans
had a strange and tragic role to play in this story. Ramsay claimed that
by "natural" law indigenous nations had been the rightful owners of the
land; thus, while nations like England claimed ownership of vast tracts
of land, only those towns where land was "appropriately" purchased
from indigenous owners were destined to survive.[1] More often, however,
the hand of providence was seen at work in the decline and supposed
disappearance of Indians. Ironically, many authors seemed sympathetic
and even acknowledged the role of white settlement in this process, yet
their solution was that any remaining Indians should become not-Indi-
ans—that is, they should become civilized by living like whites. Such a
solution effectively reinforced the value placed on social homogeneity.
These grand narratives, relating to the originary independence of the
colonists and the transfer of property leading to the preordained exit of
Indians, carried over into the explosion of local history writing in the
nineteenth century.

Early patriotic narratives, generalizing the exceptional American
character and origins, were seriously complicated from the outset by the
relationship of the new republic to the indigenous and the enslaved. The
problematic details of those relations were evident to local communities
either through local events or knowledge in circulation of more distant
events that they could relate to their own circumstances (cf. Sahlins 2005).
These issues were neither abstract nor distant to the Eastern Long Island
towns. A descendant of the Sylvester family who played a prominent role
in shaping the future of New York in the new American republic was
Ezra L'Hommedieu of Southold, an attorney who served New York State
in a number of official capacities.[2] As a member of the Indian Affairs
Commission, Ezra had a direct hand in establishing the state's aggressive
approach to the Haudenosaunee nations following the American Revolution. Although the Mohawk, Tuscarora, Oneida, Onondaga, Cayuga,
and Seneca nations had been a strong confederacy before the conflict,
they were politically divided by decisions to support the colonists or the
British or to remain neutral. Arguably taking advantage of this lingering
division, and often blatantly ignoring the 1790 federal mandate that treaties with Indian nations could only be negotiated by the federal government, New York state governors George Clinton and John Jay directed
the Indian Affairs commissioners to negotiate with individual nations to
appropriate the vast majority of their lands. This was done in exchange
for reserved lands (smaller than the nations asked for), guaranteed fishing

and hunting rights which were acknowledged to be of limited utility as white settlement disrupted their resources, and yearly cash or provisions payments to offset the expected loss of those resources (Hough 1861; Starna 2002; Graymont 1976; Prucha 1962). Notably, the commissioners relied on the assumption that Haudenosaunee and other Indians were to be citizens, or at least wards of the state, and were resistant to treating them as sovereign nations. As individual citizens, the state would find it easier to coax Indians into selling land.[3]

The commissioners' efforts were not restricted to the distant Haude-nosaunee. L'Hommedieu also was privy to, or directly involved in, the movement of the Brothertown Indians to land offered up by the Oneida (Hough 1861; SMA Group II-B). Brothertown, or Brotherton, was a group of southern New England and Long Island Indians, including a number of Montaukett, led by the Reverend Samuel Occom. By the 1760s, a number of Christian Indian communities who wished to remain sover-eign or at least independent despaired of the encroachment and negative influence of white settlers. Occom, a Mohegan teacher and minister, had gone to the Montaukett to work and eventually married Mary Fowler, a daughter of one of the tribe's prominent families descended from the sachem Wyandanch. Along with David Fowler, Occom negotiated with the Oneida to the north for a parcel of land on which Montauketts, Mohegans, Pequots, Narragansetts, and others could start anew with plenty of land and without being surrounded by whites who threat-ened the sovereignty of the communities. Of note, the agreement also included a prohibition on land rights by anyone of any African descent. This clause was partly the result of decades of anxiety over a shrinking land base owing to Indian intermarriage with "outsiders," a trend that often resulted in the loss of land from the Indian community (Silver-man 2010, 101–105, 135). Ironically, this desire to build a homogenous and harmonious village isolated from destructive influences was much like the separatist motivations of the early colonists, yet the common aim was not respected by the fledgling United States in the long term. Though delayed in their move by the Revolutionary War, the Brother-town community members succeeded in moving to Oneida land, only to find that the state had already placed pressure on the Oneida to give up more land, pressure that was passed along to the newly arrived town (Sil-verman 2010; Jarvis 2010). The circumstances of Brothertown revealed the hypocrisy of American writers who suggested that Indians would be viewed as equals upon adopting the trappings of "civilized" Chris-tian life, for this community was Christian, lived in a settled village, and practiced farming and literary arts; yet they were still ultimately forced out of their Oneida land only a few decades later. Ezra L'Hommedieu was involved in dealings with the Brothertown community at least as late as 1796, when he was provided a receipt for medicines sent to them (SMA Group II-B, E. L'Hommedieu 1796).

L'Hommedieu was also involved in the conflicts of indigenous communities who still lived in the East Long Island area, despite their often reported demise. Those Montaukett who did not join the Brothertown community lodged complaints to the commissioners about their poor treatment at the hands of the Easthampton townspeople in 1807. These complaints were dismissed for a variety of reasons, including the alleged inability of the Montaukett to remember their agreements over land use negotiated with the town and the implication that trespasses had been committed by Indians with blacks and mulattoes (SMA Group II-B, Grievances of Montauk Indians, 1791; Strong 2001). It must be argued, however, that racial categorization merely provided a convenient reason to excuse the town from honoring its commitments to the Montaukett. L'Hommedieu's involvement in these paternalistic maneuvers localized his close knowledge of the evolving state of Indian affairs in the communities around Shelter Island. Between the racial prohibitions of the Brothertown project and the racial assignations arising from the Montaukett complaints, the issues of diversity and prejudice were certainly in circulation on the East End. These issues were omens of the course of federal law a century later.

Slavery also seriously complicated the issues of liberal rights in the early republic. The enslaved of New York City and Long Island in particular, numbering well over twenty thousand by the start of the revolutionary war, were presented with a British occupation in which they were offered the opportunity to gain their freedom in exchange for military enlistment. American colonists offered no such deal, and many were appalled at the protection given to black Loyalists by the departing British at the end of the war (Hodges 2005; Rael 2005). This was not an opportunity given to the enslaved of Sylvester Manor. Most likely Thomas Dering, when evacuating Sylvester Manor before the occupation, took enslaved persons with him, as he was listed in a 1776 town census as having five slaves (reprinted in Mallmann 1990, 62–63), some of whom were inherited by his children after his death in 1785. Emancipation of the enslaved in New York was undertaken in a rather protracted fashion over the course of more than forty years, "suggesting both the degree to which New York was beholden to slavery and the limitations of antislavery sentiment in the early national period" (Hodges 2005, 113–114). Beginning in 1785, voluntary manumission was legalized but subject to strict conditions: the enslaved person had to be between the ages of twenty-one and fifty and had to be certified by the appropriate authorities as capable of self-support, or without certification by posting a £200 bond in the event the state needed to provide care (Kruger 1985, 726–727). The 1799 Act for Gradual Emancipation freed the children of the enslaved born after the passage of the law, after an extended period of indenture. Slavery as a whole was not finally abolished until 1827, yet even that law came with a caveat: the enslaved born before 1799 were freed, but those born after were still subject to their terms of indenture from the time the law was enacted in 1817 (Kruger 1985; Rael 2005; Moss 1993, 152–158).

Thus by the end of the eighteenth century, New York State and the new United States were already struggling with the gulf between the stated ideals of individual rights and the reality of how those rights were negotiated (or not) with the indigenous and the enslaved. In historical narratives Americans, predominantly white Americans, attempted to reconcile this gulf. They did so not by ignoring paradoxical issues, but by selectively reshaping the representation of certain persons or groups, often subtly relegating them to the past, at a sufficient temporal remove that problems could be acknowledged but not confronted. Yet even as local nineteenth-century historians attempted to push troublesome diversity of people and perspectives into the past, the nation became ever more diverse, and issues attributed to race and race relations became more pressing.

Reconstituting memory in the nineteenth century

"History," wrote Benjamin Thompson for his 1843 edition of *The History of Long Island*, "as a distinct species of literature, teaches the most important lessons of wisdom and virtue, and by a method the most striking and durable, that of EXAMPLE." But his own work, he felt, was of a slightly different nature. "Local history must necessarily be more minute in its investigations and vastly more particular in its details; requiring a more patient and laborious inquiry, and a more faithful delineation of those matters, which being of less general importance, have either been passed over with neglect, or made the subjects of intentional misrepresentation and falsehood" (Thompson 1843, 1: xiii–xiv).

The local historians of Long Island and Shelter Island drew on those "important lessons" expressed in the grand themes of history written at the broader national or state level and reproduced them at the local level. Because of the particularity of local details, these themes were often strained to fit the circumstances. General histories of the new nation relate to the characterization of colonial communities as independent, liberal, and equal, yet the details of local histories, rife with racial diversity, inequality, and conflict, were somehow reconciled to them. I am concerned with three main operations performed through these narratives. First, antebellum states of the northeast were keen to appropriate their colonial past as the epitome of the liberal civic ideal. The detailed descriptions of "First colonists" and town founders suggest that both innate love of freedom, especially freedom of religion, and isolated frontier conditions forged the earliest of democratic communities, upon which the principles of the nation were founded. This story tends to simplify both the range of goals and desires that the early European colonists brought with them and their extensive networks into the image of the isolated and self-sufficient village. Second, contemporary nineteenth-century communities portrayed Native Americans as people of the past, either long gone or teetering on the edge of extinction. Like the first story, this tale, often ignoring the obvious continued presence of indigenous communities, used racial intermixture as evidence to condemn their cultures to the past. While Native people are necessarily a part of the history, often acknowledged to have contributed much to the colonists, their presence was narratively extinguished by a variety of means (O'Brien 2010). Third, in a fashion similar to the effacement of the indigenous, the practice of slavery and the descendants of the enslaved are either completely absent from local histories or noted to be a thing of the past. Given the moral rhetoric surrounding the politics of slavery in the United States, both before and after the Civil War, New York and New England historians were slow to admit to any involvement in an institution that they would later popularly condemn. Although this trope operates in a negative sense, by avoidance, I argue that the absence is palpable in the histories, an act of "disowning" (Melish 1998).

A combination of factors contributed to a boom in publications of local history beginning in the 1840s. Printing presses capable of mass production and a surge in literary consumption encouraged the production of even more regionally specific writings, perhaps led by the example of more general and popular histories (Pfitzer 2008). Other developments may have included the publication of Sir Charles Lyell's *Principles of Geology*, describing principles of stratigraphy and uniformitarianism, beginning in 1830. Local histories very often began with a description of the physical environment, some employing rather technical descriptions of the glacial formation processes (e.g., Thompson 1843, vol. 1). While not considered a part of human history per se, the burgeoning study of geology and its emphasis on slow, continuous change through centuries of time brought attention to the antiquity of humankind and ultimately contributed to Darwin's theory of evolution. Moreover, geology and geography, with their attentiveness to the land and the "natural state" seemed to have prompted associations with Native Americans, as though they were part of the natural environment. Given the diverse communities of the new nation, amateur historians and natural philosophers were concerned with the progressive history of "races" and "civilizations," situating the three narrative tropes described above within the grand narrative of cultural evolution. Although a scientific outlook would not fully come to the forefront of historical writing until later in the nineteenth century, many of the younger elite before midcentury were ironically turning to Europe for formal education in the sciences, a trend that contributed to the establishment of new universities in the United States and graduate programs in those schools, like Harvard, already established (Menand 2001; Trigger 2006; Baker 1998). This intellectual current included one young man who later became a proprietor of Sylvester Manor, Eben Norton Horsford. Although he studied and taught chemistry, at the end of his life he was consumed in extensive historical research, especially of the Manor and its early inhabitants, much of which I explore in detail.

A few published histories of Long Island reflected this budding preoccupation with race and civilization, coupled with the idea of temporal succession. By beginning with descriptions of the "natural" environment, some local historians were led naturally into discussions of Indians, who were thought to have lived in this pure state of nature without altering it in any fashion. Benjamin Thompson, in prefacing the second edition of his *History of Long Island from its Discovery and Settlement to the Present Time* (1843, vol. 1), described his aim "to ascertain and describe every important fact which forms a link in the chain of events, and thereby to present to an enlightened and liberal public an accurate and connected history" (xv). His assumption of progress is apparent, but nowhere is it presented as blatantly as in the preface to the first (1839) edition:

When it is remembered that only two centuries have elapsed since this fair isle, now so far advanced in population and wealth, was the abode of a race of men scarcely elevated in the scale of intelligence above the wild beasts with which the country at that time abounded, it cannot but be a matter of some importance, as well as curiosity, to trace the progress of this strange eventful history . . . (preface included in Thompson 1843, 1: vii)

His narrative begins with descriptions of the physical geography including soil and climate, and proceeds to "discovery," a term warranted because "[n]o traces of a *civilized* people have ever been discerned upon this island" (71; emphasis added). With Thompson's decision to sandwich the description of the "savage" race between sections on the discovery by Europeans on the one side and the Dutch government on the other, he located Native Americans within history but placed them narratively within control of the colonizing Europeans. Indeed such a sentiment is evident in his speculation that no Indian uprisings occurred because "white people, by forming distinct settlements in different parts of the island, and separating the tribes, probably prevented any such combination being formed" (77).

Not all local histories conformed to this textual format to write the story of progressive civilization. Some were more concerned to establish a historical precedence of community life on which the new Republic was modeled (Conforti 2001; Cheng 2008). An interesting account of this was written by one of the earliest of local chroniclers, Silas Wood, who noted in the opening of his 1824 "Sketch of the Country" that Long Island had been, when first seen by European colonists, "in a great measure bare of timber" which he attributed directly to active indigenous landscape management by burning of the undergrowth. As an example of the towns' emphasis on improvement, he detailed many anxious efforts through legal enactments to conserve the scarce timber by strictly limiting brush- and tree-cutting. Although this may have constituted the first small steps in building the American political character, Wood had to continue on to the reversal of those laws, when the colonists came to understand how those outlawed indigenous practices had provided feed for animals and reduced their own work (Wood 1824, 5–7). Aside from this brief nod to the environmental savvy of the indigenous, Wood proceeded directly to the topic of the "settlement of Long-Island" by European colonists. His narrative style was less literary and more like a laundry-list of facts and dates, but he was occasionally prone to waxing more poetic, as when he described the larger political import of these settlements:

Being too remote from the mother country to derive any aid from there, and without connections here, the whole powers of government devolved on the inhabitants of each town. Self-preservation rendered it absolutely necessary that they should assume the exercise of these powers. . . . Thus each town at its first settlement was a pure democracy. The people in each town exercised the sovereign power: all questions were determined by the voice of the major part of the people assembled in the town meeting. In this manner they formed such laws and regulations as they judged necessary for the security, peace, and prosperity of their infant settlement. (15)

The birth of a nation, writ small, was thus claimed. This description had the early English settlements forged in complete isolation, in a political wilderness, even if the landscape was nicely groomed for them. In this manner, Wood transformed his description of first settlements into the embodiment of modern liberal principles. It was such an admirable performance that Thompson closely paraphrased it in his 1843 history (1: 109). Wood continued to reference the primordial exceptionalism of Long Islanders throughout his work; for example, "English colonists of Long-Island, even at this early period, held the doctrine that taxation and representation were inseparable" (Wood 1824, 45), in opposition to the newly imposed authority of the Duke of York's laws in 1670.

Other writers managed to evoke the image of isolation and wilderness, even while necessarily acknowledging the extensive networks to which towns were actually connected. Nathaniel Prime (1845) did recount that most East Long Island towns were established by English colonists who had first lived in the Massachusetts, New Haven, or Connecticut colony and considered themselves under the authority of the Connecticut colony by proximity (61). Yet Prime managed to also link nature and politics elsewhere in declaiming the independence of the new towns:

Having purchased their lands of the original proprietors of the soil, and secured a corresponding grant from the patentee, without any restrictions on their civil rights, they found themselves absolutely in a state of nature, possessing all the personal rights and privileges which the God of nature gave them, but without the semblance of authority one over another. From the necessity of the case they were thrown back upon the source of all legitimate authority, *the sovereign people*; and entered into a social compact, in which every man had an equal voice and equal authority. (77)

David Gardiner's *Chronicles of the Town of Easthampton* (1871; orig. 1840) likewise described the colonization of the town, including Gardiner's Island, as exercises in "cultivating the wilderness" while cut off from support. Yet he noted that not only had the land previously been planted but also the planting fields had been so well prepared that they "required only a moderate skill" to produce from; in addition, the earliest colonist Lion Gardiner was routinely in communication with both Connecticut governors and Wyandanch, the Montaukett sachem with whom he had forged a relationship in the wake of the Pequot War (13–17). Gardiner's tenure was descriptively marked by an onslaught of *firsts* (as theorized in O'Brien 2010): "first white child born in Connecticut . . . first English child born within the present state of New York . . . first rude beginning of cultivation . . . first domestic animals . . . first gatherings of their plantings" (Gardiner 1871, 17).

Long Islanders had perhaps extra incentive to emphasize their deep primordial ties to the liberal social ideals of the nation. As noted earlier, Long Island was occupied by the British nearly throughout the duration of the Revolutionary War. Although some Loyalists, like the Derings of Sylvester Manor, were able to escape to friendlier territories, many remained behind to suffer the British labor demands, revocation of rights, commandeering of property, crops, livestock, and timber, and outright destruction. Adding insult to injury, when the occupation was over, the new State of New York levied taxes to compensate the Patriots who had fled, partly at the expense of those who had remained. This act sent the message that Long Islanders had been less than true patriots, a categorization that decades later apparently still rankled. Wood was so outraged, even in 1824 (55), that he wrote the imposition of the taxes "fully proved that an abuse of power was not peculiar to the British parliament." Thompson (1843, 1: 213) mourned "their *misfortune*, and not their *fault*, that they were not within the American lines," and the unkind treatment of Long Islanders by the new nation. In explicitly distancing themselves from the Loyalists, Long Islanders may also have been implicitly distancing themselves as well from enslaved African Americans and the majority of the Haudenosaunee who had aligned themselves with the British.

Although many of these narratives registered their community's disapproval of Puritan religious persecution as a motivating factor in their established principles of freedom, several authors also betrayed that this freedom was exercised by pursuing similar forms of exclusion to address the "problems" of diversity. After proclaiming the "pure democracy" of early Long Island towns, Wood (1824, 16) wrote, with no trace of irony:

The several towns in Suffolk [county, East Long Island], adopted every precaution in their power, for the preservation of good morals and good order in their settlements.

To prevent the contagion of evil example, they excluded from their society, all such as they judged would be likely to injure it.

For this purpose they prohibited the sale of land to any, but such as were approved of by the people in their town meeting, or by a committee chosen by them, for that purpose.

Many towns were more explicit in their exclusions, such as Southampton's 1653 general court order barring Indians from entering the town (Thompson 1843, 1: 330). Social homogeneity was preferred, according to Prime (1845, 131) in his account of Southold: "Those sagacious pioneers were fully convinced, that it was far better and much easier to prevent the ingress of undesirable citizens, than to correct and reform them, after they had come in."

Thus the theme of the first colonists and first towns being isolated and independent, "laboratories" for brewing the liberal ideal, may alternatively be read as the creation of exclusionary enclaves. This theme is framed in no small part by stories of the extinction of Indians and the absence or ending of slavery, equated therefore with the absence of African Americans. These racialized persons were barred, both literally through the laws enacted and later narratively, through a failure to acknowledge facts in the archive or through simply writing their demise.

Indeed, in the more general histories of Long Island, slavery was rarely mentioned specifically. Thompson's narrative avoids it altogether except in recounting the "Negro Plot" of 1741 in New York City. His comment betrayed the embarrassment of having to acknowledge the northern institution of slavery: "At this gloomy period, the population of the city was twelve thousand, of whom one-sixth part were slaves; a strange comment, surely, upon the professions of those who had left Europe for the sole purpose of enjoying perfect freedom in America" (Thompson 1843, 1: 181). In a footnote Thompson also remarked upon the change wrought in the African race since the peoples' arrival in America, to the "obedient" and "submissive" people he knew them to be at that time. This note epitomized the widespread sentiment of white New Yorkers and New Englanders: African Americans may have been freed from slavery there, but they were still considered a servile underclass not equal to the enterprising white citizenry. Joanne Pope Melish (1998) has ably argued that this type of discrimination was underwritten by the gradual emancipation laws implemented in the antebellum northeast, keeping some African Americans of New York in bondage as late as 1837. Thus, Thompson was able to express his moral outrage at the injustice of slavery in the abstract while also denying the emancipated African Americans a socially equal place in the reality.

Other authors failed to offer even this level of acknowledgment. Prime (1845, 122) found no reason to raise the issue of slavery, despite his inclusion of a table of population statistics that enumerated "white" and "colored" separately, the colored population amounting to more than 6 percent of Suffolk County and nearly 8 percent of Long Island in its entirety. Neither was the advent of emancipation worth his discussion. Gardiner (1870), in his recounting of Easthampton history, referred to slaves in a small number of instances but not to slavery as an institution, either legal or outlawed. Instead, the earliest mention of any enslaved person was in reference to a 1719 drowning case, leaving the nineteenth-century reader perhaps to wonder (though perhaps not) why there were slaves in a state without slavery. This process of forgetting northern slavery might have taken much longer to become fully incorporated. Centennium-inspired efforts by many county or state historical societies to compile and publish document collections show that hundreds or thousands of records relating to slavery in the northeast were to be found in the same archives local historians were drawing upon, yet even then little attention was given to incorporating this aspect of the colonial past into historical narratives in New York or New England. Many of the most outspoken antislavery activists came from the northeast, but for them slavery was a southern institution.

In one other backhanded arena African Americans warranted mention in nineteenth-century Long Island area histories. Often in discussing the demise of Indian communities, authors used the introduction of African blood as evidence of compromised Indian-ness. Blood figured greatly in discussions of race by local historians, as a means of signaling the conflation of biology with character or culture. Prime (1845, 101) lamented that there was "here and there an individual who, by his complexion and straight black hair, gives some evidence of aboriginal descent, the remains of all the original tribes of [Long] island." These physical characteristics were crucial markers of race for Prime and his contemporaries, who used the same yardstick to decide that "there are a few remnants similarly amalgamated with African blood." The origin of those apparent African forebears was of no interest to Prime, however, because the answer, whether from plantations or fugitive action or even freeholders in ethnically diverse towns, presumably did not fit the image he sought.

Unlike enslaved and free African Americans, Native Americans were quite consistently represented in local histories.[4] As noted earlier, often a general discussion of aboriginal culture was given its own section, implicitly tied to descriptions of the natural environment. In some cases, authors included anecdotal historical narratives about well-known sachems in their interactions with colonists or other tribes. Curiously, of the sachems of East Long Island, Wyandanch was best represented, to the point where he was repeatedly reported to have been the Grand Sachem of Long Island (Paumanoc), although period documents plainly indicate that he only became so after the death of the politically higher-ranked Youghco (Poggaticut) who led the Manhanset (see Prime 1845, 100; Thompson 1843, 1: 92, 95; Adams 1918, 22). This reassignment is not so surprising when one considers the role in which Wyandanch was most famous with European colonists. As sachem of the Montaukett, Wyandanch had offered his alliance to the English directly after the dreadful battle of the 1637 Pequot War in which a Pequot fort had been burned with many Pequot families trapped inside. As a sign of his faithfulness, he had offered to track down and capture any Pequot who had fled to Long Island, bringing their heads as proof to Lion Gardiner. While this story was commonly cited by local historians, they rarely mentioned that his offer was subject to Youghco's approval. Yet, in 1644, Youghco had also offered his friendship to the United Colonies court representing all of the Long Island tribes of which he was leader, including Wyandanch's Montaukett.

A telling narrative about the elder Youghco, written by David Gardiner, suggests why Wyandanch was valorized to such a greater degree. Gardiner was a descendant of Lion Gardiner, a man instrumental in the Pequot War who had remained friends with Wyandanch for the remainder of the latter's life. Gardiner, in recounting the death of Youghco, wrote:

Poggatacut had exhibited uniformly less friendship for the English, and had generally discountenanced by his advice that preference in his brother. Beyond what was necessary to protect himself against the enmity of the white men, he had never shown them any favor. He cautiously avoided much intercourse with them, and whenever Wyandanch sought his advice, had uniformly, when the question was between the Indian and the English, sided with the former.

When he could covertly protect them without danger to himself
from the vengeance of the whites, the Indians were certain to receive
his assistance. He therefore often prevented that punishment for
their crimes which was sought at the hands of Wyandanch, by an
exercise in their favor of his authority as great sachem. (Gardiner
1871, 33)

The faintly damning description subtly insinuates that Youghco was
primarily interested in his own preservation. Prime (1845, 91) wrote that
Youghco was only regarded as "supreme chief" because of his age, while
Wyandanch was *"the white man's unwavering friend"* (100, emphasis in
original). These descriptions highlight the kind of resolution that local
historians were able to come to in writing about Native Americans in
more favorable, romanticized terms: by favoring figures like Wyandanch, they could represent Indians as loyal friends to the colonists,
unlike Youghco or the more famous Mohawk Joseph Brant, or Seneca
Red Jacket. Readers of Long Island histories of this period repeatedly
saw a variation on the phrase, "Long Island Indians were less troubling/
less disruptive/more content than their cousins to the north." Pequots,
Narragansetts, and Wampanoag had pursued war with the colonists;
Haudenosaunee had sided with the British; but Long Island Indians were
no trouble.

An important and consistent part of these descriptions, however,
was how local historians reported the near-extinction of Indians. For
Wood (1824, 23), citing evidence from shell middens, this process began
even before white colonization, and thus his assessment was that "at the
time of the first [white] settlement of the Island, none of the tribes were
large, most of them inconsiderable in number and some quite small."
He attributed the decline in population to "perpetual wars" to which
Indians were "addicted." A few pages later Wood generously offered the
Indian "tradition" (closer to myth than science, he seemed to suggest)
that population declines were due to disease (27). Whatever the reason
for their demise, he declared that only a few scattered families were left.
Thompson (1843) abruptly ended a long account of the intertribal wars
and political maneuvers in the mid-seventeenth century by skipping forward nearly one hundred years and leaving the impression that Long
Island Indians had no historical impact after 1669. "In 1761 the Indians
had so diminished on Long Island, as in some places to have entirely
disappeared, while in others they were greatly reduced .... This number was further reduced, in 1783, by the emigration of a considerable

number of their tribe to Oneida County with the Rev. Sampson Occom" (1843, 1: 92–93). Despite the fact that none of the Long Island historians could legitimately declare Indians gone, Prime (1845, 101) confidently predicted "the present prospect is, that in a few more years the race will be extinct, and their reserved lands will fall, for want of a claimant, into the hands of the white man." There was no greater sign of the extinguishment of a race, to Prime, than to have one's land fall to others. It is no wonder then that so many whites could believe that Indians were no more.

Although the Long Island historians could not legitimately declare Indians extinct (but this did not stop all writers from doing so), they relied on stories of political death as a proxy. The existence of a Grand Sachem of Long Island—that is, in the colonial period Youghco and Wyandanch—was taken as the marker of political viability, and thus recounting their deaths was a means of signaling Indians' effective extinction. This narrative ploy may have derived in part from a genuine misunderstanding of the form of political succession practiced by Eastern Algonquians. Historical writers may have assumed that tribes were monarchies following a royal lineage, much like England; while tribal leadership often did pass through families, those inheritances still had to be popularly approved (see discussion in chapter 2). Thus the passing of the office from Youghco to Wyandanch and then to Wyandanch's son Weoncombone, who died young and without issue, seemed to local historians to be the end of a royal line.[5] Anecdotes of Youghco's death in 1653 focused on the outpouring of grief and extraordinary measures taken by his people in his burial. Gardiner's account (presumably in the original publication of 1840) was paraphrased or replicated verbatim in numerous local histories:

The decease of the sachem Poggaticut was an important event with the Indians. His remains were transported for burial from Shelter Island to Montauk. In removing the body, the bearers rested the bier to the side of the road leading from Sag Harbor to Easthampton, near the three mile stone, where a small excavation was made to designate the spot. From that time to the present, more than one hundred and eighty years, this memorial has remained as fresh, seemingly as if but lately made. No leaf, no stone, nor other thing, has been suffered to remain in it. The Montaukett tribe, though reduced to a beggarly number of some ten or fifteen drunken and degraded beings, have retained to this day the memory of this event, and no individual of them now passes the spot in his wanderings, without removing whatever may have fallen into it. The place is to them holy ground, and the exhibition of this pious act does honor to the finest feelings of the human heart. The excavation is about twelve inches in depth, and eighteen in diameter, and will probably continue undisturbed, until the active spirit for improvement which is abroad shall have reached this district. . . . (Gardiner 1871, 34)

As an anecdote signaling the death of Indian political power, this was a dangerous story because Gardiner betrayed the extraordinary depth of cultural transmission and historical memory of the Montaukett, giving evidence of a social solidarity. Gardiner, however, added a few key qualifiers. First, he was sure to mention the reduced and depraved condition of those who remember. And second, by noting that the memorial would continue only until the "spirit for improvement" or progress eliminated it, dismissed the practice as a ragged trace of the past, an anachronism. Later authors noted that the predicted destruction of the memorial indeed came to pass (Lamb 1887; Mallmann 1990).

Wyandanch's death, allegedly from poisoning in 1659, seemed to have ended the political personhood of the East Long Island Indians, at least in the estimation of local historians. The circumstances of his death were repeated in several histories; Prime especially lamented the loss of such a loyal friend to the English and the lack of an adequate memorial of him (1845, 100–101). These histories did not dwell particularly upon his passing, yet no Indian individuals figure with any significance in the subsequent chronologies, until Sampson Occom, who would lead a symbolic remainder out of Long Island. Even in recounting the events of King Philip's War, local historians represented Long Island Indians as having quietly stayed on the sidelines, despite the New York council records censuring Indians of Easthampton and Shelter Island for paying tribute to the Narragansett (Fernow 1883, 14: 697). The effective demise of the Montaukett was written into the landscape and narrated by several local historians, in the legend of three large depressions located across East Long Island and Shelter Island which were supposedly the footprints, pointing west, of the last Grand Sachem's departure (Prime 1845, 92; Adams 1918, 39; Lamb 1887, 387).

Sylvester Manor histories

Shelter Island, where available archival evidence tells us of both a Grand Sachem who was uncooperative with the English and one of the largest holdings of an enslaved population in the colonial northeast, thus represents a troublesome addition to the grand narratives of nineteenth-century historians. Histories of Shelter Island's colonial origins reproduced the themes of isolation and liberal idealism, but far more obliquely. Although Shelter Island was accounted for in the larger Long Island histories by Wood, Thompson, and Prime, the details of its settlement were limited to the transfer of property. These authors offered greater detail on the mid-eighteenth century, from a period when the town was incorporated, and those records and decisions moved beyond the Sylvester family. The earlier writers were not privy to the anecdotal details of the plantation, although notes in Prime's history (1845, 168) indicate that he was in contact with at least one Sylvester descendant. The silence of the Manor's past continued into the latter half of the nineteenth century, when the property had come under the protection of Eben Norton Horsford, who became an obsessive researcher and promoter of history, including that of the Sylvesters.

Horsford married into the Gardiner family, descendant of the Sylvesters by the L'Hommedieu side. Recently returned from his studies in Germany, he married Mary Gardiner and took a position at Harvard as a professor of chemistry in 1847 (Rezneck 1970). After Mary's death in 1855, Horsford married her sister, Phebe, in 1860. Mary and Phebe were the daughters of Samuel Smith Gardiner who purchased the property of Sylvester Manor in a time of financial distress for the estate, thereby effectively retaining it within one Sylvester line of descent. Gardiner and his family took up residence there, and upon his death he left the estate to daughter Phebe in 1859, shortly before she married Horsford (SMA Group III-A, Gardiner v. Dering 1828; Mallmann 1990, 116). Although the Horsfords were primarily resident in Cambridge, they used the Manor as a summer home.

After Professor Horsford's retirement from Harvard in 1863, owing to the large fortune generated by his invention of an improved chemical leavener (baking powder), his interests turned to historical research (Rezneck 1970). Although he never published a narrative of Sylvester Manor's history, his research contributed to others who did, and he articulated his own historical perspective through a commemorative landscape on the Manor property. More than two hundred years after the plantation was established, Horsford began the effort to reconstitute a coherent narrative of the place, drawing together the scraps of archival materials, anecdotal histories, stories from family and community, and even landscape and archaeological materials. The narratives that resulted were inflected by some of the same concerns held by earlier local historians as well as issues circulating in the nation following the Civil War. By this point, American anxieties over diversity had only become more pronounced. Not only had emancipation promised to bring African Americans to more communities, but also tremendous numbers of immigrants were arriving--Irish and Eastern Europeans into the urban east coast and East Asians into the west.

Perhaps contributing to Horsford's historical researches, his first wife Mary enshrined some of her own perspectives on the Native American past in a book of poetry, *Indian Legends and Other Poems* (1855). Several themes in her poems, including the Revolutionary War and the opposing interests of the United States and Indian nations, suggest at least some knowledge or inspiration from her grandfather, Ezra L'Hommedieu, in his work with the state Indian Affairs commission. Two poems in particular are illustrative of the perspectives at play among Sylvester descendants at that time. The first, "The Phantom Bride," was preceded by a note explaining the story on which it was based: "a young American lady was murdered, while dressed in her bridal robe, by a party of Indians" whom her betrothed had entrusted to protect her (16–22). For their betrayal, the Indians were doomed never to be successful in battle again:

'Neath the murmuring pine trees they laid side by side,
The gallant young soldier, the fair, murdered bride:
And never again from that traitorous night,
The red man dared stand in the battle's fierce storm,
For ever before him a phantom of light,
Rose up in the white maiden's beautiful form,
And when he would rush on the foe from his lair,
Those locks of pale gold floated past on the air.

This of course reads as an allegory for the betrayal of certain Haudenosaunee nations in siding with the British. One might also interpret the appearance of the form of the girl and the presence of her golden hair even in the air whenever the "red man" emerges from his lair as the curse that white people would be ever present and encroaching on his land.

A second poem, "The Last of the Red Men," required little interpretive skill (27–34). Beginning with "I saw him in vision,—the last of that race/ Who were destined to vanish before the Pale-face," the poem described a figure representative of the race who observes his own displacement by his "foe" before sending himself to oblivion by paddling over the "Thunder of Waters" (presumably Niagara Falls). As he does so, he speaks out:

On, on, mighty Spirit!
I welcome thy spray
As the prairie-bound hunter
The dawning of day;
No shackles have bound thee,
No tyrant imprest
The mark of the Pale face
On torrent and crest

His banners are waving
O'er hilltop and plain,
The stripes of oppression
Blood-red with our slain;
The stars of his glory
And greatness and fame,
The signs of our weakness,
The signs of our shame.

The hatchet is broken,
The bow is unstrung;
The bell peals afar
Where the war-whoop once rung:
The council-fires burn
But in thoughts of the Past
And their ashes are strewn
To the merciless blast.

Such a statement reputedly coming from the figure representing the whole of the Indian "race" placed the American nation in a constitutive opposition to them, suggesting that the flag itself ("stripes of oppression" and "stars of his glory") was composed of signs of Indian defeat upon which American greatness was founded. Council fires were consigned to mark only the absent past. Although there is a note of sympathy in the portrayal, the message is clear: American progress depended upon Indian disappearance. And unlike Prime's insistence on valorizing local Indians like Wyandanch, Mary Horsford deployed the opposite tactic: she abstracted the issue by referring to distant, exoticized tribes while ignoring the local. One could not argue that she was unaware of the local conditions; her family's long-time servant, Isaac Pharo, was a Montaukett man indentured to her father as a child. Professor Horsford would later write in his historical notes that Isaac was "one of the last of the Royal family of the Chief of the Montauks" (SMA, Group IV-A, 3: file 21).

Professor Horsford's research into Sylvester Manor's past seems to have begun in his retirement, though he and his second wife Phebe were apparently still dividing their time between Shelter Island and Cambridge, Massachusetts. Most of the notes and copied material do not indicate the date of the research, but much was likely completed in the late 1870s or early 1880s, perhaps inspired by the centennial celebrations of the nation. Horsford acquired quantities of genealogical information relating to his own family line (managing to connect himself to William the Conquerer) and the Sylvester line. While not all of his sources are recorded, he conducted some of his own archival researches and seems to have hired legal researchers to find and copy wills, indentures, and other official documents. He also collected numerous transcriptions of the trials of persecuted Quakers (SMA Group IV-A, Horsford undated: files 20–21, 1–6).

The most immediate consequence of Horsford's work was the placement on the property and dedication of a sculpted stone monument to Nathaniel Sylvester, for his protection of persecuted Quakers during his tenure at the Manor. A public ceremony to mark its dedication was held in 1884 (figure 5.1). Set in a small burial ground surrounded by slate headstones dating to the eighteenth century, the monument is made from a sculpted and engraved marble top, on sandstone legs fashioned to resemble architectural columns, standing on a raised stone dais. The monument performs several kinds of associations in its looks and text. First, it memorializes Nathaniel Sylvester for "Sheltering ever the Persecuted for Conscience sake," incorporating the names of many outspoken and cruelly punished Quakers who had spent time at the Manor. This commemoration subtly references the same sort of origins story of the ideal liberal society that early antebellum histories crafted. The story of Nathaniel Sylvester's arrival and establishment of the plantation fits into a narrative of the pursuit of liberty if one focuses, for example, on his protection of persecuted Quakers and defiance of both English and Dutch colonial authorities. But neither Nathaniel's desire to create Sylvester Manor as an entailed estate like those of the English gentry nor his status as one of the largest slaveholders in the northern colonies in the mid-seventeenth century fits this tribute. The exclusion of European associations was desirable in the years following the war, in the youth of the nation. By 1884, however, Horsford and broader swathes of the American public had resurrected a nostalgic vision for the British past, even for royal connections.

(a)

(b)

FIGURE 5.1. Monuments, (a) Quaker memorial monument dedication in 1884 (photo courtesy of Fales Library and Special Collections), and (b) monument detail (photo by John Matsunaga).

A second block of text at the base of the monument establishes that connection for Sylvester Manor: First, the list of the proprietors of the property begins with the Manhanset and proceeds through the King and the Earl of Sterling (forgetting that the King never purchased the land, a critical difference in the early republic) and follows down the line to Eben Norton Horsford. Second, a selective genealogy connects Horsford back to not just Sylvester, but to Thomas Brinley, his father-in-law, who was the King's auditor. This neatly pruned family tree is accompanied by the Brinley coat of arms. For that matter, the focus on Quakers may also have served, for Horsford, as a connection to royalty, as he wrote in his notes:

> What had Shelter Island to do with procuring the King's Mandamus? . . . it is fair to presume that it was within the power of their father Thomas Brinly, to assist in securing the audience of the King for the Quaker, Ed. Burroughs, which resulted in the Royal Mandamus, which Shattuck bore into the presence of Endicott, and which put a final end to the executions, and stayed, for a time, imprisonment and the whippings. (SMA Group IV-A, Horsford undated: file 20)

Though not documented by Horsford, later writers commented that the glade in which the monument sits was called Woodstock, after Thomas Brinley's estate in England (Lamb 1887, 387; Duvall 1952).

Quaker persecution and the liberal ideals of the plantation were not the only objects of Horsford's study. He also explored Native American pasts, but usually he sought particular themes disconnected from the Manor's own significant past. His notes and draft narratives on the Manhanset show his reliance on anecdotes from historical narratives and local lore as well as a bit of speculative exploration of the landscape at Sylvester Manor. His anecdotal evidence focused on the involvement of the Manhanset in wars and their military prowess, compiled under a section titled "Record of war on Shelter Island" (SMA Group IV-A, Horsford undated: file 21). Much of the information there would have been easily found in the earlier Long Island histories; for example, he described the relationship of Lion Gardiner to Wyandanch and the efforts of the Narragansett to control the Long Island Indians. Through these stories, he replicated the idea that the Paumanoc tribes were loyal to the English and maintained peaceful relations, and yet he was also fascinated by the notion that the Manhanset were a large tribe of fierce warriors. These stories were not contradictory to Horsford, as he believed that "[t]he

Indian ways not improbably came to an end about the commencement of occupancy by Sylvester." On Shelter Island, he imagined that Indian tenure was of the ancient past, and he marveled at the apparent antiquity of their occupation in citing a report likely found in Thompson's extensive description of Long Island geology:

> The finding already mentioned at a depth of 57 feet when digging a well of an Indian pestle with beach sand and shells shows [. . .] that portions of the Island were inhabited by Indians before the . . . glaciers . . . shows that this Island is indefinitely older as a site of human habitation than the adjacent continental shore and land. . . . There is a fragment of a very crude pestle in the Manor house the history of which has lapsed—but which has the rough construction that would place it among the less finished works of this class and possibly among the class of ruder, earlier samples of stone implements. (SMA Group IV-A, Horsford undated: file 21)

As in tracing his own lineage to William the Conquerer, Horsford appeared to value the very antiquity of the Manhanset, though he did not remark upon the possibility that both lineages might have extended unto the present.

Other evidence was to be found in the landscape itself. A visitor to the Manor guided this discovery: Frank Cushing, a Bureau of Ethnology anthropologist who was well known among the academic community for his earlier groundbreaking ethnological work with the Zuni, came to the Manor sometime after 1884. Horsford described how he and Cushing explored the North Peninsula (as it is now known to archaeologists), where Cushing pointed out the traces of an Indian village. At that time, the peninsula was kept clear of trees, and Cushing claimed to see on the ground the traces of a stockade wall, a pathway through the middle of the stockade enclosure, and remains of "kitchen middens" which he demonstrated by turning up spadesful of pottery, charcoal, bone, and corn (SMA Group IV-A, Horsford undated: file 21). Indeed, when our team of archaeologists systematically tested this area more than a hundred years later, many of the same items, plus stone tools and shell middens, were found, though no sign of a stockade wall or pathway was. In his notes, Horsford wrote that this must have been the village of Youghco. Radiocarbon dating from two of the shell middens shows that this site was, in fact, several hundred years older than Youghco's time, though there was no way for Horsford to know this. Perhaps in his readings of other histories, he did not realize that

Youghco was also referred to as Poggaticut, as he distinguished this village from that known to be Poggaticut's village in Sachem's Neck, on the southeast side of the island. Most important for Horsford was that the evidence of corn agriculture, in addition to the abundant natural resources of the bay, supported the notion that the Manhanset were a large military force.

These traces apparently impressed Horsford. In an oddly off-handed comment in his notes, he wrote, "It has not seemed improper to give the name of Youghco a permanent record on this part of the Island. It has accordingly been inscribed upon the even surface of a large rock on the shore of Dering water a hundred and fifty yards towards its mouth from the monument to Nathaniel Sylvester." Unlike the monument to Nathaniel Sylvester, however, there was no public ceremony dedicating the stone. Indeed, few people today even know that the monument exists, much less that Professor Horsford placed it there. And small wonder: it is located in the marshy margin, a wooded stand thick with undergrowth on one side and the creek on the other, with no path to lead one to it. The unshaped stone, laid flat to the ground, is difficult to see unless the viewer is quite close and is literally inscribed only with the name of Youghco (figure 5.2)—no location in time, no associations of tribe, family, or territory. As a commemoration, it leaves Youghco timeless, embedded within the "natural" world, particularly separated from the history of the plantation, and certainly excluded from the modern world. This would have been perfectly appropriate in Horsford's mind, as he felt that the Manhanset tenure ended as Sylvester history began, or perhaps even earlier; the "Succession of Proprietors" engraved upon the Quaker monument listed four between the Manhanset and Nathaniel Sylvester. Given what we know to have existed in the archives available to him at the time and his willingness to seek information on the past, his representation of the Manhanset in the singular, mortal body of Youghco seems obtuse, though it was a blindness borne of predominant attitudes.

Horsford's investigations and representations of the enslaved Africans and African-Americans at the plantation are similarly ambivalent. Within his own research notes and manuscript drafts, the subject of slavery was never broached. Yet he was aware at some level of its significance in the history of the Manor estate. The only mention of African Americans in his notes follows immediately after his indication of the Youghco monument, as though the thought of the monument reminded him of another:

FIGURE 5.2. Youghco stone monument, below with detail of engraved text (photo by author).

The enclosure devoted to the burial of the early negro servants and their later descendants, near the entrance to John's House wood— why it is so called is no longer answerable—has been indicated by an inscription on a large boulder in its natural position, which reads as follows—Burying Ground/Of the Colored People/Of the Manor/ From 1651. This marks also the last resting place of Isaac Pharo. (SMA Group IV-A, Horsford undated: file 21)

Indeed, though the "colored people of the Manor" merited little mention and no investigation, the stone that commemorates their place in the

(a)

(b)

FIGURE 5.3. Stone monument engraved "Burying Ground of the Colored People of the Manor from 1651," (a) historic photo of burial ground, probably late nineteenth century (courtesy of Fales Library and Special Collections) and (b) detail of engraving (photo by John Matsunaga).

history of the estate is much more centrally accessible for viewing, located between the main roadway to the Manor house and the fence enclosing the burial ground. Like the Youghco stone, this marker is coarse and unshaped but for the engraved text. But the stone rises from the ground, presenting its engraved face toward the roadway, visible from a distance and inviting attention to the text to all who pass. Unlike the Youghco stone, this one links the "colored people" with the Manor and temporally with the early plantation (for those viewers cognizant of the Manor's history). The text of the stone pins the enslaved open-endedly to the earliest plantation history, as if to deny more recent involvement with slavery.

Though the stone created an association of the "colored people" with the plantation, Horsford also noted "later descendants" buried there. He referred to the inclusion of Isaac Pharo in the burial ground, known to the family as "the last of the Royal family of the Chief of the Montauks" and as a servant to them for nearly his entire life. Whether Isaac was in fact descended from Wyandanch himself, it should not have escaped notice that the Gardiners had been connected to the Montauketts for a very long time. Given their long association, what might have been meant by the family's burial of Isaac there? Was Horsford asserting that this Montaukett man was descended from the "early negro servants," or did he consider both African and Indian ancestry as "colored"? His comment casts the categorization of the "colored" servants into considerable ambiguity. Both the temporal and the race-categorical ambiguity, however, are mainly restricted to Horsford's private notes rather than the more accessible monument.

These three monuments taken together comprise a kind of coded historical narrative about the plantation embedded in the physical landscape of Sylvester Manor, from which the plantation has been effaced. This narration performed a separation, or a severing of associations, between three groups whose distinctiveness is constitutively reinforced by the separation. Unlike the spatial configuration of the plantation core found in the archaeological remains, where relationships were negotiated at close proximities, the placement of the monuments at some distance from one another suggests physical and social distance and denies the possibilities of interaction. The temporal marking of the monuments reinforces the separation: the Quaker monument declares Euro-American possession for nearly all time, enslaved Africans were of only the distant time of the early plantation, and Youghco of the Manhanset is completely out of time. The appearance of each monument, of sculpted or coarse stone, reinforces these implied distinctions. One thing is shared among these monuments: they are all statements made in a medium intended to be permanent.

This is not the only occasion on which Professor Horsford resorted to monuments to establish his own vision of history. He had also spent considerable research time in the last decade of his life pursuing the evidence of Viking "discovery" and occupation of New England many centuries before Columbus's arrival. To do so he attempted to demonstrate the Norse origins of Algonquian placenames in Massachusetts, scoured early explorers' accounts and maps for observations of abandoned Norse settlements, and even engaged in archaeological survey and excavations. In one such excavation, he and his daughter Cornelia claimed to have found the remains of Leif Eriksson's own house, right there in their Cambridge neighborhood. Inconveniently, he thought, an English colonist had built atop these remains, filling the Norse cellar with colonial artifacts (Horsford 1893), though an archaeologist today might suggest that the site *was* colonial and not Norse at all. Unlike his work on Sylvester Manor's history, Horsford's copious research on the precedence of the Norsemen was published as a number of books (Horsford 1886; 1888; 1892), which were quite popular for a time. But he was also a driving force and patron in a campaign to commission a statue of Leif Ericksson, which was erected in 1887 in Boston to public fanfare and a speech by Horsford himself on why Ericksson should rightfully be considered the first European to set foot in the Americas. His fascination with Norse discovery seems to fit with his appreciation of deep antiquity and origins. But numerous scholars (Fleming 1995; Mancini 2002; Headly 2003) have also connected the popular appropriation of Norse antiquity by Anglo New Englanders in the late nineteenth century with their distress over the influx of Irish and Southern and Eastern European immigrants, who were either Catholic or Jewish. As J. M. Mancini observed:

> The mainstreaming of Viking history in the last quarter of the nine-teenth century served a similar purpose as that served by the larger trend towards racializing history. At a moment of increasing fear that the nation was committing race suicide, the thought of Viking ghosts roaming the streets of a city increasingly filled with Irish, Italian, and Jewish hordes must have been comforting to an Anglo-Saxon elite whose political power, at least, was decidedly on the wane. (Mancini 2002, 877)

As the four hundredth anniversary of the Catholic, Genoese Columbus's landfall approached in 1892, Horsford's research into an earlier, whiter, and (it was argued) Protestant discoverer of America met with an appreciative audience. Despite the research into Viking occupation of New England being quite discredited in the years since the statue's placement, it remains standing in Boston today. Such is the power of monumental historical statements.

Telling stories: the forgotten return

Had Horsford written the history of Sylvester Manor, rather than committing it to stone on the landscape, he might have found it a bit more difficult to categorically separate the indigenous and the enslaved from the narrative. What if he were to incorporate the stories and legends handed down over the generations? It is unlikely that Professor Horsford, who was committed to scientific approaches (even badly used), would have done so. But two local historians who did write about Sylvester Manor and Shelter Island before the turn of the twentieth century had less concern with the use of such stories, and their narratives were liberally salted with personal anecdotes. These authors, Martha Lamb and the Reverend J. E. Mallmann, both collected lore directly from the Horsford family, as evidenced by their archived correspondence. Mallmann, minister of Shelter Island's Presbyterian Church, also collected anecdotes from many in the Island community. The inclusion of these transmitted stories, folksy and subjective though they must be, shows that the exclusion of the enslaved and the indigenous was not accomplished as the grand narratives of earlier historians or Horsford's commemorative landscape would suggest.

In 1887, Martha J. Lamb visited Sylvester Manor at the invitation of Professor Horsford. Well-known in New York City society, Mrs. Lamb was a noted writer, editor, and historian of New York. She was the owner and editor of the *Magazine of American History*. Wealth and high society likely connected Mrs. Lamb with Professor Horsford, as well as their mutual interest in history. She came away from her "little journey and delightful visit" to the Manor with quantities of material she used a few months later to publish an article titled "The Manor of Shelter Island: Historic Home of the Sylvesters" (SMA Group IV-A, Lamb correspondence 1887; Lamb 1887). She wrote with an engaging narrative style and romantic embellishments, rather than a perhaps drier academic approach. She herself characterized her work as "popular" when she later wrote to Horsford; she was hoping to contribute something to his Norumbega/Norse colonization project: "My object will be to carry the popular judgement and verdict" (SMA Group IV-A, Lamb correspondence 1889). The content of the article, while undoubtedly also incorporating Lamb's own research, recounts a number of stories and details that suggest family stories told to her at the time of her visit. Her resulting portrait was a rather different representation of Sylvester Manor than the typical New England/Long Island American origin stories. She instead painted the Sylvesters as a kind of American royalty or at least celebrity, as indicated by her closing line: "Few dwellings in America have welcomed more celebrities under its roof, and there are none extant more rich in varied and romantic associations" (Lamb 1887, 389).

Mrs. Lamb's narrative thus focuses upon the famed aspects of the Manor's history: the Brinley connection to royalty, the protection of Quakers, the relationship to the Winthrops of Connecticut, and the varied roles of Sylvesters and descendants in colonial and early Republic history. The influence of Horsford's own interests was quite apparent in her choices of topic. Such was her focus (and the biases of her time) that she also displayed a remarkable carelessness with regard to the significance of representing slavery at the Manor. For example, in describing the Boston court's persecution of Quakers, she described their efforts to sell certain Quakers into slavery in quite unreflexive terms: "[they] offered them to one sea captain after another for the markets of Virginia and Barbados. No buyer could be found; the inhumanity was too glaring" (Lamb 1887, 369). Yet the inhumanity of the situation was apparently reserved for whites, as Lamb glibly described Nathaniel Sylvester's acquisition of "as many negro slaves as he could employ to advantage in the beginning" (366). Instead, "negro slaves" were more of a status symbol in her estimation, and we might speculate if slavery at the Manor was described to her in similar terms. For example, she relayed the anecdote of Benjamin L'Hommedieu meeting Patience Sylvester, daughter to Nathaniel:

> One pleasant Sunday morning soon after his arrival, L'Hommedieu was attracted by an extremely novel object moving over the sparkling waters of the bay. As it came nearer he observed two remarkably handsome young women in a barge, with a canopy over it, and six negro slaves rowing it. The vision haunted him. He went to church that morning, and, despite Puritanical customs, permitted his eyes to remain open during prayer. (380)

This is an account unlikely to have been found in the archives. Rather it has the flavor of a long-cherished family story. Although whimsical, the detail gives an immediate picture of enormous wealth, such that six slaves may be spared to the task of rowing two young ladies to church, and evokes the exotic in the enslaved rowers.

Nor was there any attempt to depict slavery as part of the distant past. Mrs. Lamb actually *overstated* the number of the enslaved on Shelter Island at the time of the Revolutionary War. Town censuses from 1771 and 1776 put their numbers at 27 and 33 respectively, while Lamb claimed there were "not less than two hundred. . . . They have gradually dwindled away, but many of their descendants remain, and are, as a rule, industrious and respected." Included with the article was an unsourced, undated sketch labeled "ONE OF THE LAST OF THE SLAVES ON THE SYLVESTER MANOR," narratively removing the enslaved from contemporary concern (figure 5.4).

Lamb gave even less concern to discussing the role of the Manhanset in Shelter Islands's history. This reversal of the typical narrative of colonial

FIGURE 5.4. Drawing reproduced in Lamb 1887, thought to be Julia Dyd Havens.

origins disregards the usual considerable care given to describing the relationship and timing of Indian departure to colonist's settlement as a means of justifying their ultimate exclusion. Mrs. Lamb did make an obligatory gesture, in unusually rosy terms, to the Manhanset's original presence:

> The island had long been the headquarters of the Manhansett tribe of Indians, whose sachems appear to have been more enlightened and sagacious than most of their dusky contemporaries. They were pleased rather than otherwise to have white people come among them; they cared little for the soil which they never tilled, but they were tenacious about their rights in the matter of hunting and

fishing—particularly fishing. This granted, they were the best of friends and really a protection to the pioneers. (Lamb 1887, 361)

Oddly, her description touches upon two aspects of the plantation that are reasonably accurate given the benefit of evidence from the recent archaeology and broader archival research: Sylvester did apparently make an effort to protect Manhanset fishing rights, and a relationship of protection may have existed, as hinted by the wampum production in the plantation core. But Mrs. Lamb was also repeating the old story, used by the English colonists, to justify the appropriation of Indian land because Indians were not planting, thus not improving, the land. She did later note the village site north of the Manor house, which Horsford and Cushing had explored, as well as the story of the departing footsteps. Despite these token references likely told to her by Horsford, Mrs. Lamb apparently had little interest in including any Manhanset in the story of Sylvester Manor.

Even as a strangely star-struck story, Mrs. Lamb's article was the first detailed, focused account of Sylvester Manor ever published. Little wonder that subsequent histories of Shelter Island used her work as a source, particularly for the romantic anecdotes that could not be found in public archives. The story of Benjamin L'Hommedieu's first glimpse of Patience Sylvester on a slave-powered barge, for example, was quoted in its entirety in two later volumes on Shelter Island's history (Mallmann 1990; Duvall 1952). These anecdotes were uncritically accepted as part of the available historical evidence and repeated. As these narratives were compiled with others, however, the inherent complexity of the evidence from the past strained the grand messages in more general histories.

The most complete and well-known Shelter Island history written after Mrs. Lamb's article was an ecclesiastical history by the Presbyterian minister, Reverend Jacob E. Mallmann, originally published in 1899. His history went well beyond simply the church and its records, as he collected information from other municipal and ecclesiastical histories of the area, town and county records, and biographies of key figures collected from their descendants whenever possible. In 1897 Mallmann began a correspondence with Phebe Horsford following her requests to dedicate her support for church renovations to her late husband, Professor Horsford. The renovations demanded a rededication, which the church took as a moment to reflect upon its foundations. Soon enough the reverend was asking specific questions about the Sylvesters and their descendants and seeking photographs of places and people. Phebe, though elderly and ill by that time, responded willingly, sending him also copies of Martha Lamb's article and Thompson's Long Island history and referring him to her daughter Lilian who was more knowledgeable of family history (SMA Group IV-C, P.D.G. Horsford 1897 and undated). Mallmann was meticulous about the inclusion of his findings and most often identified where his information came from, sometimes quoting entire documents or letters written to him with biographical information.

Mallmann's main aim, of course, was to compile a full account of the spiritual history of Shelter Island. In his zeal for historical research, however, he began to put together more sources of information on Shelter Island's past than anyone had done before, and unsurprisingly some of it was contradictory. In some cases he astutely, but not consistently, noted the discrepancies. He was, for example, the first local historian to observe that the purchase of Shelter Island from the Manhanset was not an uncontested transfer. He recounted the complaint lodged by the Manhanset to the United Colony court that they had never sold the land, as the claim of the land by the King and its subsequent sale down the line to Sylvester and his partners had taken place without their consent, let alone recompense. Knowledge of this did not prevent him, only eight pages later, from summarizing the incorrect succession of proprietors as Horsford had upon his monument: beginning with the Manhanset, passing to the King, to the Earl of Sterling, to James Farrett, to Stephen Goodyear, to the Sylvesters. Mallmann's central interest in recounting the Manhanset complaint had little to do with the injustice of the situation; he was rather intrigued with Checkanoe, the Indian who had represented them at court and was believed to have been a translator for John Eliot, the famed Puritan proselytizer to New England Indians. Eyes on a higher plane, Mallmann enthused, "This young Indian's literary ability is an evidence to me that God has made of one blood all nations that dwell upon the face of the earth" (1990, 20).

In other cases, the reverend was less obtuse. Like so many others, he had interpreted the original record of Manhanset quitclaim to Shelter Island literally and declared that upon this settlement of the case, the Manhanset had departed, to where nobody knew. Several chapters later, as he was recounting the building of the island's first meeting-house in 1743, he had cause to relate something else on the island at the time--Indians: "This conflicts somewhat with a previous statement that upon the purchase of the island from the Indians the latter left the island" (1990, 73). In a rare moment of vagueness, Mallmann referred to unspecified evidence that a substantial village of Manhanset had lived on Sachem's

Neck until 1790 when a major portion of the dwellings were destroyed in a fire. Still further information, found in the sermons of one of his predecessors, revealed that some of these Indians had been on the island as late as 1835. At this point in his narrative, Mallmann offered his last last-of-the-Indians story from the sermon he quoted, on the conversion of the elderly, last-of-the-Manhanset Betty Tobs Caesar.

> More than fourscore years had made its deep furroughs on her brow. She had often sold herself to letchery and rum. It may be said for many, many years that no one cared for her soul. But God's time came, when all her race had been laid in the grave, and all those whom she had known in her youth were beneath the clods of the valley, then it was that God's word was spirit and life. . . . (1990, 73–74)

More than likely, descendants of the Manhanset still lived among the related Shinnecock and Montaukett (and likely do today as well), but Reverend Mallmann perhaps mourned the apparent extinction of their history. Where was the record of their existence in the intervening years? At Sylvester Manor, at least, it remained underground.

Mallmann's account also acknowledged the institution of slavery on Shelter Island, though in his representation of emancipation he declared a moral position that was lacking in earlier references. Aside from later eighteenth-century town records, these references were likely family anecdotes given to him by Sylvester descendants, and it was perhaps not politic to comment upon the morality of slavery. He noted, for example, that Nathaniel Sylvester, upon his first arrival to Shelter Island, "brought with him, besides his wife and brothers, several servants and some slaves from Barbadoes" (21), though no records of this group are known of today. Mallmann also recounted the story (alluded to in chapter 2) of Thomas Dering and two enslaved men:

> Among other possessions Mr. Dering owned a number of slaves, one of whom, by the name of Cato, was once caught in his wine cellar imbibing. Mr. Dering had him immediately brought before him for punishment, and, in order to make his punishment as effective as possible, both on the guilty one and the rest of the slaves, had them all summoned, with all the whites whom he had in his employ, in the large servants' kitchen. Among the other slaves was one named Comus, who was remarkable for his keenness of intellect as well as for his immense stature, he being six feet six inches tall. While the sin and punishment of Cato was being discussed, this giant of a slave

rose up and asked permission to plead for Cato, and having received permission from his master, proceeded as follows: "Massa, you have pigs and you have corn, 'spose them pigs get in and eat some of that corn. The pigs are yours, and is not the corn yours just the same, if the pigs have eaten it? Now Cato is yours and the cider he drank was yours before, and is it not still yours after he has drank it? I do not see why Cato should be punished." Mr. Dering rose and said: "Comus, thou reasoneth well. Cato, thou art discharged." (59–60)

It is a story loaded with moral ambiguities: slaves accept their status as property in order to argue innocence of theft, and Dering honors the rights of the enslaved who liken themselves to animals. Folklorists might recognize this anecdote as a "John and Old Master" tale, a genre popular in the late nineteenth century, which featured battles of wit and intelligence between enslavers and enslaved, in which neither was more likely to triumph than the other (Dickson 1974). The story may not have been about Dering at all.[6]

Perhaps unconstrained by personal anecdotes, when Mallmann recounts the legal statutes of gradual emancipation enacted in New York, he is more expressive of both a moral and patriotic position. He identified the number of slaves recorded in the 1776 town census and the heads of household to whom they were enslaved. He then cited the principles of the Declaration of Independence as the direct cause of the passage of the first act toward the abolishment of slavery, that of voluntary manumission in 1788. Mallmann then wrote of every instance of manumission occurring in the town records subsequent to the act, beginning in 1795 and ending in 1821. These bracketing instances were of persons who had spent at least part of their enslavement at Sylvester Manor, with the family of Sylvester Dering, though the reverend did not comment on this fact. This too may have been too personal or contentious a recollection, given that Sylvester Dering had been an esteemed church elder (1990, 75–76). However inspiring these manumissions may have been, the narrative does not include any indication of what happened to these individuals upon gaining their freedom, and the "last of the slaves" were never heard from again. Slavery, like Indians, was thus relegated to the disconnected past.

Professor Horsford's commemorative monuments to Nathaniel Sylvester, Youghco, and the enslaved accomplished what local histories could not: he set a vision of colonial history in stone by using the physical dimensions of the landscape to tell a temporal and racial story. If all were memorialized, however, what is forgotten? Through his stone inscriptions, Horsford created the impression of very distinct categories of persons who occupied the Manor estate with minimal to no interaction with one another, by reason of time, race, and social standing. Thus, the possibility of relationships, in a world where categories were not yet set in stone, was denied and forgotten.

Separation itself is a form of forgetting by severing associations. While Horsford felt compelled to create all three monuments, the separate stones in segregated locales may have made it easier to forget the enslaved and the indigenous. Allowing the coarse Youghco stone to lie in a remote "natural" location, with the woods and underbrush creating their own barriers, Horsford assured that no one who stumbled across it would connect Youghco himself with Sylvester Manor. Likewise, though more might see the monument to the enslaved, few would wonder how many generations of African Americans served the estate, as they were confined to the distant past by the chiseled date of 1651. Perhaps most important to Horsford, by keeping that monument separate from that of Nathaniel Sylvester for his aid to the Quakers, he could prevent questions of why an estate honoring Quakers, known in the eighteenth century for their outspoken opposition to slavery, also marks its engagement in slavery.

The narrative histories of Long Island, Shelter Island, and Sylvester Manor demonstrate the efforts that were made to write these distinctions into history. That is, the histories do not reveal fully the interactions and relationships on the plantation that the monuments deny, but by the inclusion of small details, in which some appear anomalous, those narratives introduced ruptures to the history encoded in the monuments, just as the appearance of particular artifacts ruptured our archaeological expectations. They do so because particular elements of collective memory, found in unremarked archival sources and anecdotal history, were read or heard at a moment when their significance *could* be introduced. Late nineteenth-century concerns regarding the status and condition of both Indian communities and African Americans provided the context in which such details catch the eye of the historian, particularly if the historian is not personally invested in the narrative as Horsford might have been. These elements of collective memory thus find a place in a new time, as Certeau (1984, 86) suggests: "Like those birds that lay their eggs only in other species' nests, memory produces in a place that it does not belong to." Far from being completely effaced, such details may haunt a history, introducing doubt or an attentiveness to absences. Where *did* the Indians go, readers might wonder, in the years between 1652, when they supposedly departed, and nearly one hundred years later when their existence was next noticed in Shelter Island narratives? What exactly did the enslaved do, and where did they end up? And what happened to introduce the implied relationship between the enslaved and the indigenous, given the continual reference to racial mixture? These gaps in the narratives arise with particular force in the context of race relations and our ideas about citizenship and sovereignty today.

6 / Unimagining Communities

Artifacts, unseen archives, and anecdotal histories thus act to introduce doubt, to disrupt the grand narratives of race. They await our willingness to see them and our ability to recognize them as ruptures. If we give attention to the haunting figures and conspicuous historical silences and juxtapose those silences with the reconstructed archaeological facts and the unremarked archival materials, then could we reassemble different stories? In my own narrative, I have tried to focus on the many elisions, failures to record or preserve, selective silences, outright destructions, and narrative erasures that have rendered us unable to gain a clear perspective on the plantation at Sylvester Manor. When these issues are presented with the archaeological material—the abandoned materiality of the plantation—we are able to see traces of what other stories might have been. But even our new interpretations will slide into the racialized historical episteme that has been constructed around the colonial and plantation foundations of the United States if we do not attend to the ongoing effects of racial discourse to contemporary perspectives. In many ways, this is not a story about race; rather, it is a story about how race came to shape the way histories were and are told. It is a story told not just by the amateur or local white historians but also by scholars and descendants of all the plantation residents. There is a difference, however, in *why*. Such narratives are not just passive reflections; instead, they bring coherence to a sense of identity for the authors and their readers.

My concern here is not just how social memory is created, but how exclusion and forgetting are crucial aspects of that creation. Certain remnants of the past are either ignored as sources or are even later redacted or reshaped when communities deem them inappropriate for the story they want to tell about themselves. It may seem paradoxical to investigate the absences, silences, or substitutions of forgetting, for indeed if forgetting is successful we should never know. But social memory, constructed among networks of people and often embedded in materiality, is an entangled sense of history, with redundant and conflicting versions that are often quite difficult to eradicate completely. This is not to say that the remnants are clear perspectives on the past, if even there were a single "past." But the evidence we have of the Shelter Island plantation certainly exceeds the narratives told by local nineteenth-century historians, especially when we expand our concepts of what constitutes historical evidence. Hints and traces--from the ground, from the little-used corners of the archives and oral histories, and even embedded within those local histories--inscribe a shape to what was either forgotten or never imagined as *history* to begin with. What stories might be otherwise told about the plantation, if not the one comprised of racialized actors? In other words, what is at stake if race is not used to characterize separate communities?

Alternative narratives

Perhaps the most evident story is about class inequalities and labor. We forget that what the Sylvesters created in the plantation population was a majority disenfranchised labor force, significantly outnumbering their own family. At a minimum, the twenty-three enslaved Africans and African Americans accounted at Nathaniel's death in 1680 were twice the family's number, but the proportion tipped more dramatically by factoring in both the Manhanset on the island and perhaps additional white indentured servants. Maintaining social control and hierarchical order was likely a constant concern to the Sylvesters who were surrounded by the disenfranchised: on the one hand, Africans had been forcibly transported across the Atlantic and subjected to the brutality of work on a Barbados sugar plantation, and their children had been born into enslavement; on the other hand, the Manhanset had been displaced by the Sylvesters and seen their landscape radically altered, and their quiet presence and labor was continually predicated upon provision of goods and protection. Both Manhanset and enslaved Africans were not so isolated from the wider world that they did not hear of discontent and anger amongst Eastern Algonquians in the buildup to King Phillip's

War, prompted by conflicts over land. The Manhanset and Montaukett were noted particularly in colony court records for having maintained communications with the Narragansett in this period (Fernow 1883, 14: 697). These were likely frightening prospects to the Sylvesters, who must have feared a collaboration of African with Manhanset. The shared experience of a colonial labor regime, however, is an apparent point of entry to the potential benefits of collaboration for the indigenous and the enslaved, a rich field for interpretation (e.g., see Silliman 2001; Voss 2008).

The plantation was also part of an emergent capitalist economy. Capitalism, as Marx and Marxian-inspired writers have elaborated, is based in part on a kind of forgetting that occurs as objects become alienated from the labor producing them (Connerton 2009). This is certainly true of the landscape of Sylvester Manor's estate. Although the later commemorative landscape does encode contributions by a (racialized) labor class and stories of the place do anecdotally refer to the servants or slaves of the Manor, it does so in a way that refers only to the bodies present, not to either the labor performed or the value of that production. As Mrs. Lamb's nineteenth-century narrative demonstrated, the recollection of the laborers themselves served as a marker of the Sylvesters' status. Such a portrait is at odds with the archaeological remains of the working yard and the dirty, intensive, and strenuous tasks performed there, but, of course, this evidence was reduced to rubble and buried under clean landscape fill. All the material signs of the effort that produced both the place and the goods sent into global circulation to generate the wealth of the family were erased. The plantation was not precisely the commodity about which Marx was theorizing, despite the estimation of its exchange value in probate inventories and the sale of much of the land after Nathaniel's death. The wealth and property that remained, however, were translated into the trappings of a new American identity for Brinley Sylvester and his descendants. Like many others in New England, they separated themselves from a history of commercial plantation production, shipping, and merchant activity, although the very capital from those activities allowed them to refashion themselves. The Sylvesters sought to represent themselves instead as part of a small independent village--wealthy but self-sustaining. Their engagement in the religious Great Awakening, emphasizing individualism and personal faith, bolstered this reidentification. While diversity was often written out of the colonial narrative in the nineteenth century, the Sylvesters in the early eighteenth century were more concerned with suppressing unwanted associations of commercial networks, Old World class hierarchies, and labor of any variety.

Enslaved labor, African American or otherwise, suffers its own invisibility in the northern colonies, an invisibility created first by nineteenth-century historians rejecting the association with southern society. This form was demonstrated in the discussion of Long Island local histories in chapter 5. Local historians' forgetting has been perpetuated, however, by more recent scholars, especially in archaeology. What we know of plantation slavery is most associated with the work of archaeologists in southern or Caribbean colonies, on large plantation estates most likely to have survived into the present with intact archaeological deposits (Singleton 1985; Armstrong 1990; Deetz 1993; Delle 1998; Ferguson 1992; Otto 1984; Vlach 1993; Upton 1985; Wilkie and Farnsworth 2005; Handler and Lange 1978; among many others). These sites have provided a wealth of information about the experience of slavery on later, larger southern plantations, particularly in contexts of spatially separate living areas; such information allows us to associate artifact assemblages with specific groups of people. But these investigations have not proven to provide a model that can be applied to plantations of either earlier periods or of a different scale, like those with relatively lower numbers of enslaved persons and with little spatial distinction. Even in the larger plantation settings, the artifact types associated with the enslaved are not fundamentally different from what might be associated with free white laborers or even wealthier whites. Instead, there is a difference in degrees, relative access to specific resources, perhaps different traditions of preparing similar foods, and very rarely an explicit expression of cultural symbols. Such a lack of stark material difference, in the form of African cultural representations or evident trauma, has sometimes been taken to mean that the enslaved on smaller northern plantations are "invisible." Another way to phrase this conclusion, however, is that we simply do not see what we *expected* to find.

This gap in expectations, the lack of stark difference, should, however, cause us to reconsider the nature of enslavement and the ways that people might cope with it. First, enslavement does entail removing possession and property (at least those that are material) and forcing the enslaved person always to be operating within the material resources made available to them by someone else rather than to be controlling those resources independently (Kopytoff 1986; Patterson 1982). Enslavement is a denial of personal sovereignty, and we should perhaps regard the absence of difference as a repression of material independence according to English ideas of personhood. Recalling Connerton's (1989) distinction of inscribed from incorporated memory, we may expect to see deprivation of material means (separate from the person, and inscribed as "property") yet acknowledge that incorporated belongings (skills, traditional practice, or kinship) remain. Thus, the expression of resistance or acts of cultural distinction by the enslaved may appear only as subtle differences in the assemblage as a whole, particularly in materials we are given to categorizing as "European" or "Native American." In the case of Sylvester Manor, those expressions occurred through the engagement with Manhanset resources. Second, outside of overt rebellion, resistance and actions on the enslaved person's behalf are quite likely to have been covert; their meanings were hidden within otherwise ordinary forms and apparent only to those sharing their knowledge. These signs were meant to be neither publically accessible nor permanently inscribed; otherwise, they would have been poor carriers of secret knowledge and unable to define those tactically practiced spaces within the "proper places" made by plantation proprietors. Why should we expect to see those experiences easily? Thus, the invisibility of northern slavery is partially created by not only our own conceptual misunderstandings but also the desire of the enslaved not to be easily apprehended.

Another conceptual occlusion that renders northern slavery difficult to address, particularly in archaeology, is the persistent belief that slavery was a distinctive status, clearly distinguishable from other forms of servitude and disenfranchisement in its extremity and trauma and consistently and exclusively associated with Africans or African Americans. These assumptions are often conflated, such that plantation contexts become the primary location for the archaeological investigation of African American pasts (Wilkie 2004). Indeed, colonial authorities adopted specific laws restricting slavery by race, but only after many decades of Africans' presence and labor in the colonies, who in some cases gained their independence (e.g., Breen and Innes 1980), and often built community in the meantime with a diversity of people. Racial categories were rather fluid in the early decades (even centuries) of the colonies, despite their increasing deployment in historical records like censuses by white colonists. Is it such a stretch to think that some slaveholders may have taken advantage of that fluidity by identifying people of mixed heritage or Indian heritage as "negro" in order to justify holding them in bondage? Census-takers' refusal to record surnames or any name for the enslaved or Indians enabled this option. Perhaps as early as the 1680s, laborers named in the accounts of the farm at Sylvester Manor were distinguished by racial qualifiers, like Black John and "John Indian, formerly called [. . .] Jo:" (Shelter Island Account Book, East Hampton Library in Long Island Collection). Although we do not know if John Indian or the keeper of the account instigated the change of name, it surely had an impact on John's prospects.

Why, however, would we not consider other forms of coerced labor to be comparable to slavery (though not the "Middle Passage") when considering a plantation's labor force? Many Eastern Algonquians of New England and New York were subjected, through land removals and dire poverty, to what we would now call debt slavery. Despite laws prohibiting Indian enslavement, their experiences may have been just that. The Narragansett were subject to both of these processes—racial "recategorization" and debt servitude—over the course of centuries, ultimately contributing to the efforts of the state of Rhode Island to declare the tribe nonexistent in the nineteenth century (Herndon and Sekatau 1997). Further, there was ample motivation for those who held others in bondage to hide, disguise, or justify the extremity of their treatment.

As such, there is also an especially conspicuous silence surrounding Manhanset labor. I have proposed some possible reasons why, at the time, the Sylvesters may have wanted to hide the Manhanset contributions. But forgetting also occurs in the much later narratives of the colonial periods. Local historians' acknowledgment of slavery at the plantation and the later estate, while not commonly accepted as part of the history of the northern colonies, still fits within a grander historical narrative of black enslavement. The historical exploitation of Indians for labor or even enslavement does not fit. The discordance of this story betrays an implicit association of Indians with land ownership and a sovereign, *separate* status. Our mythical understanding of Native Americans is that extinguishment of land title was equivalent to the extinguishment of cultural identity, not that they would submit to being "common" laborers or part of the emergent capitalist economy. When slavery *is* connected to Native histories, the most commonly known circumstance is that of the slave-owning southeast nations (Saunt 2004; Chang 2010; Miles 2005).

These perspectives contribute to a broader characterization of Indians as timeless, primitive, and excluded from modern economic structures of either slavery or wage labor. A more recent rhetoric of sovereignty has resurrected popular assumptions of Native exclusion. In the twentieth century, individuals and tribes, after being pressed for centuries to dissolve their communities and instead assimilate as citizens, put renewed and united efforts into legal recognition as independent nations (Deloria

2006; O'Brien 2010; Lyons 2011). Like race, both the concept of legal sovereignty and the relationship of Native people to the United States have evolved through time (Deloria and Wilkins 1999). Yet these contemporary categories, with their connotations of separation extending to labor and economy, have been written anachronistically into the historical narratives. The notion of Indians as laborers was not an astonishing idea in the seventeenth or eighteenth centuries; historians routinely turn up the evidence of their roles as laborers (Gallay 2002; Usner 1992 and 1999; Newell 2003; Herndon and Sekatau 2003; Rushforth 2003; Lauber 1913). During the nineteenth century, with the pervasive rhetoric of removal and separation, this exclusion of Native Americans from the narrative of plantation labor began. This blind spot, created by a documentary silence earlier and a narrative one later, renders it difficult to more clearly characterize the nature of the Manhanset's labor status—free wage labor? enslaved? coerced workers? At the same time, the popular association of African Americans with slavery and their desire of citizenship postemancipation set both the people and the concepts (of sovereignty and citizenship) at odds (e.g., Saunt 2004).

Racialized stories also, oddly, tend to elide the complexities of gender and family structure. Certainly the local histories did not attend to the notion that the colonial plantation might have been experienced differently by enslaved men and women, parents and children, when attention was given at all to slavery. The same was true for much of what was written about indigenous communities. With archaeological remains and one of the earliest documents of the estate, Nathaniel Sylvester's 1680 will, we have a small window upon these issues. The enslaved persons he bequeathed to his children were grouped by families and referenced by their relationships as husbands, wives, daughters, and sons. Although Nathaniel did not separate wives from husbands, enslaved children were distributed widely among his own children. In particular we may recall that the enslaved daughters were directed to the unmarried Sylvester daughters, a disbursal that suggests the children were already providing domestic service. Their lives, perhaps from their births, were centered at the plantation residence. The large quantities of straight pins, used commonly for all manner of clothing closures and recovered from all the plantation deposits, might be considered an index to their experience. Part of the embodied experience of women laboring there was being clothed in a plain English style. These items leave room to also imagine that, perhaps having learned to sew as children, enslaved women had opportunities to either fashion some small expressions of their own style or even to make dolls for other children, though these would not have been preserved in any record.

What of the marriages? Scholars of American slavery have described a population of enslaved Africans with proportionately more men, whether by preference of the colonial buyers or by availability in the West African supply of captives for sale (summary in Lovejoy 1989; although this gender imbalance was at its lowest in the seventeenth century). Coastal Algonquian communities suffered the opposite gendered imbalance, stemming from a disproportionately high rate of death among men in armed conflicts or later loss at sea working as sailors and whalers (Mandell 1998). Was this the case at the plantation? The 1675 petition of an Easthampton businessman to hire four Manhanset men from the island for his whaling operation demonstrates their involvement (Fernow 1883, 14: 707–708). Consider the possibility that the Manhanset either remaining on the island or even just working at the plantation may have been women. Narragansett oral history recalls that women were more often moving between the English and indigenous worlds and were more present and visible to white colonists than men (Herndon and Sekatau 1997; see also Richmond and Den Ouden 2003). The Manhanset would have understood many of the production activities evident at the plantation as women's work, such as shellfish gathering and processing, planting, and pottery-making (Bragdon 1996). Were Manhanset women producing wampum at the plantation and making the pottery into which they added the burnt shell and quicklime made by enslaved laborers to craft pots emblematic of Algonquian communities? Were Manhanset women given cloth or English-styled clothing to wear by the Sylvesters, and pushed into domestic service? And if these women made families with some of the enslaved men, were they then pressed into the status of slave by the Sylvesters, who could categorize them as "negro" knowing they would not leave their families? The slippage from one category to another might make relatively little difference to mothers and wives, but the shift would have tremendous consequences for their children (see Miles 2005). They could not have anticipated the racial statutes to come.

Although my line of thought is drawn on speculation, it bears remembering that decades later the issue of interethnic unions became the subject of colonial legal and religious concern. By 1707 New York colony authorities legally clarified the racial distinctions of enslavement, such that the status of a child followed from the status of the mother. In the cases of Indian mothers and African American fathers, this meant that slaveholders might lose opportunities to increase their labor force in bondage. Moreover, the statute might also have discouraged Algonquian wives from residing at the farms and plantations of their husbands, as a risk to their children should the law be ignored. White colonists, particularly religious authorities, began actively discouraging marriages between Indians and African Americans (e.g., Jarvis 2010). In Rhode Island, late-eighteenth-century state law prohibited Narragansett men whose mothers were Negro from voting on tribal affairs, another method of discouraging intermarriage (Boissevain 1956, 236). Historian Brad Jarvis, writing on the Brothertown Indian movement (2010), has suggested that this might have been a colonists' strategy to force demographic decline among the coastal Algonquian tribes. I would add an additional desire behind these efforts was twofold: to prevent the loss of slave increase and more generally to prevent a collaboration that the colonists perceived as dangerous. As noted by Mathis and Weik (2005, 282), "histories tend to reflect the biases of Euro-Americans, whose fears of military alliance between Africans and Native Americans and focus on inter-group antagonisms ignores the productive interactions between them."

Both labor and gender can be lenses for examining "productive interactions." Although there is an inherent danger to exclusively thinking through intermarriage by focusing attention on racialized bodies or "reproductive interactions," gender relations may also be read as a powerful fulcrum of community. Consider how gender roles act beyond simply the sexed body, in the realm of social reproduction. That is, a gendered experience is one in which historical agents acted in the interest of creating, maintaining, and adapting groups as communities. Gender is intimately tied to the translation of culture from one generation to the next. As communities or cultures are always emergent (rather than essentialized), so too are gender roles and relations, particularly in periods of conflict and change as they must have been in the colonial plantation context. Gendered experiences--as men and women, mothers, fathers, children--would have been inflected by the stresses of coping with new people and new configurations of community as well as negotiating these across generations. For the Manhanset, was this any more of a radical change than when the region's political order had been upended over the previous century, by epidemic catastrophes and warfare? Or for enslaved Africans, when they had first endured capture and transport to Barbados, only to be moved again? It seems unlikely. More to the point, when we interpret the outcomes of colonial contexts, gender may be thought of as a lens to focus beyond the binary possibilities of maintenance of continuity or change and instead on how change happens for some things to continue (e.g., Silliman 2009; Cipolla 2011 and 2013). This is how communities survive.

I return, again and again, to the configurations of community. I do not use the term in the idealized or politics-of-identity sense (e.g., Joseph 2002); rather, I use the term *community* in the practical sense of groups with daily contacts, for whom some level of cooperation is necessary, like Siminoff's (2004) notion of "communities of interest." There are two major implications to this approach for the way in which we interpret and narrate the past. First, viewing community, or culture, as always emergent and generative might change the way that we write about the processes of adaptation resulting from colonialism. Archaeologists and historians have used terms like *ethnogenesis,* or *creolization,* or *hybridity,* as descriptions of this process (Mrozowski 2010; Dawdy 2000; Gundaker 2000; Singleton 1998; Usner 1999; Loren 2000; Deagan 1998; Voss 2005 and 2008; Van Dommelen 2005; Sidbury and Cañizares-Esguerra 2011). Each of these is meant to convey the creative and empowered (in whatever large or small way) adaptation of culture in colonial settings, rather than a draconian *acculturation* or *assimilation* approach. Even in these frameworks, however, one implicitly assumes that there are stable points of origin in the process, a culture in its "pure" or baseline form (denoted at contact), and that all changes from these points are problems to be explained (e.g., Liebmann 2013). No one would deny that many aspects of colonization—especially slavery and land disenfranchisement—were traumatic ruptures. But to have changed and adapted across generations does not mean that communities disappeared, and their creativity need not be explored in the absence of acknowledging violence and struggle (see Sweet 2011; Atalay 2006). Indeed, the greatest threats to those communities come from being *labeled* as static, unchanging cultures, or worse, as fixed races. This is accomplished, perhaps a bit unwittingly, when we assume a model of historical change as an evolutionary concatenation of stable cultural forms rather than culture (or any other social structure) arising from numerous small historically situated traditions, being added, reproduced, or forgotten continuously (cf. Foucault 1970 and 1972; Agamben 2009). Latour's (2005) own notion of hybridity accounts for this understanding of communities, in that we are always already hybrids (composed of heterogeneous elements), and through time we simply shift the sets of associations we have in those elements. This approach to culture, or groups or communities, demands that we not *assume* the composition of that community; instead, we must trace how it came to be. This is a challenge to the way historians and archaeologists approach their historical subjects.

A second major implication of community and culture viewed as generative and "always already hybrid" is that it stands in opposition to the approach taken by state authorities toward recognition and regulation of nonwhite populations. There are myriad ways in which societies use government to define and regulate social relationships, anything from what constitutes marriage and family to recognizing abuse (Hacking 1999, Ong 2003). Today, the status of *citizen* in the United States standardizes many definitions at the level of the individual. Although all American Indian people today are citizens, they may also be dual members of recognized Native nations, which have a rather different political relationship vis-à-vis the United States as domestic dependent nations (see Wilkins and Stark 2011). In any federal negotiations with recognized tribes or nations, or those petitioning for recognition, each political entity must grapple with the issue of Indian identity, whether as race, tribe, or individual. The federal legal system is not equipped, or is unwilling, to handle fluid definitions of these entities, particularly when issues of *kinship* are part of the equation in defining community (e.g., Daehnke 2007; Lowery 2010). Blood quantum, a concept created in the late nineteenth century to denote racial mixing as a measure of Indian identity, is still in use today to some extent, despite the fact that such markers are recognized as neither a biological reality nor a measure of cultural affiliation (Garroutte 2001); rather, blood quantum represents the product of often faulty genealogical record keeping. The definition, or even imaginability, of these communities is very much entangled with our approach to history. Can we conceive of culture or community as something actively produced by people who make their choices in order to retain that which is most important to them, instead of something borne of the "blood," essential and unchanging? These distinctions matter in a real way to indigenous people or any people subjected to racializing discourses, in the contemporary United States.

Science, anthropology, and race

Professor Horsford built an essentialized, unchanging version of the plantation community into the landscape of Sylvester Manor with his commemorative monuments separating the Sylvesters, the enslaved, and the indigenous by space, time, and association—a racialized taxonomy. He was the epitome of modernity in this respect. Western societies, engaging in the construction of museums and monuments at an unprecedented rate by the end of the nineteenth century, were casting representations of history and the natural world in permanent media (Lowenthal 1985 and 1996; Connerton 2009). The taxonomic approach of science was a critical part of the scholarly discourse of the emerging discipline of anthropology.

The professionalization of anthropology in the United States arose from the colonizing practices—naming, mapping, describing, categorizing—of the new nation as it took stock of its natural resources (which included Indians). The theory and science of evolution likewise contributed to early forays into the study of human physical variation to create racial taxonomies.[1] Samuel Morton, for example, working in the 1830s and 1840s, examined the metric variability of thousands of human skulls collected worldwide as evidence of difference attributable to races, which he believed to be separately evolved species. His theories were popular with the Lawrence Scientific School at Harvard University (Menand 2001), where Professor Horsford taught and retired as dean (Rezneck 1970). Many Harvard scientific scholars of this time spent a portion of their research in one or another of the new government agencies responsible for surveying, cataloging, or managing the nation's people and natural resources: the U.S. Coastal Survey, the Bureau of American Ethnology, and the Bureau of Indian Affairs, for example (Menand 2001). By the late nineteenth century, when a convergence of population issues arose, theories of human behavior and difference were eagerly sought: the emancipation of a large number of enslaved people, the influx of immigrants from Eastern Europe and the far East (on the west coast), and the perception of the "Indian problem," epitomized by the horrific events at Wounded Knee. Race served as a theory of human behavior and society, either on the premise that "blood" accounted for capacities of intelligence or ability, or as a marker of evolutionary stage, such as that from savagery to barbarism to civilization proposed by Lewis Henry Morgan (Baker 1998).[2] The founding scholars in anthropology "articulated an evolutionary paradigm imbued with ideas of progress and racial inferiority. In turn, politicians and others within specific institutions used these or similar ideas to justify the oppression of people of color" (Baker 1998, 52–53). A jarring sense of difference based in race was also brought to the wider public in popular venues like the World's Fairs, where ethnological exhibits displayed people of different cultures, including Native Americans, in a manner that made them appear most exotic (Baker 1998; Deloria 2006).

The idea of an essentialized and progressive racial hierarchy, as early anthropologists theorized and the nation embraced, was countered by that of *culture*, in its historically particular manifestation, as a better explanation of difference. This was the approach taken by Franz Boas, a seminal figure in anthropology at the turn of the twentieth century. Boas's work argued his concept of culture through two main projects: first, he stated in support of racial equality that no significant form of human difference could be purely correlated to phenotypic race (1922), and second, he argued in favor of cultural relativity and particularity whereby cultures in all of their historical, geographical, and environmental variability did not conform to a progressive, evolutionary scheme (1896). Although his work was enormously influential and he trained a generation of scholars who championed his perspective, Boas made his arguments in the face of formidable opposition. Inasmuch as his arguments were partly directed at the emerging situation in Germany (he was a German Jew), they were also aimed at other policies informed by the notion that some populations were "better" or more fit than others, for example the proponents of eugenics in the United States (Baker 1998).

Anthropologist Lee Baker has argued that part of the Boas's legacy was the scholarship produced by his students in rejection of racial difference, research that contributed to the civil rights movements in the United States. Indeed, he points out, the opinion in *Brown v. Board of Education* in 1954 cited scholarly anthropological studies in striking the first blow against Jim Crow segregation laws. The concept of cultural particularity and relativity, however, has had less traction in public policy. This has had two problematic outcomes. First, recognition of racial equality without acknowledgment of how a community's history has shaped its current circumstances can lead to policy makers' refusal to address those ongoing problems, by claiming such an approach is counter to a "color-blind" policy. This ignores the deep historical reasons why racialized groups have become consistently associated with certain socioeconomic classes and can lead to blaming those groups for their own historical circumstances (Baker 1998, 208–228). Second, a refusal to acknowledge historical difference has likely contributed to the general unwillingness of Americans to recognize both the plurality of indigenous America and the historically particular relations of individual Native nations with colonial and U.S. governments. Such an unwillingness seemingly is embedded in the federal adoption of seven ill-defined but standardized criteria for the acknowledgment of Native nations (and the federal obligations that status entails), despite the enormous variability of types of political organization, community structures, kinship, forms of historicity, and experience of colonization of these nations (Campisi 2003). The criteria focus on demonstrating both continuity and community, an ironic requirement given the efforts of states and the federal government to make Indian communities assimilate or disappear altogether. For the Eastern Algonquians of the northeast, many of whom were reduced to wards of the state before the U.S. treaty-making process began and were subsequently detribalized as the Narragansett were, either petitions for federal recognition or congressional mandates are necessary to regain the protection that has been promised, but not delivered, to them. The long-dominant discourse of blood and race has inflicted tremendous pressure on Indian communities over the last two hundred years, and many tribal communities are still struggling to disentangle the representation of their communities from its effacing effects.

Epistemic violence

If the discourse of race is so harmful, why do we still use it? Ironically, the historical exploration of racialized populations is an outgrowth of viewing archaeology as politically and publically engaged practice, a legacy of the civil rights era in academia. Contemporary communities who connect to the past through racial categories may not necessarily do so by the rhetoric of blood or biology, but rather by shared history and the experience of racism. American historical archaeologists are more and more responding to the interests of various publics to look for a past hidden in the landscape and material culture of the period. Archaeology is viewed as a way to reclaim history for groups defined in contemporary discourse who do not see themselves in the standard narratives (Wolf 1982): women, African Americans, immigrants, the working class, children, and many more (a few examples include Wilkie 2003; McDavid 2004; Mullins 2001; Clark 2005; Voss 2005; Saitta 2007; Sofaer-Derevenski 2000; Shackel 2009).

The African Burial Ground site in New York City is a prime example of the power of this approach. Located in the heart of Manhattan, this eighteenth-century cemetery, documented on historic maps as the "Negro Burial Ground," was uncovered in the process of testing and excavation prior to the construction of a federal building. The site caught the attention and interest of African American communities in New York, not because they could establish particular connections of ancestry—this was rendered impossible long ago, with the disregard for record keeping on the enslaved by colonial authorities--but because they felt there was a shared heritage. Growing out of this interest, community members pressed for a new approach to the excavations and documentation of the buried individuals, specifically that the research design address questions of how burial practices and material culture might indicate African cultural background and how lives of enslavement impacted the physical condition of the buried individuals. Bringing political pressure to bear on the situation, they were successful in their efforts; following the ultimate construction of the federal building, the remains were reburied on the site and a monument memorializing the enslaved people was built (LaRoche and Blakey 1997; Blakey 1998; Perry, Howson, and Bianchi 2006). This community chose to represent historical memory that emphasized both African heritage and the shared experience of slavery as defining the identity of those in the cemetery, in turn claiming connection of that history to contemporary African Americans.

At the same time, we mediate that desire for connection with the understanding that the subject positions have no *essential* or universal commonality. Even today, "women," "African Americans," and "immigrants" are labels for groups with widely variable experiences, desires, abilities, and constraints, and we assume this to be so in the past. Subjectivities are built out of historically specific and convergent circumstances, and it is problematic to assume that categories like gender, race, or class would have been experienced in the past in a manner commensurate with today. Yet those historically specific subjectivities may still be connected to the contemporary through social memory—identifying past experiences as a reason why we are *not like that* today. But much is also necessarily forgotten; our maintenance of belief in the "natural order of things" (to borrow from Foucault 1970) requires the exclusion of alternatives from possibility. The very processes that created identities we connect to today, and wish to possess the history of, also necessarily obscure our view of how different those subjectivities were in the past.

We are confronted with forgetting when different visions of the past come into conflict with one another. This was the case at Sylvester Manor, where archival remains first rupture our sense of northern colonies with evidence of relatively large-scale enslavement of Africans in New York. Carrying the expectation of enslaved Africans to the archaeological remains, we are further startled to find both Native American technological traditions in use on the plantation and little clear-cut differentiation of space and material culture. Why is it startling? Like Professor

Horsford's vision of plantation society, popular historical narratives present racial pasts in isolation. But descendants of the mixed-heritage communities have long negotiated the conflicts of these histories in their own lives. For example, in the Long Island town of Setauket, archaeologist Christopher Matthews (2011) found that, when instigating a collaborative project on a historic district where both African Americans and African-Native Americans had lived for generations, his community partner held a complex understanding of the significance of representation in the district's history. The project sought to emphasize the history of the community in order to forestall the dispersion of members under the pressure of impoverishment. There was tension within the community, however, over what aspects of the past—whether African American or Native American or some more complex and localized history—were most in need of elucidation to younger generations. This is a contemporary example of people's negotiations of local, contingent pasts with the more popularly disseminated past.

While the sentiment of contemporary researchers to reconstitute hidden histories comes from a desire for social justice, ironically we still perpetuate a problematic view of race when we seek those histories in the usual places and fail to see the traces that challenge those expectations. Among American archaeologists, very few have sought to research either the indigenous presence in plantation settings or the incorporation of enslaved African-Americans into indigenous communities (but see Weik 1997 and 2009; Mathis and Weik 2005). How might we change this? Numerous studies of plantation contexts have recounted the recovery of apparently Native-tradition stone tools, which were attributed to African American curation of ancient artifacts as charms (Chan 2007, 157–159; Wilkie 1997; Orser 1985). What if we were to consider other roles for those artifacts, like productions or even curations by enslaved people of indigenous ancestry? Likewise in the grim inventories of Indian burials excavated by archaeologists (until their protection by federal law in 1990), European-manufactured or otherwise non-American materials are usually cited as evidence only of Native people's acculturation or engagement in trade with white colonists. For example, in a 1920 report of excavations in a Montaukett burial ground, Saville described the recovery of a drilled cowrie shell, commonly used as currency in West Africa, without pondering its source, how it might have gotten there, or its possible significance. Could it have been a gift from an African-born fugitive or someone adopted into the community? Pondering these alternative interpretations is possible only when we overcome narrow disciplinary approaches that place Native Americans in the realm of prehistory (Lightfoot 1995) or African Americans only on plantations (Wilkie 2004) or in slums (Mullins and Jones 2011; Lucas 2004 on disciplinary temporalities). Until that happens, these kinds of examples will remain branded as anomalous, haunting figures awaiting recognition.

In some respects, the federal recognition criteria and ongoing popular equation of race with culture makes the demonstration of these historical ties between the Eastern Algonquian tribes and enslaved Africans or African Americans a dangerous proposition, as there are continuing political consequences even today. At this time, only two tribal nations are recognized on Long Island, Shinnecock (granted federal recognition in 2009)[3] and Poospatuck, while two other tribal organizations, the Montaukett and the Matinecock, still petition for recognition and the restoration of even a small land base. In all of their cases, the issue of race, particularly of intermarriage with African Americans, has been used against them. The Montaukett, when bringing the case to a New York State court to protect the last of their land in the early twentieth century, were not only denied the land but were declared nonexistent as a tribe. The defense of the case and the denial of their appeal both explicitly referenced miscegenation as justification (Strong 1998 and 2001). While the use of such criteria is now prohibited in recognition petitions, the effective detribalization placed the Montaukett in the position of having to petition today to regain their recognition, a process made all the more difficult by a century of struggling to maintain their community without resources. The question of race and continuity has likely played an implicit role, not least in public perceptions, in the cases of numerous other Eastern Algonquian tribes, including the Wampanoag, the Nipmuc, and the Eastern Pequot (see Campisi 1991 and 2003; Garroutte 2001; McMullen 2002; McKinney 2006; Mrozowski et al. 2009). Miscegenation has been used as a causal explanation for the dissolution of communities, yet historically the incorporation of "outsiders" to Eastern Algonquian communities has often been the only option left to maintain and reproduce themselves, after their land and livelihoods have been taken away and their populations decimated by disease, war, and dangerous occupations. These are two different historical narratives: one conflates race with culture and community, and one does not. Without a more widespread acknowledgment of how one version comes to overwrite the other, as we have seen at Sylvester Manor, Native communities will continue to be blamed for simply surviving.

Sylvester Manor may not have been an entirely typical setting among the colonies of the mid-seventeenth century. Nathaniel Sylvester brought together an unusually diverse set of people, ideas, and aims in the plantation: Dutch and English merchant capitalism, the engagement in slave trade and large-scale Barbados plantations, a desire for independence yet a deep network of connections, alliances with Native Americans yet an apparent refusal to acknowledge them. All these sorts of communities and processes were in formation in the new colonies, though rarely all in the same place. But from the experience, perhaps through trial and error, of the plantation's multicultural setting, we can see the Euro-American ideas about how to build social order reproduced through the generations. The enslavement of African Americans endured in the northern colonies as did Native communities, despite their steady disenfranchisement. Racial formation continued to evolve, despite histories that assume the primordial incommensurability of Europeans, Indians, and Africans. The archaeology at Sylvester Manor, the archives, and the oral traditions of many descendant communities open a door onto this messy, creative, conflicted, adaptive, and uncertain beginning, and the continuous evolution of racial representations create structures of control over those descended from indigeneity and enslavement. The perspectives they bring should cause us to rethink the certainty of race today.

Epilogue

The Manor today is undergoing yet another radical transformation. Since Alice Fiske passed away, the descendant family has chosen not to keep the estate solely as private property. Recognizing the great historical value of the place—in all of its iterations—they have moved toward more public preservation and maintenance, in part by returning to some of the roots of the enterprise: food production. Now it is the Sylvester Manor Educational Farm, a nonprofit community supported agriculture (CSA) farm, where the aesthetic of the formal ornamental garden is complemented by the beans, lettuce, strawberries, and eggs. As Bennett Konesni, a tenth-generation Sylvester descendant, put it, the goal now is a place "which harnesses the energy of a working farm to support preservation of our historic buildings and grounds," citing the inclusion of many vegetables and fruits in the original plan of the formal garden as evidence of this complementarity (personal communication). The laborers are interns, young and idealistic people who are devoted to sustainable farming, rather than indentured or enslaved people who lacked better, or any, options. These farmers are mindful that they are not simply refashioning the place for the future, but they are also cautiously caring for the past, learning as they dig into the soil for planting to recognize the small remnants of past lives. More historical and archaeological research is in the future of Sylvester Manor.

The focus on food has allowed the family and managing interests to pursue a preservation plan that does not privilege any particular period. Visitors are likely to hear about the history stretching from the

Manhanset generations who initially inhabited and continued to work the plantation land, the generations who built and expanded the current Manor house, and those who marked the landscape with monuments. Hopefully the connection will be made between the labor of the plantation, making food and wampum, and the wealth of the later generations, including the means and the privilege in preserving the place for historical posterity. The stories that can be told from this place will, I hope, confront the assumptions many Americans still carry about racialized histories, the role of slavery in the northern colonies, and the enduring and active presence of American Indians in history.

Notes

Notes to Chapter 1

1. Throughout this book I use a number of different terms to refer to particular groups, reflecting different scales and politics. The terms "Indian" and "American Indian" were embedded in historical records, but more recently they have been taken on by Native Americans for self-identification and political solidarity. Often I refer also to particular tribes or confederacies (for example, Manhanset or Paumanoc) or most broadly to Native peoples or indigenous people. Similarly, I refer to enslaved Africans or enslaved African Americans; I have tried to keep distinct whenever possible, these terms with reference to African-born versus American-born persons. I have tried very hard, however, to avoid using the term "slave" in order to emphasize that no one is ever encompassed by such an identity (e.g., LaRoche and Blakey 1997). By enslaved, I hope to convey that the condition is actively imposed by an enslaver.

2. It also signals a contemporary willingness of at least part of American society to remember or reconstitute parts of the past that were once excluded.

Notes to Chapter 2

1. Tooker (1911, 183) proposed that the very word "paumanack" means "land of tribute."

2. Earlier I referred to "Iroquois" as the term commonly used for the archaeologically defined culture; Haudenosaunee is the term that the contemporary and historically documented tribes prefer, and thus will be used for the remainder of the book.

3. Such legendary visits have been imprinted on the landscape at Sylvester Manor. Alice Fiske, the most recent past proprietor, claimed that an elm tree that had grown on the southeast lawn was a scion of Mary Dyer's hanging tree.

Notes to Chapter 3

1. My interpretations of the plantation landscape from the archaeological remains present a synthesis of the tremendous work collaboratively undertaken by researchers and students at UMass Boston. The following discussion is an extension of earlier work presented in a special issue of *Northeast Historical Archaeology*, particularly Mrozowski, Hayes and Hancock 2007a; Mrozowski et al. 2007b; Hayes 2007; Kvamme 2007; Proebsting 2007; and Piechota 2007.

2. Another possible initial use of the pit, suggested by David Landon, was as a saw-pit, to accommodate the use of long two-person saws (S. Mrozowski, personal communication). Certainly there would have been a need to saw lengthy planks for flooring or siding.

Notes to Chapter 5

1. Ironically the "natural law" argument was used in the first Supreme Court case (*Johnson v. McIntosh*) to address the issue of indigenous land rights and to argue that tribes' rights to oversee the disposition of their lands was superseded by the discovering or conquering nation (Pommersheim 2009: 261).

2. Cousin to the Dering family, L'Hommedieu was a grandson of Patience Sylvester, daughter to Nathaniel and Grissel who had married and made her home close to Shelter Island in Southold. Her descendants had remained in the area, often intermarrying with Shelter Island families.

3. Hints of an interesting relationship between L'Hommedieu and Captain Joseph Brant (also known as Thayendanegea or Tekanawata, an outspoken representative of the Mohawk nation and negotiator for other Haudenosaunee) appear in the letters sent by Brant to Governor Clinton and other commissioners. Brant seems to have taken frequent opportunity to mention that L'Hommedieu owed him payment of "ancient Tribute." The compiler of the Commission's documents, Hough, speculated that this was a bit of a joke referring to a time when East Long Island Indians were subject to the Mohawk as tribute-payers, and, because L'Hommedieu was in possession of property in that area, he was obligated to pay (Hough 1861, 461).

4. Both, of course, were on the minds of social activists of the 1800s, who often protested both slavery and Indian removals, referencing both issues in the call to extend inclusion through citizenship to all (Kerber 1975).

5. Also a daughter, Quashawam, was named to the leadership position with the support of colonial authorities, but she was either ignored by the other tribes at that time or overlooked by later historians because she was female. Whatever the reason, Quashawam was not considered by historians to represent a figure of political authority (Strong 1996, 69; Siminoff 2004, 19, 20n).

6. My thanks to Mac Griswold for pointing this out to me.

Notes to Chapter 6

1. Biological anthropology today, in the era of genetics, is still centered by evolution and has contributed volumes of empirical studies that demonstrate that our commonly used racial categories have no valid genealogical coherence.

2. Morgan and Eben Horsford were correspondents for at least fifteen years, a correspondence that lends weight to the idea that Horsford was very much tied to the

intellectual circles pondering the connections of race and culture at that time (SMA Group IV-A, L.H. Morgan correspondence).

3. More than thirty years after their petition was submitted, the Shinnecock were finally recognized, only after the tribe brought suit against the Department of the Interior (*New York Times*, "U.S. Eases Way to Recognition for Shinnecock," December 16, 2009).

Bibliography

Adams, James Truslow. 1918. *History of the Town of Southampton (East of Canoe Place)*. Bridgehampton: Hampton Press.

Adebayo, A.G. 1994. Money, Credit, and Banking in Precolonial Africa: The Yoruba Experience. *Anthropos* 89: 379–400.

Agamben, Giorgio. 2009. *The Signature of All Things: On Method*. New York: Zone Books.

Ales, Marion Fisher. 1979. "A History of the Indians on Montauk, Long Island." In *The History and Archaeology of the Montauk Indians: Readings in Long Island Archaeology and Ethnohistory*, 3: 13–125. Stony Brook: Suffolk County Archaeological Association.

Alexander, L.T. 1979. "Clay Pipes from the Buck Site in Maryland." In *The Archaeology of the Clay Tobacco Pipe: II. The United States of America*, edited by Peter Davey, 37–61. Oxford: BAR International Series 60.

Alexander, L.T. 1983. "Clay Tobacco Smoking Pipes from the Caleb Pusey House." In *The Archaeology of the Clay Tobacco Pipe: VIII. America*, edited by Peter Davey, 195–233. Oxford: BAR International Series 175.

Armstrong, Douglas V. 1990. *The Old Village and the Great House: An Archaeological and Historical Examination of Drax Hall Plantation, St. Ann's Bay, Jamaica*. Urbana: University of Illinois Press.

Atalay, Sonya. 2006. No Sense of the Struggle: Creating a Context for Survivance at the NMAI. *American Indian Quarterly* 30(3&4): 597–618.

Baker, Lee D. 1998. *From Savage to Negro: Anthropology and the Construction of Race, 1896–1954*. Berkeley: University of California Press.

Barsh, Russel Lawrence. 2002. "'Colored' Seamen in the New England Whaling Industry: An Afro-Indian Consortium." In *Confounding the Color Line:*

The Indian-Black Experience in North America, edited by James F. Brooks, 76–107. Lincoln: University of Nebraska Press.

Beauchamp, William M. 1901. Wampum and Shell Articles Used by the New York Indians. *Bulletin of the New York State Museum* 41(8): 321–480. Reprinted 1978, AMS Press, New York.

Beaudry, Mary C. 2006. *Findings: The Material Culture of Needlework and Sewing.* New Haven: Yale University Press.

Beckles, Hilary. 1990. *A History of Barbados: From Amerindian Settlement to Nation-State.* Cambridge: Cambridge University Press.

Berlin, Ira. 2003. *Generations of Captivity: A History of African-American Slaves.* Cambridge: The Belknap Press of Harvard University Press.

Bernstein, David J. 1993. *Prehistoric Subsistence on the Southern New England Coast: The Record from Narragansett Bay.* San Diego: Academic Press, Inc.

Bernstein, David J. 2002. "Late Woodland Use of Coastal Resources at Mt. Sinai Harbor, Long Island, New York." In *A Lasting Impression: Coastal, Lithic and Ceramic Research in New England Archaeology,* edited by Jordan E. Kerber, 27–40. Westport: Praeger.

Bernstein, David J. 2006. Long-Term Continuity in the Archaeological Record from the Coast of New York and Southern New England, USA. *Journal of Island and Coastal Archaeology* 1: 271–284.

Blakey, Michael L. 1998. The New York African Burial Ground Project: An Examination of Enslaved Lives, A Construction of Ancestral Ties. *Transforming Anthropology* 7(1): 53–58.

Boas, Franz. 1896. The Limitations of the Comparative Method of Anthropology. *Science* 4(103): 901–908.

Boas, Franz. 1922. *The Mind of Primitive Man.* New York: The Macmillan Company.

Boissevain, Ethel. 1956. The Detribalization of the Narragansett Indians: A Case Study. *Ethnohistory* 3(3): 225–245.

Bradley, James W. 1987. *Evolution of the Onondaga Iroquois: Accommodating Change, 1500–1655.* Syracuse: Syracuse University Press.

Bragdon, Kathleen J. 1996. *Native People of Southern New England, 1500–1650.* Norman: University of Oklahoma Press.

Breen, T. H. 2004. *The Marketplace of Revolution: How Consumer Politics Shaped American Independence.* Oxford: Oxford University Press.

Breen, T. H., and Stephen Innes. 1980. *"Myne Owne Ground": Race and Freedom on Virginia's Eastern Shore, 1640–1676.* New York: Oxford University Press.

Budak, Michael K. 1991. The Function of Shell Temper in Pottery. *The Minnesota Archaeologist* 50(2): 53–59.

Burggraf, James. 2006. "Aboriginal Manufacture of Wampum on Long Island in the Mid 17th Century." In *Native Forts of the Long Island Sound Area, Readings in Long Island Archaeology and Ethnohistory,* Vol. 8, edited by

Gaynell Stone, 225–229. Stony Brook, N.Y.: Suffolk County Archaeological Association/Nassau County Archaeological Committee.

Calder, Isabel MacBeath. 1934. *The New Haven Colony.* New Haven: Yale University Press.

Calogero, Barbara L.A. 2002. "A Petrographic Assessment of Stone Tool Materials in New England." In *A Lasting Impression: Coastal, Lithic and Ceramic Research in New England Archaeology,* edited by Jordan E. Kerber, 85–103. Westport: Praeger.

Campisi, Jack. 1991. *The Mashpee Indians: Tribe on Trial.* Syracuse: Syracuse University Press.

Campisi, Jack. 2003. Reflections on the Last Quarter Century of Tribal Recognition. *New England Law Review* 37(3): 505–515.

Ceci, Lynn. 1990a. Radiocarbon Dating "Village" Sites in Coastal New York: Settlement Pattern Change in the Middle to Late Woodland. *Man in the Northeast* 39: 1–28.

Ceci, Lynn. 1990b. *The Effect of European Contact and Trade on the Settlement Pattern of Indians in Coastal New York, 1524–1665.* New York: Garland Publishing.

Certeau, Michel de. 1984. *The Practice of Everyday Life.* Translated by Steven Rendall. Berkeley: University of California Press.

Chan, Alexandra A. 2007. *Slavery in the Age of Reason: Archaeology at a New England Farm.* Knoxville: University of Tennessee Press.

Chang, David A. 2010. *The Color of the Land: Race, Nation, and the Politics of Landownership in Oklahoma, 1832–1929.* Chapel Hill: University of North Carolina Press.

Cheng, Eileen Ka-May. 2008. *The Plain and Noble Garb of Truth: Nationalism and Impartiality in American Historical Writing, 1784–1860.* Athens: University of Georgia Press.

Chilton, Elizabeth S. 1996. *Embodiments of Choice: Native American Ceramic Diversity in the New England Interior.* Ph.D. diss., Dept. of Anthropology, University of Massachusetts, Amherst.

Chilton, Elizabeth S. 1998. "The Cultural Origins of Technical Choice: Unraveling Algonquian and Iroquoian Ceramic Traditions in the Northeast." In *The Archaeology of Social Boundaries,* edited by Marion T. Stark, 132–160. Washington, D.C.: Smithsonian Institution Press.

Chilton, Elizabeth S. 1999a. "One Size Fits All: Typology and Alternatives for Ceramic Research." In *Material Meanings: Critical Approaches to the Interpretation of Material Culture,* edited by Elizabeth S. Chilton, 44–60. Salt Lake City: University of Utah Press.

Chilton, Elizabeth S. 1999b. "Ceramic Research in New England: Breaking the Typological Mold." In *The Archaeological Northeast,* edited by Mary Ann Levine, Kenneth E. Sassaman, and Michael S. Nassaney, 97–111. Westport: Bergin and Garvey.

Chireau, Yvonne P. 2003. *Black Magic: Religion and the African American Conjuring System*. Berkeley: University of California Press.

Cipolla, Craig N. 2011. Commemoration, Community, and Colonial Politics at Brothertown. *Midcontinental Journal of Archaeology* 36(2): 145-172.

Cipolla, Craig N. 2013 (in press). *Becoming Brothertown: Native American Ethnogenesis and Endurance in the Modern World*. Tucson: University of Arizona Press.

Clark, Bonnie J. 2005. Lived Ethnicity: Archaeology and Identity in Mexicano America. *World Archaeology* 37(3): 440-452.

Cobb, Charles R., and Melody Pope. 1998. Sixteenth-Century Flintknapping Kits from the King Site, Georgia. *Journal of Field Archaeology* 25(1): 1-18.

Conforti, Joseph A. 2001. *Imagining New England: Explorations of Regional Identity from the Pilgrims to the Mid-Twentieth Century*. Chapel Hill: University of North Carolina Press.

Connerton, Paul. 1989. *How Societies Remember*. Cambridge: Cambridge University Press.

Connerton, Paul. 2009. *How Modernity Forgets*. Cambridge: Cambridge University Press.

Crain, Edward E. 1994. *Historic Architecture in the Caribbean Islands*. Gainesville: University Press of Florida.

Cronon, William. 1983. *Changes in the Land: Indians, Colonists, and the Ecology of New England*. New York: Hill and Wang.

Cummings, Abbott Lowell. 1964. *Rural Household Inventories, Establishing the Names, Uses, and Furnishings of Rooms in the Colonial New England Home, 1675-1775*. Boston: Society for the Preservation of New England Antiquities.

Daehnke, Jon D. 2007. A 'strange multiplicity' of voices: Heritage stewardship, contested sites and colonial legacies on the Columbia River. *Journal of Social Archaeology* 7(2): 250-275.

Dallal, Diane. 2004. "The Tudor Rose and the Fleur-de-lis: Women and Iconography in Seventeenth-Century Dutch Clay Pipes Found in New York City." In *Smoking and Culture: The Archaeology of Tobacco Pipes in Eastern North America.*, edited by Sean Rafferty and Rob Mann, 207-239. Knoxville: University of Tennessee Press.

Davidson, James M. 2004. Rituals Captured in Context and Time: Charm Use in North Dallas Freedman's Town (1869-1907), Dallas, Texas. *Historical Archaeology* 38(2): 22-54.

Dawdy, Shannon Lee. 2000. Understanding Cultural Change Through the Vernacular: Creolization in Louisiana. *Historical Archaeology* 34(3): 107-123.

Day, Joan. 1991. "Copper, Zinc and Brass Production." In *The Industrial Revolution in Metals*, edited by Joan Day and R. F. Tylecote, 131-199. London: The Institute of Metals.

Deagan, Kathleen. 1983. "The Mestizo Minority: Archaeological Patterns of Intermarriage." In *Spanish St. Augustine: The Archaeology of a Colonial*

Creole Community, edited by Kathleen Deagan, 99–124. New York, Academic Press.

Deagan, Kathleen. 1998. "Transculturation and Spanish American Ethnogenesis: The Archaeological Legacy of the Quincentenary." In *Studies in Culture Contact: Interaction, Culture Change, and Archaeology,* edited by James Cusick, 23–43. Carbondale: Center for Archaeological Investigations, Occasional Paper No. 25, Southern Illinois University.

Deagan, Kathleen A., and Darcie A. MacMahon. 1995. *Fort Mose: Colonial America's Black Fortress of Freedom.* Gainesville: University Press of Florida.

DeCorse, Christopher R. 2001. *An Archaeology of Elmina: Africans and Europeans on the Gold Coast, 1400–1900.* Washington, D.C.: Smithsonian Institution Press.

Deetz, James. 1988. American Historical Archeology: Methods and Results. *Science* 239(4838): 362–367.

Deetz, James. 1993. *Flowerdew Hundred: The Archaeology of a Virginia Plantation, 1619–1864.* Charlottesville: University Press of Virginia.

Deetz, James. 1996. *In Small Things Forgotten: An Archaeology of Early American Life.* Revised and expanded edition. New York: Anchor Books/Doubleday.

Delgado, Richard, and Jean Stefancic. 2001. *Critical Race Theory: An Introduction.* New York: New York University Press.

Delle, James A. 1998. *An Archaeology of Social Space: Analyzing Coffee Plantations in Jamaica's Blue Mountains.* New York: Springer.

Deloria, Philip J. 2006. *Indians in Unexpected Places.* Lawrence: University Press of Kansas.

Deloria, Vine, Jr., and David E. Wilkins. 1999. *Tribes, Treaties, and Constitutional Tribulations.* Austin: University of Texas Press.

Dickson, Bruce D., Jr. 1974. The "John and Old Master" Stories and the World of Slavery: A Study in Folktales and History. *Phylon* 35(4): 418–429.

Dunn, Richard S. 1972. *Sugar and Slaves: The Rise of the Planter Class in the English West Indies, 1624–1713.* New York: W.W. Norton and Company.

Duvall, Ralph G. 1952. *The History of Shelter Island, 1652–1932, with a supplement, 1932–1952.* Shelter Island Heights, New York.

Earle, Timothy K. 1987. Chiefdoms in Archaeological and Ethnohistorical Perspective. *Annual Review of Anthropology* 16: 279–308.

Ehrhardt, Kathleen L. 2005. *European Metals in Native Hands: Rethinking Technological Change 1640–1683.* Tuscaloosa: University of Alabama Press.

Emerson, Matthew C. 1999. "African Inspirations in a New World Art and Artifact: Decorated Pipes from the Chesapeake." In *"I, Too, Am America": Archaeological Studies of African-American Life,* edited by Theresa A. Singleton, 47–74. Charlottesville: University Press of Virginia.

Feathers, James K. 2006. Explaining Shell-Tempered Pottery in Prehistoric Eastern North America. *Journal of Archaeological Method and Theory* 13(2): 89–133.

Fennell, Christopher C. 2007. *Crossroads and Cosmologies: Diasporas and Ethnogenesis in the New World*. Gainesville: University Press of Florida.

Ferguson, Leland G. 1992. *Uncommon Ground: Archaeology and Early African America, 1650–1800*. Washington, D.C.: Smithsonian Institution Press.

Ferguson, Leland G. 1999. "'The Cross Is a Magic Sign': Marks on Eighteenth-Century Bowls from South Carolina." In *"I, Too, Am America": Archaeological Studies of African-American Life*, edited by Theresa A. Singleton, 116–131. Charlottesville: University Press of Virginia.

Ferme, Mariane C. 2001. *The Underneath of Things: Violence, History, and the Everyday in Sierra Leone*. Berkeley: University of California Press.

Fisher, Linford D. 2012. "It Provd But Temporary, & Short Lived": Pequot Affiliation in the First Great Awakening. *Ethnohistory* 59(3): 465-488.

Fleming, Robin. 1995. Picturesque History and the Medieval in Nineteenth-Century America. *The American Historical Review* 100(4): 1061–1094.

Foote, Thelma Wills. 2004. *Black and White Manhattan: The History of Racial Formation in Colonial New York City*. Oxford: Oxford University Press.

Forbes, Jack D. 1993. *Africans and Native Americans: The Language of Race and the Evolution of Red-Black Peoples*. Urbana: University of Illinois Press.

Forty, Adrian. 1999. "Introduction." In *The Art of Forgetting*, edited by Adrian Forty and Susanne Küchler, 1–18. Oxford: Berg.

Foucault, Michel. 1970. *The Order of Things: An Archaeology of the Human Sciences*. New York: Vintage Books.

Foucault, Michel. 1972. *The Archaeology of Knowledge and the Discourse on Language*. New York: Vintage Books.

Foutch, Amy. 2004. "Shelltopia, Mortar, Wampum, Too Many Snails, & $50 Worth of Pennies: An Analysis of the Shell Assemblage at Sylvester Manor." NSF funded REU report, submitted to the Andrew Fiske Center for Archaeological Research, University of Massachusetts, Boston.

Franklin, Maria. 2001. "The Archaeological Dimensions of Soul Food: Interpreting Race, Culture, and Afro-Virginian Identity." In *Race and the Archaeology of Identity*, edited by Charles E. Orser Jr., 88–107. Salt Lake City: University of Utah Press.

Fredrickson, George M. 1988. *The Arrogance of Race: Historical Perspectives on Slavery, Racism, and Social Inequality*. Hanover, Mass.: Wesleyan University Press.

Fredrickson, George M. 2002. *Racism: A Short History*. Princeton: Princeton University Press.

Fuller, Myron L. 1914. *The Geology of Long Island New York*. Washington, D.C.: United States Geological Survey, Professional Paper 82.

Funari, Pedro Paulo A. 1999. "Maroon, race and gender: Palmares material culture and social relations in a runaway settlement." In *Historical Archaeology: Back from the Edge*, edited by Pedro Paulo A. Funari, Martin Hall, and Sian Jones, 308–327. London: Routledge.

Gallay, Alan. 2002. *The Indian Slave Trade: The Rise of the English Empire in the American South, 1670–1717.* New Haven: Yale University Press.

Gardiner, David. 1871. *Chronicles of the Town of Easthampton, County of Suffolk, New York.* New York: Bowne & Co.

Garman, James C. 1998. Rethinking "Resistant Accommodation": Toward an Archaeology of African-American Lives in Southern New England, 1638–1800. *International Journal of Historical Archaeology* 2(2): 133–160.

Garroutte, Eva Marie. 2001. The Racial Formation of American Indians: Negotiating Legitimate Identities within Tribal and Federal Law. *American Indian Quarterly* 25(2): 224–239.

Gary, Jack. 2007. Material Culture and Multi-Cultural Interactions at Sylvester Manor. *Northeast Historical Archaeology* 36: 100–112.

Genovese, Eugene D. 1974. *Roll, Jordan, Roll: The World the Slaves Made.* New York: Vintage Books.

Gero, Joan M. 1991. "Genderlithics: Women's Roles in Stone Tool Production." In *Engendering Archaeology: Women and Prehistory,* edited by Joan M. Gero and Margaret W. Conkey, 163–193. Oxford: Blackwell.

Goddard, Ives. 1978. "Eastern Algonquian Languages." In *Handbook of North American Indians, Vol. 15: Northeast,* edited by Bruce Trigger, 70–77. Washington, D.C.: Smithsonian Institution.

Gomez, Michael A. 1998. *Exchanging Our Country Marks: The Transformation of African Identities in the Colonial and Antebellum South.* Chapel Hill: University of North Carolina Press.

González-Ruibal, Alfredo. 2008. Time to Destroy: An Archaeology of Supermodernity. *Current Anthropology* 49(2): 247–279.

Goodby, Robert G. 1994. *Style, Meaning, and History: A Contextual Study of 17th Century Native American Ceramics From Southeastern New England.* Ph.D. diss., Brown University. University Microfilms, Ann Arbor.

Goodby, Robert G. 1998. "Technological Patterning and Social Boundaries: Ceramic Variability in Southern New England, A.D. 1000–1675." In *The Archaeology of Social Boundaries,* edited by Miriam T. Stark, 161–182. Washington, D.C.: Smithsonian Institution Press.

Goodby, Robert G. 2002. "Reconsidering the Shantok Tradition." In *A Lasting Impression: Coastal, Lithic, and Ceramic Research in New England Archaeology,* edited by Jordan E. Kerber, 141–154. Westport: Praeger.

Graymont, Barbara. 1976. New York State Indian Policy After the Revolution. *New York History* 57: 438–474.

Griswold, Mac. 2013. *THE MANOR: Three Centuries at a Slave Plantation on Long Island.* New York: Farrar, Straus & Giroux.

Gross, Ariela J. 2008. *What Blood Won't Tell: A History of Race on Trial in America.* Cambridge: Harvard University Press.

Grumet, Robert S. 1996. "Introduction." In *Northeastern Indian Lives, 1632–1816,* edited by Robert S. Grumet, 1–12. Amherst: University of Massachusetts Press.

Gundaker, Grey. 1998. *Signs of Diaspora, Diaspora of Signs: Literacies, Creolization, and Vernacular Practice in African America*. New York: Oxford University Press.

Gundaker, Grey. 2000. Discussion: Creolization, Complexity, and Time. *Historical Archaeology* 34(3): 124–133.

Hacking, Ian. 1999. *The Social Construction of What?* Cambridge: Harvard University Press.

Halbwachs, Maurice. 1992. *On Collective Memory*. Chicago: University of Chicago Press.

Hall, Gwendolyn Midlo. 2005. *Slavery and African Ethnicities in the Americas: Restoring the Links*. Chapel Hill: University of North Carolina Press.

Halliburton, R., Jr. 1977. *Red over Black: Black Slavery among the Cherokee Indians*. Westport: Greenwood Press.

Hancock, Anne P. 2002. *The Changing Landscape of a Former Northern Plantation: Sylvester Manor, Shelter Island, New York*. Unpublished master's thesis, University of Massachusetts, Boston.

Handler, Jerome S. 2009. The Middle Passage and the Material Culture of Captive Africans. *Slavery and Abolition* 30(1): 1–26.

Handler, Jerome S., and Frederick W. Lange. 1978. *Plantation Slavery in Barbados: An Archaeological and Historical Investigation*. Cambridge: Harvard University Press.

Harrison, Faye V. 1995. The Persistent Power of "Race" in the Cultural and Political Economy of Racism. *Annual Review of Anthropology* 24: 47–74.

Harrison, Faye V. 1998. Introduction: Expanding the Discourse on "Race." *American Anthropologist* 100(3): 609–631.

Harrison, Simon. 2004. Forgetful and Memorious Landscapes. *Social Anthropology* 12(2): 135–151.

Hasenstab, Robert J. 1999. "Fishing, Farming, and Finding the Village Sites: Centering Late Woodland New England Algonquians." In *The Archaeological Northeast*, edited by Mary Ann Levine, Kenneth E. Sassaman, and Michael S. Nassaney, 139–153. Westport: Bergin and Garvey.

Hauser, Mark, and Douglas V. Armstrong. 1999. "Embedded Identities: Piecing Together Relationships through Compositional Analysis of Low-Fired Earthenwares." In *African Sites Archaeology in the Caribbean*, edited by Jay B. Haviser, 65–93. Princeton: Markus Wiener Publishers.

Hauser, Mark W., and Christopher R. DeCorse. 2003. Low-Fired Earthenwares in the African Diaspora: Problems and Prospects. *International Journal of Historical Archaeology* 7(1): 67–98.

Hayes, Katherine. 2008. *Race Histories: Colonial Pluralism and the Production of History at the Sylvester Manor Site, Shelter Island, New York*. Ph.D. diss., Dept. of Anthropology, University of California, Berkeley. ProQuest.

Hayes, Katherine. 2013 (in press). "Small Beginnings: Experimental Technologies and Implications for Hybridity." In *The Archaeology of Hybrid Material*

Culture, edited by Jeb Card. Carbondale: Center for Archaeological Investigations Occasional Paper No. 39, Southern Illinois University.

Headley, Janet A. 2003. Anne Whitney's *Leif Eriksson*: A Brahmin Response to Christopher Columbus. *American Art* 17(2): 40–59.

Heath, Barbara J., and Jack Gary, editors. 2012. *Jefferson's Poplar Forest: Unearthing a Virginia Plantation*. Gainesville: University Press of Florida.

Heath, Dwight B., editor. 1963. *Mourt's Relation: A Journal of the Pilgrims at Plymouth*. Originally published in 1622. New York: Corinth Books.

Herndon, Ruth Wallis, and Ella Wilcox Sekatau. 1997. The Right to a Name: The Narragansett People and Rhode Island Officials in the Revolutionary Era. *Ethnohistory* 44(3): 433–462.

Herndon, Ruth Wallis, and Ella Wilcox Sekatau. 2003. "Colonizing the Children: Indian Youngsters in Servitude in Early Rhode Island." In *Reinterpreting New England Indians and the Colonial Experience*, edited by Colin Calloway and Neal Salisbury, 137–173. Boston: The Colonial Society of Massachusetts.

Hilden, Patricia J. Penn. 2001. "'Til Indian Voices Wake Us . . . '" In *For the Geography of a Soul: Emerging Perspectives on Kamau Brathwaite*, edited by Timothy Reiss, 403–430. Trenton: Africa World Press.

Hodges, Graham Russell Gao. 2005. "Liberty and Constraint: The Limits of Revolution." In *Slavery in New York*, edited by Ira Berlin and Leslie M. Harris, 91–109. New York: The New Press.

Hodges, Graham Russell, and Alan Edward Brown, editors. 1994. *"Pretends to Be Free": Runaway Slave Advertisements from Colonial and Revolutionary New York and New Jersey*. New York: Garland Publishing, Inc.

Hoff, Henry A. 1994a. The Sylvester Family of Shelter Island. *The New York Genealogical and Biographical Record* 125(1): 13–18.

Hoff, Henry A. 1994b. The Sylvester Family of Shelter Island (concluded). *The New York Genealogical and Biographical Record* 125(2): 88–93.

Hogendorn, J. S., and H. A. Gemery. 1988. Continuity in West African Monetary History? An Outline of Monetary Development. *African Economic History* 17: 127–146.

Horsford, Eben Norton. 1886. *John Cabot's Landfall in 1497, and the Site of Norumbega. A Letter to Chief-Justice Daly, President of the American Geographical Society*. Cambridge: John Wilson and Son, University Press.

Horsford, Eben Norton. 1888. *Discovery of America by Northmen: Address at the Unveiling of the Statue of Leif Eriksen, Delivered in Faneuil Hall, October 29, 1887*. Boston: Houghton, Mifflin and Company.

Horsford, Eben Norton. 1892. *The Landfall of Leif Erikson A.D. 1000 and the Site of His Houses in Vineland*. Boston: Damrell and Upham.

Horsford, Eben Norton. 1893. *Leif's House in Vineland*. Boston: Damrell and Upham.

Horsford, Mary Gardiner. 1855. *Indian Legends and Other Poems.* New York: J.C. Derby.

Hoskins, Janet. 1998. *Biographical Objects: How Things Tell the Stories of People's Lives.* New York: Routledge.

Hough, Franklin B., editor. 1861. *Proceedings of the Commissioners of Indian Affairs, Appointed by Law for the Extinguishment of Indian Titles in the State of New York,* Volumes I and II. Albany: Joel Munsell.

Howlett, Katherine. 2002. *Is Gender Etched in Stone? A Lithic Analysis of a Contact Period Native American Site.* Unpublished master's thesis, University of Massachusetts, Boston.

Huey, Paul R. 1988. *Aspects of Continuity and Change in Colonial Dutch Material Culture at Fort Orange, 1624–1664.* Ph.D. diss., University of Pennsylvania. University Microfilms, Ann Arbor.

Jacobs, Jaap. 2009 *The Colony of New Netherland: A Dutch Settlement in Seventeenth-Century America.* Ithaca: Cornell University Press.

Janowitz, Meta F. 1993. Indian Corn and Dutch Pots: Seventeenth-Century Foodways in New Amsterdam/New York. *Historical Archaeology* 27(2): 6–24.

Jarvis, Brad D.E. 2010. *The Brothertown Nation of Indians: Land Ownership and Nationalism in Early America, 1740–1840.* Lincoln: University of Nebraska Press.

Johnson, Marion. 1970. The Cowrie Currencies of West Africa, Part I. *Journal of African History* 11(1): 17–49.

Johnson, Eric S. 1993. *"Some by Flatteries and Others by Threatenings": Political Strategies Among Native Americans of Seventeenth-Century Southern New England.* Ph.D. diss., University of Massachusetts, Amherst. University Microfilms, Ann Arbor.

Johnson, Eric S. 1996. "Uncas and the Politics of Contact." In *Northeastern Indian Lives 1632–1816,* edited by Robert S. Grumet, 29–47. Amherst: University of Massachusetts Press.

Johnson, Eric S. 1999. "Community and Confederation: A Political Geography of Contact Period Southern New England." In *The Archaeological Northeast,* edited by Mary Ann Levine, Kenneth E. Sassaman, and Michael S. Nassaney, 155–168. Westport: Bergin and Garvey.

Johnson, Matthew. 1996. *An Archaeology of Capitalism.* Oxford: Blackwell Publishers.

Johnston, J. H. 1929. Documentary Evidence of the Relations of Negroes and Indians. *The Journal of Negro History* 14(1): 21–43.

Joseph, Miranda. 2002. *Against the Romance of Community.* Minneapolis: University of Minnesota Press.

Karr, Ronald Dale, editor. 1999. *Indian New England 1524–1674: A Compendium of Eyewitness Accounts of Native American Life.* Pepperell: Branch Line Press.

Kelly, Kenneth G. 2001. "Change and Continuity in Coastal Benin." In *West Africa during the Atlantic Slave Trade: Archaeological Perspectives*, edited by Christopher R. DeCorse, 81–100. London: Leicester University Press.

Kelly, Kenneth G. 2004. "The African Diaspora Starts Here: Historical Archaeology of Coastal West Africa." In *African Historical Archaeologies*, edited by Andrew M. Reid and Paul J. Lane, 219–241. New York: Kluwer Academic/ Plenum Publishers.

Kenmotsu, Nancy. 1991. "Gunflints: A Study." In *Approaches to Material Culture Research for Historical Archaeologists*, compiled by George L. Miller, Olive R. Jones, Lester A. Ross, and Teresita Majewski, 197–221. Ann Arbor: The Society for Historical Archaeology.

Kennedy, Jonathan Ryan. 2008. *Multi-Cultural Meals: A Zooarchaeological Study of the Plantation Core at Sylvester Manor.* Unpublished master's thesis, Historical Archaeology, University of Massachusetts, Boston.

Kent, Barry C. 1983. More on Gunflints. *Historical Archaeology* 17(2): 27–40.

Kerber, Linda K. 1975. The Abolitionist Perception of the Indian. *Journal of American History* 62(2): 271–295.

Kerber, Linda K. 1997. The Meanings of Citizenship. *The Journal of American History* 84(3): 833–854.

Kingery, W. David, Pamela B. Vandiver, and Martha Prickett. 1988. The Beginnings of Pyrotechnology Part II: Production and Use of Lime and Gypsum Plaster in the Pre-Pottery Neolithic Near East. *Journal of Field Archaeology* 15(2): 219–244.

Kopytoff, Igor. 1986. "Cultural Biography of Things: Commoditization as Process." In *The Social Life of Things: Commodities in Cultural Perspective*, edited by Arjun Appadurai, 64–91. Cambridge: Cambridge University Press.

Kruger, Vivienne L. 1985. *Born to Run: The Slave Family in Early New York, 1627 to 1827.* Ph.D. diss., Columbia University. University Microfilms, Ann Arbor.

Küchler, Susanne. 2002. *Malanggan: Art, Memory and Sacrifice.* Oxford: Berg.

Kvamme, Kenneth L. 2001. Final Report of Geophysical Investigations Conducted at Sylvester Manor, Shelter Island, New York, 2000. Submitted to the Andrew Fiske Memorial Center for Archaeological Research, Department of Anthropology, University of Massachusetts, Boston.

Kvamme, Kenneth L. 2007. Geophysical Explorations at Sylvester Manor. *Northeast Historical Archaeology* 36: 51–70.

Lamb, Martha J. 1887. The Manor of Shelter Island, Historic Home of the Sylvesters. *Magazine of American History* 18(5): 361–389.

LaRoche, Cheryl J., and Michael L. Blakey. 1997. Seizing Intellectual Power: The Dialogue at the New York African Burial Ground. *Historical Archaeology* 31(3): 84–106.

Latour, Bruno. 2005. *Reassembling the Social: An Introduction to Actor-Network-Theory.* Oxford: Oxford University Press.

Lauber, Almon Wheeler. 1913. Indian Slavery in Colonial Times Within the

Present Limits of the United States. *Studies in History, Economics and Public Law* 54(3): 253–604.

Lavin, Lucianne. 1998. The Windsor Tradition: Pottery Production and Popular Identity in Southern New England. *Northeast Anthropology* 56: 1–17.

Lavin, Lucianne. 2002. "Those Puzzling Late Woodland Collared Pottery Styles: An Hypothesis." In *A Lasting Impression: Coastal, Lithic, and Ceramic Research in New England Archaeology*, edited by Jordan E. Kerber, 155–178. Westport: Praeger.

Lepore, Jill. 1999. *The Name of War: King Philip's War and the Origins of American Identity*. New York: Vintage Books.

Lewis, Kenneth E. 1985. "Plantation Layout and Function in the South Carolina Lowcountry." In *The Archaeology of Slavery and Plantation Life*, edited by Theresa A. Singleton, 35–65. Orlando, Fla.: Academic Press, Inc.

Liebmann, Matthew. 2008. The Innovative Materiality of Revitalization Movements: Lessons from the Pueblo Revolt of 1680. *American Anthropologist* 110: 360–372.

Liebmann, Matthew. 2013 (in press). "Parsing Hybridity: Archaeologies of Amalgamation in Seventeenth-Century New Mexico." In *The Archaeology of Hybrid Material Culture*, edited by Jeb Card. Carbondale: Center for Archaeological Investigations Occasional Paper No. 39, Southern Illinois University.

Lightfoot, Kent G. 1995. Culture Contact Studies: Redefining the Relationship Between Prehistoric and Historical Archaeology. *American Antiquity* 60(2): 199–217.

Lightfoot, Kent G., and Robert M. Cerrato. 1988. Prehistoric Shellfish Exploitation in Coastal New York. *Journal of Field Archaeology* 15(2): 141–149.

Lightfoot, Kent G., Robert Kalin, and James Moore. 1987. *Prehistoric Hunter-Gatherers of Shelter Island, New York: An Archaeological Study of the Mashomack Preserve*. With contributions by Robert Cerrato, Margaret Conover, and Stephanie Rippel-Erickson. Berkeley: Contributions of the University of California Archaeological Research Facility no. 46.

Lightfoot, Kent G., and Antoinette Martinez. 1997. "Interethnic Relationships in the Native Alaskan Neighborhood: Consumption Practices, Cultural Innovations, and the Construction of Household Identities." In *The Native Alaskan Neighborhood: A Multiethnic Community at Colony Ross*, Volume 2 of The Archaeology and Ethnohistory of Fort Ross, California, edited by Kent G. Lightfoot, Ann M. Schiff, and Thomas A. Wake, 1–22. Berkeley: Archaeological Research Facility, University of California.

Lightfoot, Kent G., Antoinette Martinez, and Ann M. Schiff. 1998. Daily Practice and Material Culture in Pluralistic Social Settings: An Archaeological Study of Culture Change and Persistence from Fort Ross, California. *American Antiquity* 63(2): 199–222.

Little, Elizabeth A. 2002. Kautantouwit's Legacy: Calibrated Dates on Prehistoric Maize in New England. *American Antiquity* 67(1): 109–118.

Little, Elizabeth A., and Margaret J. Schoeninger. 1995. The Late Woodland Diet on Nantucket Island and the Problem of Maize in Coastal New England. *American Antiquity* 60(2): 351–368.

Lizee, Jonathan Michael. 1994 *Prehistoric Ceramic Sequences and Patterning in Southern New England: The Windsor Tradition*. Ph.D. diss., University of Connecticut. University Microfilms, Ann Arbor.

Lizee, Jonathan M., Michael D. Glascock and Hector Neff. 1995. Clay acquisition and vessel distribution patterns: neutron activation analysis of late Windsor and Shantok tradition ceramics from southern New England. *American Antiquity* 60(3): 515-530.

Loren, Diana DiPaolo. 2001. Social skins: Orthodoxies and practices of dressing in the early colonial lower Mississippi Valley. *Journal of Social Archaeology* 1(2): 172–189.

Loren, Diana DiPaolo. 2008. *In Contact: Bodies and Spaces in the Sixteenth- and Seventeenth-Century Eastern Woodlands*. Lanham: AltaMira Press.

Loren, Diana DiPaolo. 2010. *The Archaeology of Clothing and Bodily Adornment in Colonial America*. Gainesville: University Press of Florida.

Lovejoy, Paul E. 1989. The Impact of the Atlantic Slave Trade on Africa: A Review of the Literature. *The Journal of African History* 30(3): 365–394.

Lowenthal, David. 1985. *The Past Is a Foreign Country*. Cambridge: Cambridge University Press.

Lowenthal, David. 1996. *Possessed by the Past: The Heritage Crusade and the Spoils of History*. New York: Free Press.

Lowery, Malinda Maynor. 2010. *Lumbee Indians in the Jim Crow South: Race, Identity, and the Making of a Nation*. Chapel Hill: University of North Carolina Press.

Lucas, Gavin. 2002. Disposability and Dispossession in the Twentieth Century. *Journal of Material Culture* 7(1): 5–22.

Lucas, Gavin. 2004. Modern Disturbances: On the Ambiguities of Archaeology. *Modernism/modernity* 11(1): 109–120.

Luedtke, Barbara E. 1985. *The Camp at the Bend in the River: Prehistory at the Shattuck Farm Site*. Boston: Massachusetts Historical Commission Occasional Publications in Archaeology and History.

Luedtke, Barbara E. 1992. *An Archaeologist's Guide to Chert and Flint*. Los Angeles: Institute of Archaeology, University of California Los Angeles, Archaeological Research Tools 7.

Luedtke, Barbara E. 1993. Lithic Source Analysis in New England. *Bulletin of the Massachusetts Archaeological Society* 54(2): 56–60.

Luedtke, Barbara E. 1997. "Lithic Procurement and Use on the Boston Harbor Islands." Paper presented at the Annual Meeting of the Society for American Archaeology, Nashville, Tenn., April 2–6, 1997.

Luedtke, Barbara E. 1998. Worked Ballast Flint at Aptucxet. *Northeast Historical Archaeology* 27: 33–50.

Luedtke, Barbara E. 1999. What Makes a Good Gunflint? *Archaeology of Eastern North America* 27: 71–79.

Lyons, Scott Richard. 2011. Actually Existing Indian Nations: Modernity, Diversity, and the Future of Native American Studies. *American Indian Quarterly* 35(3): 294–312.

Mallmann, Jacob E. 1990. *Historical Papers on Shelter Island and its Presbyterian Church.* Reprint, originally published 1899. Bowie: Heritage Books.

Mancini, J.M. 2002. Discovering Viking America. *Critical Inquiry* 28(4): 868–907.

Mandell, Daniel R. 1998. Shifting Boundaries of Race and Ethnicity: Indian-Black Intermarriage in Southern New England, 1760–1880. *The Journal of American History* 85(2): 466–501.

Mandell, Daniel R. 2005. "'The times are exceedingly altered': The Revolution and Southern New England Indians." In *Eighteenth Century Native Communities of Southern New England in the Colonial Context*, edited by Jack Campisi, 160–190. The Mashantucket Pequot Museum and Research Center, Occasional Paper No. 1.

Mandell, Daniel R. 2008. *Tribe, Race, History: Native Americans in Southern New England, 1780–1880.* Baltimore: Johns Hopkins University Press.

Mathis, Ruth, and Terrence Weik. 2005. "Not just Black and White: African Americans reclaiming the Indigenous past." In *Indigenous archaeologies: Decolonizing theory and practice*, edited by Claire Smith and H. Martin Wobst, 281–297. London: Routledge.

Matthews, Christopher N. 2011. Lonely Islands: Culture, Community, and Poverty in Archaeological Perspective. *Historical Archaeology* 45(3): 41–54.

McBride, Kevin A. 1994. "The Source and Mother of the Fur Trade: Native-Dutch Relations in Eastern New Netherlands." In *Enduring Traditions: The Native Peoples of New England,* edited by Laurie Weinstein, 31–51. Westport: Bergin and Garvey.

McCashion, John H. 1979. "A Preliminary Chronology and Discussion of Seventeenth and Early Eighteenth Century Clay Tobacco Pipes from New York State Sites." In *The Archaeology of the Clay Tobacco Pipe: II. The United States of America,* edited by Peter Davey, 63–149. Oxford: BAR International Series 60.

McDavid, Carol. 2004. "From 'Traditional' Archaeology to Public Archaeology to Community Action: The Levi Jordan Plantation Project." In *Places in Mind: Public Archaeology as Applied Anthropology,* edited by Paul A. Shackel and Erve J. Chambers, 35–56. New York: Routledge.

McKee, Larry. 1992. "The Ideals and Realities Behind the Design and Use of 19th Century Virginia Slave Cabins." In *The Art and Mystery of Historical Archaeology: Essays in Honor of James Deetz,* edited by Anne Elizabeth Yentsch and Mary C. Beaudry, 195–213. Boca Raton, Fla.: CRC Press.

McKinney, Tiffany M. 2006. "Race and Federal Recognition in Native New

England." In *Crossing Waters, Crossing Worlds: The African Diaspora in Indian Country*, edited by Tiya Miles and Sharon P. Holland, 57–79. Durham, N.C.: Duke University Press.

McManus, Edgar J. 1966. *A History of Negro Slavery in New York*. Syracuse: Syracuse University Press.

McManus, Edgar J. 1973. *Black Bondage in the North*. Syracuse: Syracuse University Press.

McMullen, Ann. 2002. "Blood and Culture: Negotiating Race in Twentieth-Century Native New England." In *Confounding the Color Line: The Indian-Black Experience in North America*, edited by James F. Brooks, 261–291. Lincoln: University of Nebraska Press.

Melish, Joanne Pope. 1998. *Disowning Slavery: Gradual Emancipation and "Race" in New England, 1780–1860*. Ithaca: Cornell University Press.

Menand, Louis. 2001. *The Metaphysical Club*. New York: Farrar, Straus and Giroux.

Messer, Peter C. 2005. *Stories of Independence: Identity, Ideology, and History in Eighteenth-Century America*. DeKalb: Northern Illinois University Press.

Meyers, Allan D. 1999. West African Tradition in the Decoration of Colonial Jamaican Folk Pottery. *International Journal of Historical Archaeology* 3(4): 201–223.

Miles, Tiya. 2002. "Uncle Tom Was an Indian: Tracing the Red in Black Slavery." In *Confounding the Color Line: The Indian-Black Experience in North America*, edited by James F. Brooks, 137–160. Lincoln: University of Nebraska Press.

Miles, Tiya. 2005. *Ties That Bind: The Story of an Afro-Cherokee Family in Slavery and Freedom*. Berkeley: University of California Press.

Mills, Barbara J., and William H. Walker, editors. 2008. *Memory Work: Archaeologies of Material Practices*. Santa Fe, N.M.: School for Advanced Research Press.

Mills, Charles W. 2008. "White Ignorance." In *Agnotology: The Making and Unmaking of Ignorance*, edited by Robert N. Proctor and Londa Schiebinger, 230–249. Stanford: Stanford University Press.

Mintz, Sidney W. 1985. *Sweetness and Power: The Place of Sugar in Modern History*. New York: Penguin Books.

Moore, Christopher. 2005. "A World of Possibilities: Slavery and Freedom in Dutch New Amsterdam." In *Slavery in New York*, edited by Ira Berlin and Leslie M. Harris, 29–56. New York: The New Press.

Morse, Jedidiah. 1790. *Geography made easy: being an abridgement of the American geography. . . . To which is added, a geographical account of the European settlements in America; and of Europe, Asia and Africa. Illustrated with eight neat maps and cuts. Calculated particularly for the use and improvement of schools in the United States. By Jedidiah Morse, A.M. Minister of the congregation in Charlestown, near Boston. Second edition, abridged* by the author. Boston (accessed through Eighteenth Century Collections Online. Gale. University of Minnesota. 8 Dec. 2011).

Moss, Richard Shannon. 1993. *Slavery on Long Island: A Study in Local Institutional and Early African-American Communal Life.* New York: Garland Publishing, Inc.

Mouer, L. Daniel, Mary Ellen N. Hodges, Stephen R. Potter, Susan L. Henry Renaud, Ivor Noël Hume, Dennis J. Pogue, Martha W. McCartney, and Thomas E. Davidson. 1999. "Colonoware Pottery, Chesapeake Pipes, and 'Uncritical Assumptions.'" In *"I, Too, Am America": Archaeological Studies of African-American Life,* edited by Theresa A. Singleton, 83–115. Charlottesville: University Press of Virginia.

Mrozowski, Stephen A. 1994. The Discovery of a Native American Cornfield on Cape Cod. *Archaeology of Eastern North America* 22: 47–62.

Mrozowski, Stephen A, 2010. Creole Materialities: Archaeological Explorations of Hybridized Realities on a North American Plantation. *Journal of Historical Sociology* 23(1): 16-39.

Mrozowski, Stephen A., Katherine Hayes, and Anne P. Hancock. 2007a. The Archaeology of Sylvester Manor. *Northeast Historical Archaeology* 36: 1-15.

Mrozowski, Stephen A., Katherine Hayes, Heather Trigg, Jack Gary, David Landon, and Dennis Piechota. 2007b. Conclusion: Meditations on the Archaeology of a Northern Plantation. *Northeast Historical Archaeology* 36: 143-156.

Mrozowski, Stephen A., Holly Herbster, David Brown, and Katherine L. Priddy. 2009. Magunkaquog Materiality, Federal Recognition, and the Search for a Deeper History. *International Journal of Historical Archaeology* 13: 430-463.

Mullins, Paul R. 2001. "Racializing the Parlor: Race and Victorian Bric-a-Brac Consumption." In *Race and the Archaeology of Identity,* edited by Charles E. Orser, 158–176. Salt Lake City: University of Utah Press.

Mullins, Paul R., and Lewis C. Jones. 2011. Archaeologies of Race and Urban Poverty: The Politics of Slumming, Engagement and the Color Line. *Historical Archaeology* 45(1): 33–50.

Nassaney, Michael S. 2004. Native American Gender Politics and Material Culture in Seventeenth-century Southeastern New England. *Journal of Social Archaeology* 4(3): 334–367.

Neiman, Fraser D. 1986. "Domestic Architecture at the Clifts Plantation: The Social Context of Early Virginia Building." In *Common Places: Readings in American Vernacular Architecture,* edited by Dell Upton and John M. Vlach, 293–314. Athens: University of Georgia Press.

Newell, Margaret Ellen. 2003. "The Changing Nature of Indian Slavery in New England, 1670–1720." In *Reinterpreting New England Indians and the Colonial Experience,* edited by Colin G. Calloway and Neal Salisbury, 106–136. Boston: The Colonial Society of Massachusetts.

Noël Hume, Ivor. 2001. *If These Pots Could Talk: Collecting 2000 Years of British Household Pottery.* Hanover: Chipstone Foundation.

O'Brien, Jean M. 1997. *Dispossession by Degrees: Indian Land and Identity in Natick, Massachusetts, 1650–1790.* Lincoln: University of Nebraska Press.

O'Brien, Jean M. 2010 *Firsting and Lasting: Writing Indians Out of Existence in New England.* Minneapolis: University of Minnesota Press.

Omi, Michael, and Howard Winant. 1994. *Racial Formation in the United States: From the 1960s to the 1990s.* Second edition. New York: Routledge.

Ong, Aihwa. 2003. *Buddha Is Hiding: Refugees, Citizenship, the New America.* Berkeley: University of California Press.

Orser, Charles E. Jr. 1985. Artifacts, Documents and Memories of the Black Tenant Farmer. *Archaeology* 38(4): 48–53.

Orser, Charles E., Jr., and Annette M. Nekola. 1985. "Plantation Settlement from Slavery to Tenancy: An Example from a Piedmont Plantation in South Carolina." In *The Archaeology of Slavery and Plantation Life,* edited by Theresa Singleton, 67–94. Orlando, Fla.: Academic Press.

Otto, John S. 1984. *Cannon's Point Plantation, 1794–1860.* Orlando, Fla.: Academic Press.

Parm, Melissane. 2005. "The Forging of Political Economy: The Mashpee Indians, Gideon Hawley and the Balance of Power, 1788–1796." In *Eighteenth Century Native Communities of Southern New England in the Colonial Context,* edited by Jack Campisi, 191–211. The Mashantucket Pequot Museum and Research Center, Occasional Paper No. 1.

Pascoe, Peggy. 2009. *What Comes Naturally: Miscegenation Law and the Making of Race in America.* Oxford: Oxford University Press.

Patterson, Orlando. 1982. *Slavery and Social Death: A Comparative Study.* Cambridge: Harvard University Press.

Pearce, Jacqueline. 1992. *Post-Medieval Pottery in London, 1500–1700: Border Wares.* London: HMSO.

Pels, Peter. 1997. The Anthropology of Colonialism: Culture, History, and the Emergence of Western Governmentality. *Annual Review of Anthropology* 26: 163–183.

Peña, Elizabeth S. 2001. The Role of Wampum Production at the Albany Almshouse. *International Journal of Historical Archaeology* 5(2): 155–174.

Perdue, Theda. 2009. "Native Americans, African Americans, and Jim Crow." In *IndiVisible: African-Native American Lives in the Americas,* edited by Gabrielle Tayac, 21–33. Washington, D.C.: Smithsonian.

Perry, Warren R., Jean Howson, and Barbara A. Bianco, editors. 2006. *New York African Burial Ground Archaeology Final Report, Volume I.* Report prepared by Howard University, Washington, D.C., for the United States General Services Administration Northeastern and Caribbean Region.

Pfitzer, Gregory M. 2008. *Popular History and the Literary Marketplace, 1840–1920.* Amherst: University of Massachusetts Press.

Piechota, Dennis. 2007. The Laboratory Excavation of a Soil Block from Sylvester Manor. *Northeast Historical Archaeology* 36: 83–99.

Plane, Ann Marie, and Gregory Button. 1993. The Massachusetts Indian Enfranchisement Act: Ethical Contest in Historical Context. *Ethnohistory* 40(4): 587–618.

Pommersheim, Frank. 2009. *Broken Landscape: Indians, Indian Tribes, and the Constitution*. Oxford: Oxford University Press.

Porter, Kenneth W. 1932. Relations Between Negroes and Indians Within the Present Limits of the United States. *The Journal of Negro History* 17(3): 287–367.

Prime, Nathaniel S. 1845. *A History of Long Island, From Its First Settlement by Europeans, to the Year 1845, with Special Reference to Its Ecclesiastical Concerns*. New York: Robert Carter.

Proebsting, Eric L. 2007. The Use of Soil Micromorphology at Sylvester Manor. *Northeast Historical Archaeology* 36: 71–82.

Prucha, Francis Paul. 1962. Thomas L. McKenney and the New York Indian Board. *The Mississippi Valley Historical Review* 48(4): 635–655.

Rael, Patrick. 2005. "The Long Death of Slavery." In *Slavery in New York,* edited by Ira Berlin and Leslie M. Harris, 91–109. New York: The New Press.

Rafferty, Sean, and Rob Mann, editors. 2004. *Smoking and Culture: The Archaeology of Tobacco Pipes in Eastern North America*. Knoxville: University of Tennessee Press.

Ramsay, David. 1791. *The History of the American Revolution. By David Ramsay, In two volumes*. London. (accessed on Eighteenth Century Collections Online. Gale. University of Minnesota. 8 Dec. 2011).

Regan, Janet, and Curtis White. 2010. "Hammersmith through the Historical Texts." In *Saugus Iron Works: The Roland W. Robbins Excavations, 1948–1953*, edited by William A. Griswold and Donald W. Linebaugh, 27–55. Washington, D.C., National Park Service, U.S. Dept. of the Interior.

Rehren, Thilo, and Marcos Martinón-Torres. 2008. *"Naturam ars imitata*: European Brassmaking between Craft and Science." In *Archaeology, History and Science: Integrating Approaches to Ancient Materials*, edited by Thilo Rehren and Marcos Martinón-Torres, 167–188. Walnut Creek, Calif.: Left Coast Press.

Rezneck, Samuel. 1970. The European Education of an American Chemist and Its Influence in 19th-Century America: Eben Norton Horsford. *Technology and Culture* 11(3): 366–388.

Rice, Prudence M. 1987. *Pottery Analysis: A Sourcebook*. Chicago: University of Chicago Press.

Richmond, Trudie Lamb, and Amy E. Den Ouden. 2003. "Recovering Gendered Political Histories: Local Struggles and Native Women's Resistance in Colonial Southern New England." In *Reinterpreting New England Indians and the Colonial Experience*, edited by Colin G. Calloway and Neal Salisbury, 174–231. Boston: The Colonial Society of Massachusetts.

Ricoeur, Paul. 2004. *Memory, History, Forgetting*. Translated by Kathleen Blamey and David Pellauer. Chicago: University of Chicago Press.

Ritchie, William A. 1980. *The Archaeology of New York State: Revised Edition*. Harrison, New York: Harbor Hill Books.

Ritchie, Duncan. 2002. "Late Woodland Lithic Resource Use and Native Group Territories in Eastern Massachusetts." In *A Lasting Impression: Coastal, Lithic and Ceramic Research in New England Archaeology*, edited by Jordan E. Kerber, 105–123. Westport: Praeger.

Robinson, Paul A. 1996. "Lost Opportunities: Miantonomi and the English in Seventeenth-Century Narragansett Country." In *Northeastern Indian Lives 1632–1816*, edited by Robert S. Grumet, 13–28. Amherst: University of Massachusetts Press.

Rothschild, Nan A. 2003. *Colonial Encounters in a Native American Landscape: The Spanish and Dutch in North America*. Washington: Smithsonian Books.

Rouse, Irving. 1947. Ceramic Traditions and Sequences in Connecticut. *Bulletin of the Archaeological Society of Connecticut* 21: 10–25.

Rowlands, Michael. 1993. The role of memory in the transmission of culture. *World Archaeology* 25(2): 141–151.

Rowlands, Michael. 1999. "Remembering to Forget: Sublimation as Sacrifice in War Memorials." In *The Art of Forgetting*, edited by Adrian Forty and Susanne Küchler, 129–145. Oxford: Berg.

Rubertone, Patricia E. 2001. *Grave Undertakings: An Archaeology of Roger Williams and the Narragansett Indians*. Washington, D.C.: Smithsonian Institution Press.

Rubin, Julius H. 2005. "Samson Occom and Christian Indian Community and Identity in Southern New England After the Great Awakening." In *Eighteenth Century Native Communities of Southern New England in the Colonial Context*, edited by Jack Campisi, 114–159. The Mashantucket Pequot Museum and Research Center, Occasional Paper No. 1.

Rushforth, Brett. 2003. "A Little Flesh We Offer You": The Origins of Indian Slavery in New France. *William and Mary Quarterly* 3rd series, 60(4): 777–808.

Ruttenberg, Nancy. 1993. George Whitefield, Spectacular Conversion, and the Rise of Democratic Personality. *American Literary History* 5(3), Eighteenth-Century American Cultural Studies (Autumn): 429–458.

Sahlins, Marshall. 2005. Structural Work: How Microhistories Become Macrohistories and Vice Versa. *Anthropological Theory* 5(1): 5–30.

Saitta, Dean J. 2007. *The Archaeology of Collective Action*. Gainesville: University Press of Florida.

Sassaman, Kenneth E. 1998. "Lithic Technology and the Hunter-Gatherer Sexual Division of Labor." In *Reader in Gender Archaeology*, edited by Kelly Hays-Gilpin and David S. Whitley, 159–171. Reprint, originally published 1992. London: Routledge.

Saunt, Claudio. 2002. "'The English Has Now a Mind to Make Slaves of Them

All': Creeks, Seminoles, and the Problem of Slavery." In *Confounding the Color Line: The Indian-Black Experience in North America*, edited by James F. Brooks, 47–75. Lincoln: University of Nebraska Press.

Saunt, Claudio. 2004. The Paradox of Freedom: Tribal Sovereignty and Emancipation during the Reconstruction of Indian Territory. *Journal of Southern History* 70(1): 63–94.

Saunt, Claudio. 2005. *Black, White, and Indian: Race and the Unmaking of an American Family*. Oxford: Oxford University Press.

Saville, Foster H. 1920. A Montauk Cemetery at Easthampton, Long Island. Museum of the American Indian: Heye Foundation, *Indian Notes and Monographs* 2(3): 63–102.

Sayers, Daniel O., P. Brendan Burke, and Aaron M. Henry. 2007. The Political Economy of Exile in the Great Dismal Swamp. *International Journal of Historical Archaeology* 11(1): 60–97.

Schaefer, Richard G. 1998. *A Typology of Seventeenth-Century Dutch Ceramics*. BAR International Series 702.

Schama, Simon. 1987. *The Embarrassment of Riches: An Interpretation of Dutch Culture in the Golden Age*. New York: Alfred A. Knopf, Inc.

Schama, Simon. 2003. *A History of Britain 2: The British Wars 1603–1776*. London: BBC Worldwide Ltd.

Schmidt, Peter R., editor. 1996. *The Culture and Technology of African Iron Production*. Gainesville: University Press of Florida.

Schneider, Tammy. 2003. "'This Once Savage Heart of Mine': Joseph Johnson, Wheelock's 'Indians,' and the Construction of a Christian/Indian Identity, 1764–1776." In *Reinterpreting New England Indians and the Colonial Experience*, edited by Colin G. Calloway and Neal Salisbury, 232–263. Boston: The Colonial Society of Massachusetts.

Shackel, Paul A. 2000. *Archaeology and Created Memory: Public History in a National Park*. New York: Kluwer Academic/Plenum Publishers.

Shackel, Paul A. 2009. *The Archaeology of American Labor and Working-Class Life*. Gainesville: University Press of Florida.

Sidbury, James, and Jorge Cañizares-Esguerra. 2011. Mapping Ethnogenesis in the Early Modern Atlantic. *William and Mary Quarterly* 68(2): 181–208.

Silliman, Stephen W. 2001. Theoretical Perspectives on Labor and Colonialism: Reconsidering the California Missions. *Journal of Anthropological Archaeology* 20: 379–407.

Silliman, Stephen W. 2009. Change and Continuity, Practice and Memory: Native American Persistence in Colonial New England. *American Antiquity* 74(2): 211–230.

Silverman, David J. 2010. *Red Brethren: The Brothertown and Stockbridge Indians and the Problem of Race in Early America*. Ithaca: Cornell University Press.

Sim, Alison. 1997. *Food and Feast in Tudor England*. New York: St. Martin's Press.

Siminoff, Faren R. 2004. *Crossing the Sound: The Rise of Atlantic American Communities in Seventeenth-Century Eastern Long Island*. New York: New York University Press.

Singleton, Theresa, editor. 1985. *The Archaeology of Slavery and Plantation Life*. Orlando, Fla.: Academic Press Inc.

Singleton, Theresa A. 1998. "Cultural Interaction and African American Identity in Plantation Archaeology. In *Studies in Culture Contact: Interaction, Culture Change, and Archaeology*, edited by James Cusick, 172–188. Carbondale: Center for Archaeological Investigations, Southern Illinois University, Occasional Paper No. 25.

Smedley, Audrey. 2007. *Race in North America: Origin and Evolution of a Worldview*. Third Edition. Boulder, Colo.: Westview Press.

Smith, Carlyle. 1950. *The Archaeology of Coastal New York. Anthropological Papers of the American Museum of Natural History*, 43(2).

Smith, Frederick. 1998. Disturbing the Peace: Constant Silvester in Barbados. *Journal of the Barbados Museum and Historical Society* 44: 38–53.

Smith, Greg C. 1995. "Indians and Africans at Puerto Real: The Ceramic Evidence." In *Puerto Real: The Archaeology of a Sixteenth-Century Spanish Town in Hispaniola*, edited by Kathleen Deagan, 335–374. Gainesville: University Press of Florida.

Smith, Linda Tuhiwai. 1999. *Decolonizing Methodologies: Research and Indigenous Peoples*. London: Zed Books Ltd.

Snow, Dean R. 1980. *The Archaeology of New England*. New York: Academic Press.

Sofaer-Derevenski, Joanna, editor. 2000. *Children and Material Culture*. London: Routledge.

Solecki, Ralph. 1950. The Archaeological Position of Historic Fort Corchaug, Long Island and its Relation to Contemporary Forts. *Bulletin of the Archaeological Society of Connecticut* 24: 3–40.

Solecki, Ralph. 2006. "Epilogue to Historic Fort Corchaug." In *Native Forts of the Long Island Sound Area*, Readings in Long Island Archaeology and Ethnohistory Vol. 8, edited by Gaynell Stone, 35–85. Stony Brook, N.Y.: Suffolk County Archaeological Association/Nassau County Archaeological Committee.

Spivak, Gayatri Chakravorty. 1999. *A Critique of Postcolonial Reason: Toward a History of the Vanishing Present*. Cambridge: Harvard University Press.

Sportman, Sarah, Craig Cipolla, and David Landon. 2007. Zooarchaeological Evidence for Animal Husbandry and Foodways at Sylvester Manor. *Northeast Historical Archaeology* 36: 127–142.

Spyer, Patricia. 2000. *The Memory of Trade: Modernity's Entanglements on an Eastern Indonesian Island*. Durham, N.C.: Duke University Press.

Stahl, Ann Brower. 2001. *Making History in Banda: Anthropological Visions of Africa's Past*. Cambridge: Cambridge University Press.

Starna, William A. 2002. "The United States will protect you": The Iroquois, New York, and the 1790 Nonintercourse Act. *New York History,* Winter: 4–33.

Stoler, Ann Laura. 2002. *Carnal Knowledge and Imperial Power: Race and the Intimate in Colonial Rule.* Berkeley: University of California Press.

Strong, John A. 1994. The Imposition of Colonial Jurisdiction over the Montauk Indians of Long Island. *Ethnohistory* 41(4): 561–590.

Strong, John A. 1996. "Wyandanch: Sachem of the Montauks." In *Northeastern Indian Lives 1632–1816,* edited by Robert S. Grumet, 48–73. Amherst: University of Massachusetts Press.

Strong, John A. 1997. *The Algonquian Peoples of Long Island From Earliest Times to 1700.* Interlaken, New York: Empire State Books.

Strong, John A. 1998. *"We Are Still Here!": The Algonquian Peoples of Long Island Today.* Second edition. Interlaken New York: Empire State Books.

Strong, John A. 2001. *The Montaukett Indians of Eastern Long Island.* Syracuse: Syracuse University Press.

Sweet, James H. 2011. The Quiet Violence of Ethnogenesis. *William and Mary Quarterly* 68(2): 209–214.

Sweet, John Wood. 2003. *Bodies Politic: Negotiating Race in the American North, 1730–1830.* Baltimore: Johns Hopkins University Press.

Taylor, Alan. 2001. *American Colonies: The Settling of North America.* New York: Penguin Books.

Thirsk, Joan. 2007. *Food in Early Modern England: Phases, Fads, Fashions 1500–1760.* London: Hambledon Continuum.

Thomas, Nicholas. 1991. *Entangled Objects: Exchange, Material Culture, and Colonialism in the Pacific.* Cambridge: Harvard University Press.

Thomas, Nicholas. 1994. *Colonialism's Culture: Anthropology, Travel, and Government.* Princeton: Princeton University Press.

Thompson, Benjamin F. 1843. *The History of Long Island; from its Discovery and Settlement to the Present Time. With Many Interesting and Important Matters; Including Notices of Numerous Individuals and Families; Also a Particular Account of the Different Churches and Ministers.* Second edition, two volumes. New York: Gould, Banks & Co.

Thorbahn, Peter F. 1988. Where Are All the Late Woodland Villages in Southern New England? *Bulletin of the Massachusetts Archaeological Society* 49(2): 46–57.

Tooker, William Wallace. 1911. *The Indian Place-Names on Long Island and Islands Adjacent, with their Probable Significations.* New York: G.P. Putnam's Sons.

Trigg, Heather B., and David B. Landon. 2010. Labor and Agricultural Production at Sylvester Manor Plantation, Shelter Island, New York. *Historical Archaeology* 44(3): 36–53.

Trigg, Heather, and Ashley Leasure. 2007. Cider, Wheat, Maize, and Firewood:

Paleoethnobotany at Sylvester Manor. *Northeast Historical Archaeology* 36: 113–126.

Trigger, Bruce G. 2006. *A History of Archaeological Thought.* Second edition. New York: Cambridge University Press.

Trouillot, Michel-Rolph. 1995. *Silencing the Past: Power and the Production of History.* Boston: Beacon Press.

Upton, Dell. 1985. White and Black Landscapes in Eighteenth-Century Virginia. *Places: A Quarterly Journal of Environmental Design* 2(2): 59–72.

USDA Soil Conservation Service. 1975. *Soil Survey of Suffolk County, New York.* Washington, D.C.: U.S. Department of Agriculture.

Usner, Daniel H., Jr. 1992. *Indians, Settlers, and Slaves in a Frontier Exchange Economy: The Lower Mississippi Valley Before 1783.* Chapel Hill: University of North Carolina Press.

Usner, Daniel H., Jr.1999. "'The Facility Offered by the Country': The Creolization of Agriculture in the Lower Mississippi Valley." In *Creolization in the Americas,* edited by David Buissert and Steven G. Reinhardt, 35–62. College Station: University of Texas at Arlington—Texas A&M University Press.

Van Dommelen, Peter. 2005. "Colonial Interactions and Hybrid Practices: Phoenician and Carthaginian Settlement in the Ancient Mediterranean." In *The Archaeology of Colonial Encounters: Comparative Perspectives,* edited by Gil J. Stein, 109–141. Santa Fe, N.M.: School of American Research Press.

Van Dyke, Ruth M., and Susan E. Alcock. 2003. *Archaeologies of Memory.* Malden, Blackwell.

Vaughan, Alden T. 1995. *Roots of American Racism: Essays on the Colonial Experience.* New York: Oxford University Press.

Vlach, John Michael. 1993. *Back of the Big House: The Architecture of Plantation Slavery.* Chapel Hill: University of North Carolina Press.

Voss, Barbara L. 2005. From *Casta* to *Californio*: Social Identity and the Archaeology of Culture Contact. *American Anthropologist* 107(3): 461–474.

Voss, Barbara L. 2008. *The Archaeology of Ethnogenesis: Race and Sexuality in Colonial San Francisco.* Berkeley: University of California Press.

Watkins, Laura Woodside. 1968. *Early New England Potters and Their Wares.* Hamden, Conn.: Archon Books.

Weik, Terrence. 1997. The Archaeology of Maroon Societies in the Americas: Resistance, Cultural Continuity, and Transformation in the African Diaspora. *Historical Archaeology* 31(2): 81–92.

Weik, Terrence. 2009. The Role of Ethnogenesis and Organization in the Development of African-Native American Settlements: an African Seminole Model. *International Journal of Historical Archaeology* 13(2): 206–238.

Wenk, Hans-Rudolph, and Andrei Bulakh. 2006. *Minerals. Their Constitution and Origin.* Cambridge: Cambridge University Press.

White, Carolyn L. 2005. *American Artifacts of Personal Adornment, 1680–1820: A Guide to Identification and Interpretation.* Lanham: Altamira Press.

Whittaker, John C. 1994. *Flintknapping: Making and Understanding Stone Tools.* Austin: University of Texas Press.

Wilkie, Laurie A. 1993. Continuities in African Naming Practices among the Slaves of Wade's Green Plantation, North Caicos. *Journal of the Bahamas Historical Society* 15(1): 32–37.

Wilkie, Laurie A. 1996. Glass-Knapping at a Louisiana Plantation: African-American Tools? *Historical Archaeology* 30(4): 37–49.

Wilkie, Laurie A. 1997. Secret and Sacred: Contextualizing the Artifacts of African-American Magic and Religion. *Historical Archaeology* 31(4): 81–106.

Wilkie, Laurie A. 2003. *The Archaeology of Mothering: An African-American Midwife's Tale.* New York: Routledge.

Wilkie, Laurie A. 2004. Considering the Future of African American Archaeology. *Historical Archaeology* 38(1): 109–123.

Wilkie, Laurie A., and Paul Farnsworth. 2005. *Sampling Many Pots: An Archaeology of Memory and Tradition at a Bahamian Plantation.* Gainesville: University Press of Florida.

Wilkins, David E., and Heidi Kiiwetinepinesiik Stark. 2011. *American Indian Politics and the American Political System.* Third edition. Lanham, Md.: Rowman and Littlefield Publishers, Inc.

Williams, Lorraine. 1973. *Fort Corchaug and Fort Shantok: A Comparative Study on Seventeenth Century Culture Contact in the Long Island Sound Area.* Ph.D. diss., New York University. University Microfilms, Ann Arbor.

Williams, Roger. 1973. *A Key into the Language of America.* Detroit: Wayne State University Press.

Wilson, C. Anne. 1991. *Food and Drink in Britain: From the Stone Age to the 19th Century.* Chicago: Academy Chicago Publishers.

Wolf, Eric R. 1982. *Europe and the People Without History.* Berkeley: University of California Press.

Wood, Silas. 1824. *A Sketch of the First Settlement of the Several Towns on Long-Island; with their Political Condition, to the End of the American Revolution.* New York: printed by Alden Spooner.

Woodson, Carter G. 1920. The Relations of Negroes and Indians in Massachusetts. *The Journal of Negro History* 5(1): 45–57.

Worrall, Arthur J. 1980. *Quakers in the Colonial Northeast.* Hanover, N.H.: University Press of New England.

Published Transcriptions and Archival Collections

Barck, Dorothy C., editor. 1927. *Papers of the Lloyd Family of the Manor of Queens Village, Lloyd's Neck, Long Island, New York,* Vol. 1. Printed from the Collections of The New-York Historical Society, New York.

Fernow, B., editor. 1881. *Documents Relating to the Colonial History of the State of New York,* Vol. 13. Albany: Weed, Parsons and Company.

Fernow, B., editor. 1883. *Documents Relating to the Colonial History of the State of New York*, Vol. 14. Albany, Weed, Parsons and Company.

Fox, George. 1709. *A journal or historical account of the life, travels, sufferings, Christian experiences and labour of love in the work of the ministry, of . . . George Fox, who departed this life in great peace with the Lord, the 13th of the 11th month, 1690.* Two volumes. London: printed and sold by J. Sowle in White-Hart-Court in Gracious-Street.

Gardener, Captain Lion. 1897. "Gardener's Narrative. Written in East Hampton, June 12, 1660." In *History of the Pequot War: the Contemporary Accounts of Mason, Underhill, Vincent and Gardener.* Reprinted from the Collections of the Massachusetts Historical Society. Cleveland: The Helman-Taylor Company.

Hoadly, Charles J., editor. 1858. *Records of the Colony or Jurisdiction of New Haven, from May, 1653, to the Union.* Hartford: Case, Lockwood and Company.

Mason, John. 1897. "A brief history of the Pequot War: especially the memorable taking of their fort at Mistick in Connecticut in 1637." [Written in 1677.] In *History of the Pequot War: the Contemporary Accounts of Mason, Underhill, Vincent and Gardener.* Reprinted from the Collections of the Massachusetts Historical Society. Cleveland: The Helman-Taylor Company.

Massachusetts Historical Society (MHS)

Winthrop Papers Collection

1654 *Nathaniel Sylvester to John Winthrop Jr., Roade Islande 27th of July 1654.*

1655 *Nathaniel Sylvester to John Winthrop Jr., . . .in Pequitt, ye 6th of October 1655.*

1674 *Nathaniel Sylvester [II] to John Winthrop Jr., In Shelter Island ye 9th of ye 3/mo 1674.*

1947 Winthrop Papers, Volume V, 1645–1649. Printed by the Massachusetts Historical Society, Boston.

1992 Winthrop Papers, Volume VI (Malcolm Freiberg editor).

O'Callaghan, E. B., editor. 1850. *The Documentary History of the State of New-York* Volume I. Albany: Weed, Parsons & Co. Public Printers.

Pelletreau, William S., editor. 1874. *The First Book of Records of the Town of Southampton with other Ancient Documents of Historic Value.* Sag Harbor, New York: John H. Hunt, Book and Job Printer.

Pulsifer, David, editor. 1859. *Records of the Colony of New Plymouth in New England: Acts of the Commissioners of the United Colonies of New England,* Vol. 1 (1643–1651) and Vol. 2 (1653–1679). Boston: The Press of William White.

Records of the Town of East-Hampton. 1887. Sag Harbor: John H. Hunt, Printer.

Shelter Island Historical Society (SIHS) Records

Budd, John, John Tuttle, Jonas Houldsworth, and John Booth. *An Inventory of the Estate of Nathaniell Sylvester taken the 22: Septembre 1680.*

Middleton, Thomas, Constant Sylvester, John Booth, and Nathaniel Sylvester. *Articles of Agreement on September 20, 1652.*

New York Superior Court, *Court Findings of Brinley Sylvester vs. William Nicoll in August 1735.*

Sylvester, Nathaniel, 1679/80 Will of Nathaniel Sylvester on March 19, 1680. Script copy in General Sylvester Dering II Document Book Vol. I, #6, Property of Shelter Island Library, on loan to Shelter Island Historical Society, Shelter Island, New York.

Shelter Island Account Book, 1658–1758. East Hampton Library, Long Island Collection.

Southold Town Records. 1882. Copied and Explanatory Notes Added by J. Wickham Case, Printed by Order of the Towns of Southold and Riverhead. New York: S.W. Green's Son.

Sylvester, Constant. 1671. Will of Constant Sylvester on 7 April 1671. MS. 24493, Fol. 341, British Museum (Joseph Hunter's Colls.).

Suffolk County Deeds, Riverhead County Clerk's Office (Riverhead, N.Y.). *Lease of Sylvester Manor on December 1, 1693.* Liber A: 161.

Sylvester Manor Archive (SMA) collection. 1649–1996. MSS 208. Fales Library and Special Collections, New York University.

RECORD GROUP I

Series A: Sylvester Family

Sylvester, Grizzell —Last Will and Testament (1685 May 7), Box 140, Folder 19.

Sylvester, Gyles - Last Will and Testament [copy of 1707 original document], 1723 June 19, Box 140, Folder 32.

Sylvester, Nathaniell (II), Bond - to Isaac Arnold and James Lloyd for Slave, 1687 September 20, Box 140, Folder 20.

Sylvester, Peter, Bond - to James Lloyd, for two slaves, 1688 September 11, box 140, Folder 21.

RECORD GROUP II

Series B: Ezra L'Hommedieu

Copy of Land Grant to Stockbridge Indians, 1788 September 2, Box 15, Folder 10.

Grievances of Montauk Indians; Commissioners Response; Expenditures Account Book, 1807, Box 15, Folder 29.

L'Hommedieu, Ezra, Received of Ezra L'Hommedieu Medicines for Brotherton Indians - Receipt by Thomas Eddy, 1796 April 18, Box 12 Folder 16.

Oneida Academy - A Plan of Education for the Indians, particularly of the Five Nations, 1791, Box 15, Folder 11.

Oversize Series B, Subseries 1: Correspondence
Whitefield, George; Letter to Thomas Dering, 1764, Box 142, Folder 32.

RECORD GROUP III
Series A: Samuel Smith Gardiner
Gardiner v. Dering: Legal documents - Samuel S. Gardiner v Esther Sarah Dering (Dower dispute case), 1828, Box 46, Folder 12.
Indenture - Isaac Pharoah ("Montock Indian") as servant to Samuel S. Gardiner, 1829, Box 46, Folder 14.

RECORD GROUP IV: HORSFORD FAMILY
Series A: Eben N. Horsford
Horsford, E. N., Drafts, notes and miscellaneous material for genealogical manuscript (undated, eight folders), Box 111, Folders 20–21; Box 112, Folders 1–6.
Lamb, Martha J., Correspondence with E. N. Horsford , 1887, 1889, Box 72, Folder 41.
Morgan, Lewis H., Correspondence with E. N. Horsford , 1865–1880, Box 65, Folder 40.

Series C: Phoebe Dayton Gardiner Horsford
Horsford, P.D.G., Correspondence from J. E. Mallman, 1897, Box 95, Folder 9.
Horsford, P.D.G, Correspondence to J. E. Mallman, undated, Box 95, Folder 10.

Taylor, John. 1710. A Short Recital or Journal of some of the Travels, Labours and Sufferings of John Taylor, Late of York, etc. London.
Trans-Atlantic Slave Trade Database. Published on CD-ROM by Cambridge University Press.
Underhill, Captain John. 1897. "Newes From America; or, A New and Experimentall Discoverie of New England; Containing, A True Relation of their War-like proceedings these two yeares last past, with a Figure of the Indian Fort, or Palizado." Original printed by J.D. for Peter Cole, London, 1638. In *History of the Pequot War: the Contemporary Accounts of Mason, Underhill, Vincent and Gardener.* Reprinted from the Collections of the Massachusetts Historical Society. Cleveland: The Helman-Taylor Company.

Index

Africans/African Americans: free blacks, 52, 136; cowrie currency, 94; and foodways, 90-91, 119; material culture and, 113, 115-117, 119–120; and mortar production, 76, 94, 98, 104-105; and pottery, 10, 98, 104-105; in Revolutionary War, 135; stone tools made by, 107; at Sylvester Manor, 10, 53–56, 76–77, 78, 164, 165, 167–168. *See also* slavery

African Burial Ground (New York City), 176–177

agriculture, 18–20, 21, 64

American Indians, 17–49; allotment and enrollment process, 14–15; archival resources on, 4–5; and citizenship, 128, 173; collaborations with African Americans, 8–9, 10–11, 105, 165, 177–178; colonizers induce demographic changes in, 22; detribalization, 12–14, 176, 179; federal criteria for recognizing, 175–176, 179; fluidity of racial categories, 10, 56, 167; Jim Crow laws applied to, 12; as laborers, 168-69; and livestock, 89; New York authorities negotiate for their land, 127–128; in plantation settings, 10, 85, 178; pottery of, 98–99; property rights of, 125, 126; representation of, 7-8, 121-22, 131, 136, 174; and slavery, 4, 14, 15–16, 51, 55, 168; sovereignty of, 11, 14, 128, 168–169; stone tools made by, 106;

war captives exchanged for enslaved Africans, 52–53. *See also* eastern/coastal Algonquians

animal remains, 70–71, 88–94

anthropology, race and, 173–176

archaeology: archaeological remains as evidence, 5, 9, 58, 59–61; historical, 5; investigation of slavery in, 166–167; as politically and publicly engaged practice, 176

artifacts, associating people with, 119–120

Barbados, 1-2, 37-38, 41, 42, 44

beads, 113, *114*

Booth, John, 36, 37, 42

brass, 112, 113, *114*

Brothertown Indians, 128–129, 171

buckles, 112, 113

buttons, 112, 113

ceramics. *See* pottery (ceramic material)

Checkanoe, 36, 158

citizenship: American Indians as individual citizens, 128; government defining and regulating, 173; race and, 11–15, 125, 126, 173

class: distinctions signaled in plantation core, 69, 78; past versus present experiences of, 177; race associated with, 175; sumptuary laws according to, 111

clothing, 111–113, *114*, 119–120
clothing fasteners, 112–113, 169
colonization: community and adaptation
   to, 172–173; Dutch and British
   settlement history, 23–26; emergence
   of new Atlantic communities, 26–36;
   professional anthropology arises from
   practices of, 174
community: colonization and, 172–173;
   gender as fulcrum of, 171–172;
   government defining and regulating,
   173; kinship as defining, 173; racial
   categories in construction of, 176–177,
   179
Connerton, Paul, 6, 101, 167
copper, 113, 115
Corchaug, 2, 18, *27*, 28
culture, race versus, 175, 179
Cushing, Frank, 148, 157

Dering, Sylvester, 126, 159
Dering, Thomas, 55, 83, 125–126, 129, 135,
   159–160
detribalization, 13, 176, 179
Duke's Laws, 44, 51, 52, 53, 134
Dutch colonies: emergence of new Atlantic
   communities, 26–36; English take
   over New Netherland Colony, 43, 51;
   settlement history, 23–26; slavery in,
   50–51; wampum used in, 92
Dutch West India Company (WIC), 25–26,
   28–29, 30, 37, 50, 51

eastern/coastal Algonquians, 17–49;
   Brothertown Indian movement,
   128–129, 171; coastal/eastern
   Algonquian tribes, 26, 27; colonists
   encourage conversion to Christianity,
   25; cultural affinities of, 17–18; in
   debt slavery, 168; detribalization,
   12–14, 176, 179; documenting by
   name, 52; emergence of new Atlantic
   communities, 26–36; excluded from
   towns, 136; federal recognition sought
   by, 176; gender imbalance among,
   170; and the Great Awakening, 125;
   King Phillip's War, 44–45, 78, 141,
   164–165; in land disputes after English
   takeover, 43; in local histories, 132,
   133, 137–141; miscegenation seen as
   cause of dissolution of, 179; political

structure, 21–23; pottery of, 98,
   99–100; sachems, 22–23, 26, 27, 35, 138;
   settlement patterns, 20–21; subsistence,
   18–20; Sylvester's decreasing tolerance
   for, 78–79; tobacco smoking by, 117;
   wampum used by, 92–93. *See also
   groups by name*
Easthampton, 2, 32, 64, 129, 135, 137, 141
English colonies: attracting settlers, 50–51;
   conflict with Dutch over eastern Long
   Island, 43; emergence of new Atlantic
   communities, 26–36; King Phillip's
   War, 44–45, 78, 141, 164–165; land
   sales on eastern Long Island, 31–32; in
   local histories of nineteenth century,
   130–141; Manhanset agreement with,
   33–34; Pequot War, 2, 29–30, 34, 138;
   settlement history, 23–26; slavery in,
   52–56; wampum used in, 92. *See also*
   New England; New York

family units, 53–54
Farrett, James, 31, 158
faunal remains, 88–94
Fiske, Alice and Andrew, 58, 65, 75, 181
flint tools, 106, 108–109, *110*
food: agriculture, 18–20, 21, 64; faunal
   remains, 88–91; pottery for storage and
   cooking, 95–98
forgetting: in creation of social memory,
   163–164; deliberate, 58; different visions
   of past lead to, 177; separation as form
   of, 161; varieties of, 6, 12

Gardiner, David, 135, 137, 138–139, 140–141
Gardiner, Lion, 30–31, 32, 135, 138, 147
Gardiner, Samuel Smith, 83–84, 142
gender: as fulcrum of community, 171–172;
   past versus present experiences of, 177;
   race as entangled with, 8; racialized
   stories elide complexities of, 169–170.
   See also women
Goodyear, Stephen, 31, 36, 37, 40, 158

Haudenosaunee, 28, 35, 92, 93, 113, 118,
   127–128, 135, 139
history: anomalous details in narratives,
   161–162; Euro-American biases in,
   171; hidden histories, 178; historical
   archaeology, 5; historical memory,
   11, 122, 141, 177; Horsford's history

of Sylvester Manor, 141–153; local histories, 130–141, 166, 168; memory and construction of historical narratives, 121–122; racializing, 153, 163; social memory as entangled sense of, 164

Horsford, Eben Norton: becomes proprietor of Sylvester Manor, 132, 142; commemorative monuments of, 145–152, 160–161, 173; history of Sylvester Manor, 142–143, 144–153; and Lamb's history, 155, 157; at Lawrence Scientific School, 174; on Viking "discovery" of New England, 152–153

Horsford, Mary Gardiner, 142, 143–144

Horsford, Phebe Gardiner, 142, 145, 157–158

indentured servants, 50, 51, 53, 164

individualism: American Indians as individual citizens, 128; eighteenth-century shift toward, 124–125; Great Awakening encourages, 165; and property rights, 126

intermarriage (miscegenation), 8, 128, 170–171, 179

kettles, 113

King Phillip's War, 44–45, 78, 141, 164–165

Konesni, Bennett, 181

lacing tips, 113, 115

Lamb, Martha J., 154–157, 158, 165

landscapes: with ambiguous boundaries, 85; archaeology of, 58–61; experience of, 57, 61; Manhanset, 61–64; Sylvester Manor plantation, 65–76

L'Hommedieu, Ezra, 127, 128, 129, 142, 143, 155, 157

lithics (stone tools), 105–111, 178. See also flint tools

livestock, 70–71, 88–90

local histories, 130–141, 166, 168

Long Island: Brothertown Indians, 128; coastal/eastern Algonquian tribes, 26, 27; colored population of, 137; conflicts of indigenous communities in eighteenth century, 129; English and Dutch contest eastern, 43; Indian settlement patterns on, 20; land sales by English, 31–32; local histories of, 130–141; Pequot War's effects on, 30–31; Restoration affects, 43; during

Revolutionary War, 125–126, 129, 135. See also Shelter Island

Mallmann, Jacob E., 37, 55, 79, 124, 154, 157–160

Manhanset: agreement with English, 33–34; coastal/eastern Algonquian tribes, 27; copper refashioning of, 113, 115; cultural ties to southern New England, 18; Horsford on, 147–148; Indian mothers with African American fathers, 170–171; as laborers, 164, 169; Lamb on, 155–157; landscapes, 61–64; last of, 159; and livestock, 89, 90; maintain communications with Narragansett, 165; in Mallmann's history, 158–159; and order removing firearms from Indians, 45; Pequot control over, 2, 28; pottery of, 98–99, 101, 105; remain in residence on Sylvester Manor, 44, 58, 63, 77–78, 79; stone tools made by, 107–108, 109; transfer Shelter Island to Sylvester, 36, 158; wampum produced by, 63, 76, 77, 78, 93, 94; wild species eaten by, 91, 119. See also Youghco (Poggaticut)

"Manor of Shelter Island, The: Historic Home of the Sylvesters" (Lamb), 154–157

marriage: gender imbalance and, 170; intermarriage, 8, 128, 170–171, 179

memory: collective, 161; community in maintenance and transmission of, 122; historical, 11, 122, 141, 177; inscribed and incorporated, 5–6, 101, 167; landscape and, 57, 58, 61; reconstituting in nineteenth century, 130–141; remembering race, 5–11; social, 10, 101, 121, 163–164, 177. See also forgetting

Miantonomi, 30, 32, 35

Middleton, Thomas, 36, 37, 43, 45

miscegenation (intermarriage), 8, 128, 170–171, 179

Mohegan, coastal/eastern Algonquian tribes, 26, 27, 27, 29, 128

Montaukett: in Brothertown movement, 128; coastal/eastern Algonquian tribes, 26, 27; conflict with Easthampton townspeople, 129; cowrie shell in burial of, 178; cultural ties to southern New England, 18; federal recognition sought by, 179; in local histories,

140–141; maintain communications with Narragansett, 165; Manhanset descendants among, 159; Narragansett harassment of, 32–33, 35, 78; Pequot control over, 2, 28; Wyandanch, 30–31, 32, 34, 128, 135, 138–139, 140, 141, 147

Narragansett: in Brothertown movement, 128; coastal/eastern Algonquian tribes, 26, 27; in debt slavery, 168; designs on eastern Long Island, 32–33, 147; detribalization of, 12–14, 176; hostility toward Montaukett, 32–33, 35, 78; in local histories, 139; Long Island Indians pay tribute to, 141; Manhanset and Montaukett maintain communications with, 165; in Pequot War, 29, 30; and racialization, 13, 171; relationship with Williams, 28, 30; settlement patterns of, 21; women move between English and indigenous worlds, 170
New England: Brothertown Indians, 128; coastal/eastern Algonquian tribes, 26, 27; construction of historical narratives of slavery and Indian removal in, 122; Dutch and British settlement history, 23–26; emergence of new Atlantic communities, 26–36; historians fail to admit involvement in slavery, 131; slavery in, 52–53; Viking "discovery" of, 152–153
New York: African Burial Ground, 176–177; construction of historical narratives of slavery and Indian removal in, 122; Dutch settlement in, 25; English take over New Netherland Colony, 43, 51; gradual emancipation in, 83, 129–130, 137, 159; historians fail to admit involvement in slavery, 131; negotiations with Indians for their land, 127–128; slavery in, 51–52, 53, 170. See also Long Island
Nicoll, William, 48, 49
Ninigret, 33–35
North Peninsula, 62, 64, 148

Occom, Samuel, 128, 140, 141

Paumanoc confederacy, 2, 18, 26, 27
Pequot: in Brothertown movement, 128; Eastern Algonquian tribes under protection of, 2, 26–27; in local

histories, 139; relations with Dutch, 28–29, 30
Pequot War, 2, 29–30, 34, 138
pewter, 96–97
Pharoah (Pharo), Isaac, 84, 144–145, 150, 151–152
pins, 112, 114, 169
pottery (ceramic material), 95–105; with pendant triangle decoration, 115; in slaughter waste-pit, 72; variation in American Indian, 22; women in making of, 170
Prime, Nathaniel, 134–140, 142, 144

Quaker memorial monument, 16, 145, 146, 149, 152, 161
Quakers, 40–41, 43, 145, 147, 154, 155

race: and citizenship and sovereignty, 11–15, 125, 126; colonial racial categorization, 3, 56; communities that connect to the past through, 176–177, 179; versus culture, 175, 179; designations for, 11–12; disruption of grand narratives of, 163; fluidity of categories, 10, 56, 167–168; gender and, 8; in local histories, 132, 137–138; perceptions of physical difference in racialized identity, 7; racializing history, 153, 163; racial slavery, 3, 7, 12, 15, 51–52, 167, 170; remembering, 5–11; researchers perpetuate problematic view of, 178; science and, 173–176; stability attributed to categories of, 4; structured experience conflated with racial identity, 85. See also African Americans; American Indians
Raleigh, Sir Walter, pipe bowls, 118, 118–119
Ramsay, David, 126, 127
religion: Dutch on baptizing enslaved, 51; Great Awakening, 125, 165; Society for the Propagation of the Gospel in New England, 25
Roberts (Robins) Island, 42–43, 89, 105

science, race and, 173–176
Setauket, 178
Shantok-type pottery, 100–101, 102, 103, 104
shellfish, 20, 21, 28, 63, 64, 76, 88, 91–92, 170
Shelter Island: in Articles of Agreement of Sylvester and his partners, 39;

coastal/eastern Algonquian tribes,
27; incorporation as town, 124, 142;
Indian settlement patterns on, 20;
Lamb's history of, 154–157, 165; local
histories of, 130–131; location of,
1; Mallmann's history of, 157–160;
Manhanset agreement with English,
33–34; Manhanset continue to occupy,
44, 58, 63, 77–78, 79; manorial status
for, 43, 47, 124; in New Haven Colony's
jurisdiction, 40; during Revolutionary
War, 125–126; sale to Goodyear, 31;
soils of, 80, 105; stone-tool materials
on, 107–108; Sylvester and partners
purchase, 36, 37, 158; Sylvester
consolidates ownership of, 45–46; Giles
Sylvester sells parcels of, 48–49, 123;
Sylvesters settle on, 1, 39; in Sylvester's
will, 46, 47; as troublesome addition to
grand narratives of nineteenth-century
historians, 141–142; Uncas visits, 42. *See
also* Sylvester Manor
Shinnecock: cultural ties to southern New
England, 18; federal recognition for,
179; and Manhanset agreement with
English, 33; Manhanset descendants
among, 159; Narragansett harassment
of, 35; Pequot control over, 2, 28
silver, 97, 115
slavery, 49–56; African Burial Ground
in New York City, 176–177; American
Indians and, 4, 14, 15–16, 51, 55, 168;
antislavery activists, 137; archaeological
investigation of, 166–167; archival
resources on, 4–5; enslaved
collaborations with American Indians,
8–9, 10–11, 105, 165, 177–178; complicate
issues of liberal rights, 129–130;
construction of historical narratives
of, 122; coping with enslavement,
166–167; under Dering and Gardiner,
83–84; in domestic service, 112;
enslavement as traumatic rupture, 172;
and foodways, 91, 119; gender and new
configurations of community in, 171;
gradual emancipation in New York, 83,
129–130, 137, 159; Horsford on, 149–151;
invisibility of northern, 9, 166, 167,
177; Lamb on, 155, *156*, 165; land rights
denied to those of African descent, 128;
and livestock, 89; in local histories, 131;

135, 136–138, 166, 168; Mallmann on,
159–160; marriage under, 47, 50, 170–171;
material culture and, 119–120, 166-167;
monument to enslaved, 149–151, *151*,
160–161; and naming, 54; as northern
institution, 3–4; Pharo descended
from, 152; popular representations of,
85; Quaker opposition to, 161; racial
slavery, 3, 7, 12, 15, 51–52, 167, 170; during
Revolutionary War, 129, 155; on sugar
plantations in Caribbean, 54–55, 164; on
Sylvester Manor, 10, 53–56, 76–77, 78,
164, 165, 167–168; Sylvester's holdings, 2,
39, 53–56, 145, 155, 159, 169; in Sylvester's
will, 46, 47, 47, 48, 53
small finds, 111–119
Southampton, 2, 32, 52, 136
Southold, 2, 32, 46, 52, 75, 105, 136
sovereignty: denial of slaves', 166; of Native
Americans, 11, 14, 128, 168–169; race,
citizenship, and, 11–15, 125, 126
Sterling (Stirling), Earl of, 31, 147, 158
stone tools, 105–111, 178
Sylvester, Brinley (nephew), 49, 79, 82, 83,
165
Sylvester, Constant (brother), 37, 43–44,
45, 54, 78
Sylvester, Giles (son), 46, 48, 79, 82, 123
Sylvester, Grissell (daughter), 47, 48, 54
Sylvester, Grissell Brinley (wife):
background of, 2, 38; children of, 2,
39–40; death of, 48, 79; marriage to
Nathaniel Sylvester, 38; settles on
Shelter Island, 1, 39; in Sylvester's will,
46, 47
Sylvester, Nathaniel, 37–49; archive of
family documents, 124; Articles of
Agreement with his partners, 38–39;
background of, 1–2, 37; burial place
of, 59; consolidates ownership of
Shelter Island, 45–46; death of, 2, 46;
decreasing tolerance for Indians, 78–79;
inherits brother's share, 43–44; Lamb
on, 154–155; as liaison between Dutch
and English, 75; livestock owned by,
88; Manhanset fishing rights protected
by, 42, 157; Manhanset transfer
Shelter Island to, 36, 37, 158; marriage
to Grissell Brinley, 38; purchases
additional properties for pasturage, 77;
as Quaker, 40–41; Quaker memorial

monument, 145, *146*, 149, 160–161; Roberts Island interest of, 42–43; servants and laborers of, 2–3; settles on Shelter Island, 1, 39; slave holdings of, 2, 39, 53–56, 145, 155, 159, 169; Southold business interests of, 105; tool inventory of, 111; and wampum production, 93–94; will of, 46–48, 124

Sylvester, Patience, 155, 157

Sylvester Manor: archaeological excavation of, 57–85; in capitalist economy, 165–166; cobble-paved surface, 65–66, *66*, *67*, 73; continuous construction and revision of core, 76; core plantation, *60*; in court cases, 41–42; diversity at, 180; effacing the plantation, 78–82; in eighteenth- and nineteenth- centuries, 83–84; extant Manor house, 49, *49*, 74, 82, 83, 124–125; Gardiner purchase, 83, 142; Horsford's history of, 141–153; interpreted results from geophysical survey, 73, *74*; Lamb's history of, 154–157, 165; Mallmann's history of, 157–160; Manhanset remain on, 44, 58, 63, 77–78; map of 1828, *84*; map of plantation period features, *67*; negotiating spatial structuring of, 9–10; "Negro Gardens," 77; original plantation infrastructure not preserved, 123–124; original Sylvester residence, 66–69, 73, 75, 79, 82, 94; overlying midden layer, *67*, 69, 79–82, 88, 90, 112; plantation landscape, 65–76; pottery at, 95, 96–97, 100–101; as Quaker friendly, 41; as setting of ongoing negotiation of social distance, 86–87; slaughter waste-pit, 70–73, *71*, 75, 79, 89; slavery at, 10, 53–56, 76–77, 78, 164, 165, 167–168; small finds at, 111–119; stone tools at, 106, 107–111; structure trench, 66–69, *67*, 91; as

Sylvester Manor Educational Farm, 181–182; technological practices shared at, 10, 105, 177–178; wampum produced at, 92; workyard, 69–70, 72, 78, 79–82, 87

Taylor, John, 41, 44

Thompson, Benjamin, 130, 132–133, 135, 136, 137, 139, 142, 148, 158

Uncas, 27, 29–30, 34, 42

United Colonies Commission, 24–25, 28, 33–34, 35, 36

Wampanoag, 26, 27, 139, 179

wampum, 27, 28, 30, 63, 76, 77, 78, 92–94, *93*, 170

Williams, Roger, 21, 24, 28, 30, 35

Winthrop, John, Jr.: in eastern Long Island land sales, 31; and slavery, 52; Sylvester as business colleague of, 1, 154; Sylvester's correspondence with, 38, 39, 42; Youghco complains about English to, 34

women: move between English and indigenous worlds, 170; enslaved, 169–170; at plantation core, 69, 112; pottery made by, 99

Wood, Silas, 133–134, 135–136, 139, 142

Wyandanch, 30–31, 32, 34, 128, 135, 138–139, 140, 141, 147

York, Duke of, 43, 51, 134

Youghco (Poggaticut): burial of, 140–141; certificate of agreement with English, 33–34, 78, 138–139; Horsford believes he finds village of, 148–149; monument to, 149, *150*, 152, 160–161; and sale of Shelter Island to Middleton, 36; and Wyandanch's agreement with English, 31; Wyandanch succeeds, 138–139, 140–141

ABOUT THE AUTHOR

Katherine Howlett Hayes is a faculty member in anthropology and affiliate faculty in American Indian Studies at the University of Minnesota. She holds a Ph.D. in anthropology from the University of California, Berkeley, and an M.A. in historical archaeology from the University of Massachusetts, Boston.

Early American Places

Colonization and Its Discontents: Emancipation, Emigration, and Antislavery in Antebellum Pennsylvania
Beverly C. Tomek

Empire at the Periphery: British Colonists, Anglo-Dutch Trade, and the Development of the British Atlantic, 1621—1713
Christian J. Koot

Slavery before Race: Europeans, Africans, and Indians at Long Island's Sylvester Manor Plantation, 1651–1884
Katherine Howlett Hayes